■ ADVANCE PRAISE
CLARIFICATION IN
AND PSYCHOTHERAPY

"This important book addresses an essential component of counseling and psychotherapy that is too often overlooked in training programs and the professional literature. With clear guidelines, and lots of clinical examples, Dr. Kirschenbaum demonstrates not only how to help clients clarify their values on issues such as relationships, love and sex, work, money, substance use, religion and spirituality, politics, and meaning in life, but also how to resolve their conflicts around such values and thus promote clients' living more consistently their highest purposes. Deeply relevant to seasoned counselors and therapists as well as students, this book not only provides practical instruction, but philosophically astute expositions of what values are, their central role in human life, and how the values clarification process can be applied with multicultural sensitivity to diverse populations. It is highly recommended for anyone who practices counseling or psychotherapy."

ANDRE MARQUIS, PH.D., Associate Professor, Dept. of Counseling and Human Development, Warner Graduate School of Education, University of Rochester; author, *Theoretical Models of Counseling and Psychotherapy*.

"Counseling and psychotherapy is by no means a 'value free' enterprise; both clients and mental health professionals have preferred values and beliefs. Furthermore, both professionals and clients may need help in understanding and clarifying their values in the therapeutic process. Dr. Kirschenbaum has developed an excellent book that not only helps mental professionals develop the skills necessary to facilitate client value clarification, but also assists professionals in understanding and clarifying their own personal values, and thereby avoiding the juxtaposition of those values onto clients in therapy.

RICHARD E. WATTS, PH.D., University Distinguished Professor of Counseling, Sam Houston State University, immediate past editor of *Counseling and Values*.

"It is not often that a book has the potential to truly modify what therapists and counselors do. This one does. Kirschenbaum presents a cogent and easily understood framework for working on values in counseling and therapy sessions, along with numerous examples of exercises that therapists and counselors can use in doing so. This book is a helpful, comprehensive, and insightful aid for working with clients' values as an integral part of counseling and therapy. It is an important resource that all counselors and therapists should read carefully and utilize its contents in their practice."

DAVID W. JOHNSON, ED.D., Psychotherapist, Professor Emeritus, Dept. of Educational Psychology, University of Minnesota, author, *Joining Together: Group Theory and Group Skills, 8th edition*.

"With this book, I finally have a resource on values clarification to offer my students who are contemplating their theoretical orientation. Dr. Kirschenbaum has influenced my integrated approach to counseling and will continue to influence my students with this valuable book. My students will be more prepared to provide mental health counseling services because they will be armed with practical values clarification strategies to complement the other approaches that our program teaches."

ROBERT H. RICE, JR., PH.D., Director of Clinical Internships, Mental Health Counseling Program, St. John Fisher College

"Dr. Kirschenbaum's new book provides a fresh look at values clarification and how concepts can be applied in a variety of counseling and psychotherapy settings. Building on his seminal work in the field, Dr. Kirschenbaum provides many useful strategies that can be used in individual and group work. It is a must read for practitioners who want useful tools for working with client values, goal setting, decision-making, and action planning."

LORRAINE J. GUTH, PH.D., Professor, Department of Counseling, Indiana University of Pennsylvania

"Howard Kirschenbaum meets a vital and insufficiently addressed need in the field of counseling and psychotherapy by making relevant an issue important to all of our clients—the values by which they live. He makes a compelling case that the process of values clarification and realization in action is critical to the client's sense of self and functioning. To a large degree, we are our values. Fundamental questions such as "What kind of person do I wish to be? "How do I want to live?" "What is the meaning and purpose of my life?" and "What values do I want to guide my life?" are key to our clients' making effective choices in their lives. Kirschenbaum, one of the founders of the values clarification movement, helps us understand that clarifying values enables clients to identify their priorities, make informed choices, and live with more conviction, meaning, and direction. Further, as clients clarify their values, they live a more grounded life, improve their mental health, and often contribute to the well-being of others as well. This book is conceptually sound, grounded in research, and convincing in its message that all clients will benefit from their therapists' sensitivity to and willingness to assist clients in sorting out and implementing their values. Perhaps the greatest strength of Kirschenbaum's book is its breadth and richness in providing practical guidelines for the therapist to help clients address their values issues."

DAVID J. CAIN, PH.D., Psychotherapist, California, editor, *Humanistic Psychotherapies: Handbook of Research and Practice.*

"This well-written text is rich with material about values clarification, an effective technique designed to help people in making life's complicated decisions and choices. This book will be a great resource for helping professionals in implementing values clarification into the counseling and psychotherapy process."

K. DAYLE JONES, Coordinator, Mental Health Counseling Program, University of Central Florida, Orlando; Chair, ACA DSM-5 Proposed Revisions Task Force.

"I began using Values Clarification with adolescent groups over 30 years ago, and now, as a therapist and Counselor Educator, was excited to see this new work focusing on usage with clients, students, and supervisees. The text is replete with strategies and case examples applicable to a wide variety of populations. Kirschenbaum describes using values clarification not only from the obvious Person-Centered perspective, but also articulates connections for usage from Cognitive Behavioral, Existential, Narrative, Solution Focused, and other perspectives where the concordance might be initially less apparent. In the final chapter, Kirschenbaum attends to the research citing the efficacy of values clarification, making this a very comprehensive and accessible handbook."

JUDI DURHAM, PH.D., Department of Counseling & Family Therapy,
Saint Joseph College, Connecticut; former President,
North Atlantic Association for Counselor Education and Supervision.

"An elegant presentation of how values clarification, counseling, and psychotherapy can merge to offer us powerful, practical new tools. A treatise both remarkably clear and wise."

MERRILL HARMIN, PH.D., Professor Emeritus, Southern Illinois
University; author, *Values and Teaching.*

"In my practice, in addition to providing my patients with relevant information, I find that asking good questions to help them clarify their values around health issues increases the likelihood of better outcomes. This book provides valuable tools for helping professionals to assist their clients to find their authentic selves and ways to realize their intentions to live healthier, fuller lives."

MARY MILLER, M.D., Internal Medicine, Connecticut, author,
Value Dilemmas for New and Expecting Parents.

"This book is a treasure trove of methods, tools, case studies, and theory, all with the most practical hands-on ways to use them. It is filled with originality, creativity, and solid foundational thinking. What a gift for a young counselor or therapist, and just as valuable to established ones. It is the culmination of a lifetime of brilliant teaching, profound counseling, and creative leadership Kirschenbaum has brought to the profession."

SIDNEY B. SIMON, ED.D., Professor Emeritus, Psychological Education,
University of Massachusetts, and coauthor of *Values Clarification:
A Handbook of Practical Strategies.*

"Dr. Kirschenbaum, one of the early developers of Values Clarification, describes in clear and accessible language how dozens of Values Clarification strategies can be effectively used in the practice of psychotherapy. These strategies rapidly cast a sharp light on unconscious areas of conflict and inconsistency, and offer a path to their resolution. In my 35 years as a psychotherapist, they have proved their usefulness over and over again."

MARIANNE PREGER-SIMON, ED.D., Psychotherapist, Whately, MA, author of
Heart by Heart: Mothers and Daughters Listening to Each Other

"The author draws upon his extensive professional experience and impeccable qualifications as one of the original authors who brought the values clarification movement into prominence in the 1970s. The current book clarifies the history of the approach, process of employing such a strategy in a professional setting, and outcomes of such a process, while offering a wealth of time-tested strategies along with suggestions for implementation. Members of the helping professions will find specific examples that relate to the topics of marriage and family, substance abuse, pastoral healing, and geriatric health, among many others. Readers will also likely gain valuable insights in the philosophical, theoretical, and research domains that underlie the use of values clarification strategies and the counseling process."

WILLIAM E. HERMAN, PH.D., Professor of Psychology,
State University of New York College at Potsdam.

"This is the most comprehensive, up-to-date, and practical book on values clarification. Straightforward examples and real-life applications make this book a must read for students and professional helpers from diverse fields. As therapist-educator, I am thrilled to have a resource that will support my students in discovering their inner selves."

STEPHEN P. DEMANCHICK, PH.D., Assistant Professor, Creative Arts Therapy,
Director, Nazareth College Play Therapy Center for Children and Families, Rochester,
NY; co-editor, Person-Centered Journal.

"Howard Kirschenbaum continues to build upon the body of knowledge concerning values in education, human development, and the helping professions and has achieved the pinnacle with this book. He has provided therapists with a wealth of knowledge and highly practical applications to enhance the decision-making process for all of our clients. It is the single most informative, balanced, and practical book on the subject of dealing with values issues in counseling and psychotherapy that I have ever read."

DANIEL M. LINNENBERG, ED.D., Assistant Professor, Counseling and Human
Development, University of Rochester; Pastor and Substance Abuse Counselor.

"For many years, I explored modes of effective, nonjudgmental pastoral counseling for parishioners, who represented a broad spectrum of social settings. I have found the values clarification approach to be a useful, democratic, nonauthoritarian way of enabling my fellow humans to discern core issues and to work towards solution that are ethically responsible and existentially practical. This new book by Dr. Kirschenbaum will be of great practical help to pastoral counselors of all faiths."

THE REVEREND J. T. LEAMON, Pastor Emeritus, United Church of Christ.

"Dr. Howard Kirschenbaum is the most qualified person I know to write this book. His background in education, psychotherapy, group training, and writing is an unbeatable combination for helping therapists and counselors do their best work. This is a remarkable tool that will enhance the skills of anyone in the field of human growth."

RABBI DOV PERETZ ELKINS, ED.D., lecturer, consultant;
author, Clarifying Jewish Values.

"For 40 years I have called myself an applied psychologist. I deal with what comes my way in many different venues. Counseling, therapy, coaching, even consulting all bleed together on a given day. I bring all the tools with me and use what works—what's needed in the moment. Values clarification works for me in all these roles, adding texture and providing tools, strategies, and ways of thinking that add meaning for my varied clients, whether students, business leaders, physicians, or other professionals. Any student of human interaction and behavior will love this book. It is a true gift for an eclectic like me."

RODNEY NAPIER, PH.D., Professor of Organizational Consulting and
Executive Coaching, University of Pennsylvania; President,
The Napier Group; author, Groups: Theory and Experience, 7th edition.

"Dr. Kirschenbaum's *Values Clarification in Counseling and Psychotherapy* provides the missing link for professional counselors to better understand how values clarification is at the center of addictions approaches, such as Motivational Interviewing and Stages of Change theory. Too often unacknowledged in the addictions field, values clarification and values-based decision making form the foundation of contemporary substance abuse counseling and prevention approaches. Dr. Kirschenbaum reawakens addictions specialists' awareness of the essential emphasis upon values in clinical theory and practice."

RICHARD L. SCHNELL, ED.D., Distinguished Service Professor Emeritus,
State University of New York at Plattsburgh; Former Chair,
NYS Board for Mental Health Practitioners; Former Treatment
Director of state-licensed substance abuse treatment agencies in New York.

"What a great resource! This book represents a very important contribution to an area of practice that has been too long neglected. Values are truly the basis of so much we do and think, yet they so often go unexamined. How many times have counselors thought that we have covered all the ground and have reached that point in the therapeutic alliance where action is warranted, only to hear, "Yes, but…"? This is a clear indication that we may have helped the client reach a cognitive understanding but missed the underlying values present in the issues that must be addressed in any steps toward change. This book clearly addresses that often overlooked and sometimes avoided crucial aspect of the therapeutic process. The case examples really help bring it to life. Regardless of one's approach, *Values Clarification in Counseling and Psychotherapy* provides an excellent framework for greater success."

E. H. MIKE ROBINSON, III, PH.D., Robert Heitzelman Eminent Scholar and Chair,
Department of Educational and Human Sciences, College of Education, University
of Central Florida; author, *Introduction to the Counseling Profession*; past president,
Association for Spiritual, Ethical, Religious and Values Issues in Counseling.

■ Values Clarification in Counseling
and Psychotherapy

Values Clarification in Counseling and Psychotherapy

Practical Strategies for Individual and Group Settings

Howard Kirschenbaum

OXFORD
UNIVERSITY PRESS

OXFORD
UNIVERSITY PRESS

Oxford University Press is a department of the University of Oxford.
It furthers the University's objective of excellence in research, scholarship,
and education by publishing worldwide.

Oxford   New York
Auckland   Cape Town   Dar es Salaam   Hong Kong   Karachi
Kuala Lumpur   Madrid   Melbourne   Mexico City   Nairobi
New Delhi   Shanghai   Taipei   Toronto

With offices in
Argentina   Austria   Brazil   Chile   Czech Republic   France   Greece
Guatemala   Hungary   Italy   Japan   Poland   Portugal   Singapore
South Korea   Switzerland   Thailand   Turkey   Ukraine   Vietnam

Oxford is a registered trademark of Oxford University Press in the UK and certain other
countries.

Published in the United States of America by
Oxford University Press
198 Madison Avenue, New York, NY 10016

Library of Congress Cataloging-in-Publication Data
Kirschenbaum, Howard.
    Values clarification in counseling and psychotherapy : practical strategies for
    individual and group settings/Howard Kirschenbaum.
    p. cm.
    Includes bibliographical references.
    ISBN 978–0–19–997218–0 (pbk. : alk. paper)
    1. Counseling psychology.   2. Psychotherapy.   3. Group psychotherapy.
    4. Values clarification.   I. Title.
    BF636.6.K565 2013
    158.3—dc23
    2012036877

9 8 7 6 5 4 3 2 1
Printed in the United States of America
on acid-free paper

To Sidney B. Simon and Merrill Harmin, my mentors in values clarification and friends of 50 years

■ CONTENTS

Values Clarification in Counseling and Psychotherapy

1 Paul's Case

A Brief Example of Values Clarification Counseling

The school counselor was sitting alone at his desk when Paul stormed into his office. He had known Paul for about a year. Paul was a high school sophomore—a bright, angry nonconformist who was working hard at finding himself and often suffered in the process. For example, the other boys in his school wore blue jeans and sneakers, while he wore black jeans and work boots. Other boys wore their hair short to medium, but he wore his long. The following dialogue is an accurate recollection of their conversation (Glaser & Kirschenbaum, 1980, p. 571).

PAUL: I've really had it with those guys! They hassle me all the time about my hair being long. What do they know, the creeps? I just want to get the hell out of here. I'm tired of being hit on by those jerks.

COUNSELOR: Sounds like you're really fed up with those guys, to the point that you'd really like to leave.

PAUL: Yeah. My hair is my business. I don't want to look like them ... they all look like carbon copies of each other. This is a free country, and a person has a right to wear his hair any way he wants to.

COUNSELOR: So your hair is an important statement of who you are? You really believe that it's your right to wear it any way you want to.

PAUL: Yeah ... but I'm getting really tired of those guys bugging me.

COUNSELOR: I hear how fed up you are. [Pause.] Let me ask, is your long hair primarily a social statement for you, or do you really like wearing it long ... the look and feel of it for you? If, for example, all the guys in the school were to let their hair grow, would you keep yours the way it is because you really like it ... or would you cut it short to make a statement about wanting to be different?

PAUL: Hmm, I never thought of that. I guess I grew it at first to spite my dad. It was the first thing I ever did that went against his orders ... that he couldn't make me change. Then after a while I got to really like it. Maybe someday I'll get bored with it, but right now I'd keep it long even if everybody else grew theirs.

COUNSELOR: So, more important than trying to make a point by wearing your hair long is the fact that you really *like* it that way.

PAUL: Yeah.

COUNSELOR: Have you thought about how you might be able to lessen their hassling?

PAUL: Yeah, I want to leave. I just can't take it. I mean, it was really bad today.

COUNSELOR: So the first thing that comes to mind is wanting to quit school.

PAUL: Yeah.

COUNSELOR: Can you think of any others?

PAUL: I could cut my hair... but I won't!

COUNSELOR: So cutting your hair is another alternative... [At this point, the counselor reached for a marker he kept handy and wrote on a board behind him "Quit" and, below that, "Cut hair."]

PAUL: I won't do it!

COUNSELOR: You feel pretty certain of that.... Might there be any other alternatives?

PAUL: [Long pause.] Well, maybe I could cut it a little—get one of those haircuts that are done by someone who knows what they're doing. I cut it now. Maybe if it was cut better it would look better.

COUNSELOR: Okay, cutting your hair just a little and well is another alternative. [He added "Professional cut" to the list.]

PAUL: But I haven't got the bucks to do it....

COUNSELOR: Uh-huh.... I can think of one or two other ideas. Would you like to hear them?

PAUL: Yeah.

COUNSELOR: Well, I had a friend with long hair who wore it tied back... and another who wore a headband to kind of keep it neat.

PAUL: Huh. I have a headband that a friend of mine once gave me. I wonder where I stashed it.

COUNSELOR: [After adding "tie back" and "headband" to the list.] Well, let's take a look at these ideas. How do you respond to each of them? And do you think they'd help to lessen the guys' hassling of you?

PAUL: I don't know. I still feel like quitting, but I think that I'd be giving in to them if I did. I think I'd feel a little funny wearing the headband—like I was playing hippie or something. I kind of like the idea of tying my hair back or getting a professional haircut...

COUNSELOR: So those two seem the best ideas to you, huh?

PAUL: Yeah. I guess that if I got it cut by someone, it would look better. It wouldn't look so homegrown.... Until I get some cash, though, I think I'll try tying it back. I have a friend who used to wear his hair that way.

COUNSELOR: So you're going to tie it back while you're figuring out a way to raise the money to get a good cut.... When do you think you'll begin tying it back—today... next week... ?

PAUL: Well,... maybe tomorrow morning.

COUNSELOR: Okay, then. Stop by and let me know how things turn out, all right?

PAUL: Yeah, thanks.

2   The Values Clarification Approach

▦ WHAT VALUES CLARIFICATION IS

Values clarification is a counseling approach designed to help people

- recognize or establish their goals, directions, and priorities;
- make choices and decisions to help them achieve their goals, directions, and priorities; and
- take action to implement their choices and decisions and thereby achieve their goals, directions, and priorities.

There are many *value-rich areas* in life that can be sources of satisfaction, joy, and meaning; sources of confusion and conflict around which people welcome or seek help; or areas that are neither particularly satisfying nor painful, but are lived in habitual, unreflective ways. These value-rich areas include, but are not limited to,

- friendship and relationships,
- work,
- money and material success,
- family,
- health (diet, drugs, exercise, etc.),
- love and sex,
- religion,
- personal tastes (clothes, hairstyle, etc.),
- leisure time,
- politics and social action,
- school,
- aging, death,
- diversity and identity issues, and
- meaning and purpose in life.

Values clarification is designed to assist people in making life's complicated decisions and choices—in *clarifying* and *actualizing* their priorities, goals, and values in these and other value-rich areas.

Values clarification can be used with people of virtually *all ages*, from a few years through old age. Values clarification can be used in a *developmental* or *preventive* way, helping people work on the value-rich areas at appropriate times in their development, as a way of helping them live richer, more meaningful lives and avoid problems that result from the lack of values clarity. Values clarification can also be used as a *remedial* counseling tool, helping people work on the issues that are currently causing them anywhere from mild to serious unhappiness or other difficulties resulting from a lack of value clarity or seeming inability to act on their goals and priorities.

Values clarification can be used to help *individuals* clarify and act on their values. It can do this in *individual counseling, group counseling,* and *psychoeducational* settings. Values clarification can also be used to help *groups and organizations* clarify their values, that is, clarify and actualize the values of the group or organization.

Values clarification can be used by many helping professionals, including counselors, psychologists, psychotherapists, social workers, pastoral counselors, physicians, nurses, educators, and teachers. It can also be used by nonprofessionals, including consultants, community organizers, youth leaders, parents, and friends, and with oneself. This book focuses on the use of values clarification in counseling and psychotherapy as they are practiced across the helping professions.

■ WHAT VALUES CLARIFICATION IS NOT

Values clarification is not, by itself, an approach to mental health counseling or psychotherapy. It is not intended to help people deal with deep-seated psychological and emotional issues in their lives. It is not intended to help them cope with strong and distressful feelings. It is not designed to help them recover from emotional hurts and traumas. It is not intended to help them with anxiety, depression, or other *DSM*-described mental health problems.

Nevertheless, *values clarification can be used as a valuable tool in many different mental health counseling and psychotherapy approaches,* from psychodynamic to cognitive behavioral to humanistic. (See chapter 10, "Values Clarification and Other Approaches to Counseling and Psychotherapy.") Likewise, it can play a helpful part in many different counseling and psychotherapeutic settings, including individual, marriage and family, rehabilitation, substance abuse, and other clinical settings. (See chapter 9, "Some Applications of Values Clarification Counseling.") Whatever the mental health approach or setting, values clarification can help clients identify goals they want to work on in counseling and therapy. It can help the counselor and client develop a therapeutic contract that incorporates the client's goals and helps the client take responsibility for his or her part in therapy. Clarifying questions and strategies can help a client gain further insight into his or her situation. And values clarification can be particularly helpful when clients have worked through their psychological and emotional difficulties to the point where they are ready to begin setting goals, making choices, implementing their recovery programs, and moving on with their lives.

To clarify this distinction further, *all counseling is not mental health counseling.* Rather, as the American Counseling Association (2010) defines it, "Counseling is a professional relationship that empowers diverse individuals, families and groups to accomplish mental health, wellness, education, and career goals." I would have added "life goals" because, in so many areas of living, individuals sometimes need help thinking through their goals and priorities, generating and evaluating different courses of action, deciding on the best direction to proceed, and developing strategies for acting on their decisions to realize their goals. In short, they are clarifying and realizing their values. *This is a normal part of living that all of us engage in.* We do it by ourselves. We do it with partners, friends, family, and colleagues. And sometimes, when we experience a particularly strong conflict between competing values or our decisions are particularly difficult, we seek professional help from counselors, be they pastoral counselors, life coaches, career counselors, mental health counselors, or psychotherapists.

Whatever the professional's job title or credentials, use of values clarification need not constitute mental health counseling. Mental health counseling, psychotherapy, and psychiatry are often understood as the diagnosis and treatment of psychological problems and mental disorders. As the positive psychology field has demonstrated, having clear values that one acts upon and realizes in one's life contributes to mental health (Frisch, 2006; Seligman et al., 2005), but being confused or conflicted over some of life's choices and dilemmas does not in itself constitute a mental health problem. If it did, just about every person would be suffering from mental health problems, for setting priorities, making difficult choices, and living by one's values are fundamental tasks of the human condition. Hence, I emphasize that values clarification is not a form of mental health counseling but can be integrated into mental health counseling and psychotherapy settings.

Finally, because values clarification historically has often been associated with programs in values education, moral education, and character education, it may also be useful to add that values clarification is not a complete or sufficient approach to values, moral, or character education. However, it can be used as a valuable tool in values, moral, and character education in homes, schools, and other youth settings. This is the subject of another book (Kirschenbaum, 1995).

■ A BRIEF HISTORY OF VALUES CLARIFICATION

Values clarification began as a counseling intervention in the 1950s. Educator Louis Raths (1963, 1972) noticed a distinct difference between the "emotional needs" and "value needs" of young people. He observed that children and youth had *emotional needs*, which he categorized as the need for belonging, achievement, economic security, freedom from fear, love and affection, freedom from intense feelings of guilt, self-respect, and understanding one's world. When these needs were unmet, he saw that young people exhibited various *emotional needs behaviors*, including becoming overly withdrawn, aggressive, submissive, or regressive or manifesting psychosomatic illness. To satisfy these unmet emotional needs, young people needed a variety of emotional supports and interventions from their caregivers—parents, teachers, youth leaders, and, if needed, mental health professionals. Raths's numerous practical dos and don'ts for meeting young people's emotional needs remain eminently useful suggestions today.

But Raths also noticed that, in addition to emotional needs, many children and youth had *value needs*. Before existentialism became widely known in the United States, Raths recognized that questions of meaning and value deserved serious attention. He saw that many youth were not clear on what was important to them or how to build lives that had meaning and satisfaction. Instead, they often demonstrated behavior patterns such as

- apathy—a lack of interest or enthusiasm for life's activities;
- flightiness—jumping from one interest or passion to another, rarely sticking with goals and commitments;
- overconforming—tending to always go along with the group;
- overdissenting—tending to always take the opposing position, not apparently out of principle, but just to be different; and
- poor decision making—choices and decisions that too often resulted in unsatisfying results for themselves and/or harm to others.

It wasn't that the young people who exhibited these behavior patterns had no preferences or goals, but that their preferences and goals never rose to sufficient clarity and importance to guide their behavior in clear, consistent, and satisfying ways. For Raths, the youth seemed to have *value indicators* but not *values*.

Value Indicators

Feelings	Goals
Likes	Choices
Dislikes	Actions
Preferences	Behaviors
Attitudes	Habits
Priorities	Patterns
Beliefs	Opinions
Etc.	

Raths thought that true *values* should synthesize these value indicators. They should have an affective component (e.g., feelings, likes, dislikes), a cognitive component (e.g., opinions, beliefs, choices), and a behavioral component (e.g., actions, patterns). There should be a consistency or congruence between one's affect, cognition, and behavior.

Raths wondered what could be done to help young people move away from the value-deficit behaviors and toward more value-driven behaviors. He observed that many young people rarely, if ever, had the opportunity to think about their lives in a supportive, yet challenging setting. So Raths began experimenting with an intervention designed to address this lack of values in the youth he worked with. He began asking young people "clarifying questions" about their lives—questions designed to help them close the gap between their feelings and choices and actual behavior, questions to encourage a process of developing and implementing a more full-blown values system. Moreover, he refrained from judging or evaluating the young people's responses. He observed that the questions alone seemed to start thought processes in motion that led to deeper reflection and ultimately action on the part of the youth. It appeared that when young people went through this process, when they began the process of thoughtfully reflecting on their value indicators, then their value needs or value-deficit behavior patterns often evolved into behavior patterns more indicative of clear values.

Value-Deficit Behaviors	Value-Driven Behaviors
Apathy	Purposefulness, enthusiasm
Flightiness	Commitment
Inconsistency	Consistency
Overconforming	Critical thinking
Overdissenting	Balance of conformity and individuality
Unsatisfying decisions	Satisfying decisions

Raths, inadvertently, was developing a new approach to counseling. Of course, he tied into a cultural tradition dating as far back as Socratic questioning, an 18th-century belief in rationalism, and Emerson's repeated reinforcement of Socrates' dictum, "The unexamined life is not worth having." More recently, counselors, psychotherapists, and teachers of all persuasions have known the value of a good, well-timed, clarifying question. But Raths went a bit further. Basing his thinking on the work of John Dewey (1909, 1939), he suggested that certain types of questions might be particularly useful in helping students examine more deeply the areas of values confusion and conflict in their lives. Raths's doctoral students Sidney B. Simon and Merrill Harmin, in the late 1950s and 1960s, amplified the theory and practice of values clarification, expanding Raths's description of *a value* as being an aspect of our life that meets seven criteria.

Prizing and Cherishing

1. Prized, Cherished—A value is something we prize and cherish; we care deeply about; it is very important to us.
2. Publicly Affirmed—A value is something we feel strongly enough about that we are willing to express it to others in appropriate circumstances; we are not ashamed of our values.

Choosing

3. Chosen from Alternatives—A value is chosen from various options. The process of choosing from alternatives helps increase the likelihood that the choice is prized and cherished.
4. Chosen after Considering Consequences—Recognizing the pros and cons and consequences of a choice for oneself, one's family, and one's community increases the likelihood of a choice that will be consistent with all one's goals and priorities.

5. Chosen Freely—Undue peer or authority pressure reduces the likelihood that one's choices will be meaningful and satisfying. Values are experienced as freely chosen, not coerced.

<u>Acting</u>

6. Acted Upon—A value is demonstrated in our behavior. We don't just talk about it; we live it.
7. Acted Upon Consistently—Values are seen consistently in our behavior patterns. The more it is a value, the more it is observed in our behavior and the fewer inconsistencies can be observed in our behavior.

Raths, Harmin, and Simon's (1966, 1978) *Values and Teaching* became an influential book in education. It demonstrated how to use the clarifying question and provided a number of value-clarifying exercises to help young people develop values, that is, aspects of their lives that meet all seven criteria. Simon and others continued to develop additional exercises and activities for values clarification, and Simon, Howe, and Kirschenbaum's (1972) subsequent book, *Values Clarification: A Handbook of Practical Strategies for Teachers and Students*, described 79 of these activities, with myriad examples. Each book sold more than 600,000 copies—truly blockbusters for professional volumes. Many other books by these and other authors followed— expanding values clarification theory, developing new activities, and applying the values clarification approach to career exploration, parenting, human sexuality, religion, health, life planning, and other settings. (For an annotated bibliography on values clarification, see Kirschenbaum, 1977b.)

Not only teachers but also school counselors, career counselors, pastoral counselors, scout leaders, group leaders, adult educators, and many other helping professionals working with youth and adults soon began to use values clarification. Because the training workshops on values clarification were primarily experiential, tens of thousands of adults in these workshops experienced the values clarification process firsthand and saw that it was a useful and powerful tool for working with adults as well as young people. It became a widely popular method to use in classrooms, in individual or group counseling settings, in psychoeducational interventions, in college teaching, and in counselor training.

But the leaders of values clarification at the time, myself included, overreached. Growing attention was being paid to the moral development of youth in the 1970s and 1980s—a perennial concern that became particularly prominent at the time because of increases in teen sex, drugs, violence, and other social problems. Rather than seeing values clarification as a useful tool that could play a helpful role in comprehensive values, moral, and character education, values clarification was offered as a complete and sufficient program of values and moral development—an answer to rising drug use, teen pregnancies, and the like. This simplistic proposition was untenable, and soon values clarification was subject to widespread criticism as an insufficient and problematic approach to youth development if it were not accompanied by more traditional approaches to instilling and modeling values. As I often observed, values clarification became so controversial that some school principals at the time would rather have been accused of having asbestos in their ceilings than using values clarification in their classrooms. Values clarification went the way of many fads and soon disappeared from popular attention.

Even though the popularity of values clarification per se faded, the methods and activities that values clarification proponents had introduced remained and even spread to become staples in the repertoire of counselors, group leaders, educators, human resource professionals, and trainers—for both youth and adults. However, although values clarification has continued to be used by many counselors and therapists over the decades, often it has been used without training or knowledge of its depth and versatility. Allied approaches, such as reality therapy and cognitive behavioral therapy, were developing simultaneously with values clarification, but those approaches were developed especially for counselors and therapists with a mental health focus, whereas values clarification was diffused over many professions. As a result, later generations of counselors and psychotherapists have been unfamiliar with values clarification, used pieces of it without knowing it, or used it relatively superficially without realizing its potential.

I was aware of these trends for many years. But in 2000, when I became department chair of Counseling and Human Development at the Margaret Warner Graduate School of Education and Human Development, University of Rochester, and began teaching basic and advanced counseling courses, values clarification and I came full circle. I found that my masters and doctoral counseling students were highly receptive to values clarification. They found it practical, helpful, and applicable to many roles in which they found themselves as community counselors, school counselors, pastoral counselors, and career counselors. My doctoral students, many of whom were experienced mental health counseling professionals, reminded and taught me how values clarification could be a useful tool in mental health counseling settings, including individual and group psychotherapy, rehabilitation counseling, marriage and family counseling, and counselor education itself.

Simultaneously, as I began attending conferences and workshops with counselors and psychotherapists around the United States and beyond, I kept on running into people who asked me, "Are you the Kirschenbaum who wrote that book on values clarification?" (It was usually the *Handbook of Practical Strategies* they were referring to.) They invariably would tell me things like "I still have that book today; I use it all the time," "I've used it so much I've had to hold it together with duct tape," and "It's so practical. How come we don't hear more about values clarification today?"

So this is a long overdue book for counseling, psychology, and related helping professions. For some counselors and therapists, it will be new—a new approach to working with clients, a new set of tools for enhancing their practice. For most, I suspect, this book will seem both new and familiar. Values clarification does have some things in common with some other counseling approaches (see chapter 10), so these things will seem familiar. One's reaction might be "Oh, I've done that for years" or "I've used that activity, but I've called it something different." At the same time, I believe readers will find much here to deepen their understanding of and repertoire for working with values, goal setting, decision making, and action planning in counseling and psychotherapy. Like the proverbial college student who exclaimed in his first writing class, "Hey, I've been speaking prose all my life and I never knew it!" many readers may feel that they have been using values clarification instinctively and, through this book, will gain insights about using it more consistently and effectively.

■ FURTHER DEVELOPMENTS IN VALUES CLARIFICATION

Because values clarification has gone through a number of changes over the years, with contributions by many authors and practitioners, there is no official theory of values clarification or complete agreement on definitions of terms. This last section of the introduction presents my own understanding of some basic concepts, practices, and terms in values clarification.

Criteria Versus Processes

Consistent with its history, the initial hypothesis of values clarification could be stated as follows:

> *Asking value-clarifying questions to a young person with values needs behaviors increases the likelihood that the person will demonstrate value-driven behaviors.*

Values Needs Behaviors	$\longrightarrow$	Value- Clarifying Questions	$\longrightarrow$	Value- Driven Behaviors

This was instructive as far as it went, but as values clarification continued to develop—being used with adults, expanding to seven criteria for a value, being more than value-clarifying questions—I suggested that a broader hypothesis was called for (Kirschenbaum, 1975). This is possible if we think of Raths, Harmin, and Simon's seven criteria for a value as *seven valuing processes.*

There is nothing wrong with defining a value as an aspect of one's life that meets the seven prizing-choosing-acting criteria. Arguably, among scores of definitions of the word *value* (see chapter 11), the Raths, Harmin, and Simon (1966) definition is one of the most detailed, comprehensive, and useful. It embraces affective, cognitive, and behavioral aspects of valuing. It challenges us to ask, "Are these beliefs *real* values? Do I really care about them? Have I examined them and chosen them? Do I act on them?" In other words, the seven criteria have a certain inspirational or motivational force to lead us toward more complete or mature values.

However, the seven criteria are not operational for the purposes of identifying or measuring values. How proud must someone be of a belief before it may be considered a value? How many alternatives must be considered before the criterion of choice among alternatives is satisfied? How often must action be repeated? And so on. It would be futile to try to set arbitrary cutoff points at which each criterion is met, when values range from favorite hobbies to enduring life principles and when each individual's situation is so different. In fact, no one but the individual can determine when the criteria for his or her values are achieved. But individuals do not clarify their values to achieve some theoretical goal of an official, seven-criteria value. Rather, they use the prizing-choosing-acting processes when they feel these processes are helpful toward clarifying and achieving their goals.

So I have come to think of the seven criteria of a value as also being *seven valuing processes*. Some have argued that there may be more than *seven* valuing processes (e.g., Kirschenbaum, 1973), but for the purposes of this book, the seven original criteria/processes of values clarification are maintained. Thinking in terms of valuing *processes* allows us to understand some of the processes in slightly different ways. This is discussed further in the following chapter.

The Core Hypothesis

Reframing the seven criteria as seven valuing processes also allows us to state what I would call the *core hypothesis* of values clarification today:

> *By using the seven valuing processes, we increase the likelihood that our living in general or a decision in particular will have positive value for us and be constructive in the social context.*

Or stated from the point of view of the professional:

> *Engaging clients in the seven valuing processes increases the likelihood that their living in general or a decision in particular will have positive value for them and be constructive in the social context.*

Value-Deficit Behaviors		Value-Driven Behaviors
Apathy		Enthusiasm
Flightiness		Purposefulness
Inconsistency $\longrightarrow$ VALUES $\longrightarrow$		Consistency
Overconforming CLARIFICATION		Balance of conformity
Overdissenting		and individuality
Poorer decisions,		Better decisions,
personally and socially		personally and socially

Hypotheses, of course, are meant to be tested; hence, the topic of research on values clarification is discussed in chapter 11. At this point, I refer to my own experience with the hypothesis in using values clarification for more than 45 years with individuals and groups in a wide variety of settings from working with students in classrooms, to doing group counseling with young adults in a detention facility, to counseling couples, to working with individuals on career choices, to two weeks ago, sitting with a friend in her nursing home room, where she was under hospice care apparently near the end, and she told me that she wanted to go home. Rather than dismiss what to many would have seemed like an unrealistic idea—she could hardly move without help—I counseled her on the pros and cons of spending her final days or weeks where she was or at home. And when, having no family, she asked me, "What do *you* think I should do?" I said, "I can't make that choice for you, Lyn. Only you can decide whether the benefits of being at home are worth the additional costs and difficulties. But I will support you in whatever choice you make." She died a few days later. Whether she let the matter drop or made a conscious decision to stay where she was, I am convinced that my taking her desire seriously (as did hospice), honoring her autonomy, and being a companion to her in thinking through her dilemma made her feel less alone and more completely and competently human in her final days.

So in my own experience, the hypothesis is supported. I do not see people making worse choices because they have examined the potential pros and cons and consequences of their options; that is, they have looked before they leaped. I do not see people making poorer decisions because they have asked themselves, "What is important to me? Is this something I believe in?" I do not see people making destructive choices because they examined the forces and pressures (peer, authority, economic, social, etc.) influencing their decision. Nor do I see people harming themselves by discovering or confronting the discrepancies between their goals and priorities, their beliefs, and how they are living their lives.

My own experience is confirmed by many thousands of practitioners—counselors, therapists, teachers, youth workers, and others—who have used values clarification in diverse settings over at least four decades. I continually hear anecdotes from counselors who say, "I have this group of drug offenders [or gang members, unwed teen mothers, etc.] who are usually very difficult to work with. They just don't like to open up to authority figures or each other. But I came in and asked them to do the 'One-Minute Autobiography' and 'What's in Your Wallet?' strategies, I told them there were no right answers, and I couldn't get them to stop talking!" Or "I have this client who doesn't say much. So I asked her to do the '20 Things I Love to Do' activity, and she loved it. That gave us so much to talk about, and pretty soon she was telling me what her real concerns were." Or "What I like about values clarification is that everyone has something to say. I give the group some 'Sentence Stems' and go around the circle. Of course, they can pass, but they hardly ever do. Even the quiet ones in the group seem to come out of their shells a bit and are accepted into the group." These are experienced professionals. If they had any clues that values clarification was fostering narcissism, selfishness, and destructive behavior in clients, they wouldn't keep using the approach. Rather, they report that not only are clients more engaged and forthcoming but also they are more civil, respectful, thoughtful, and introspective during the process and often beyond.

All this is not to say that the process of values clarification is easy or risk free. Having more alternatives can make decision making slower, more complicated, and sometimes agonizing. Living habitually is often easier than making new choices. Even people who are reflective about their decisions sometimes make choices they later regret. Acting on one's values can sometimes disrupt one's own life, the lives of those around us, and even the social and political order. Even when we believe a decision is right *for us*, how can we know if, in the long run, it will be constructive or destructive in the social context? When one decides to leave a marriage or a job, for example, the spouse or fellow employees may feel supportive, but they may also feel betrayed. When is it appropriate to put one's own needs and values above those of others, and when do the values of love for or duty to others trump one's own self-actualization? Some of the multicultural implications of these questions are discussed further in chapter 11, but for now the point is that values clarification, like life itself, is not necessarily easy, and it offers no guarantees for a Hollywood ending. The hypothesis says that using the seven valuing processes makes the desired outcomes only *more likely*. Values clarification is not a panacea.

To understand the values clarification hypothesis, it is also important to recognize that *all* the valuing processes are important. If only *some* of the valuing processes are engaged, one easily ends up with caricatures of values clarification—for example, individuals who think only of what *they* want to do, what's important to *them*, and what *they* have freely chosen but neglect to consider the consequences for others and do not stop to consider how acting on *some* of their values may interfere with achieving their *other* values.

Finally, it should be acknowledged that *the values clarification approach is not the only path to values clarification*. Faith, mindfulness, meditation, cultivating the attitudes of acceptance and gratitude, and service toward others are among other paths to clear, satisfying, socially constructive values that philosophers, religious leaders, and psychologists have advocated through the centuries. But neither are *these* panaceas. Practitioners of these disciplines may also suffer from confusion and conflict in values.

Terminology

Values Clarification or Values Realization

For the past 20 years, Sidney Simon, one of the three original leaders in the values clarification approach, has used the term *values realization* to describe his work in which he combines values clarification with other personal growth approaches (Knapp & Simon, 2000). In some ways, I think *values realization* would be a better term for values clarification.

The term *values clarification* implies becoming clear about one's values, which is certainly a major part of values clarification. But values clarification also means acting on one's values, bringing those values to fruition in one's life. The word *clarification* does not capture that aspect of values clarification. The word *realization*, however, conveys both meanings. One is to become aware of or recognize one's values. The other is to bring about, effect, implement, or actualize one's values. To realize one's values is both to recognize and to actualize them in one's life. Then again, to *realize* implies that the values were there all along, and one finally recognized them, which does not do justice to this aspect of values clarification. Clarifying is a more active process than that. It is not just realizing or recognizing, but figuring out, working on, prioritizing, and deciding. The term *clarifying* conveys that active valuing process better than *realizing*.

Terminology aside, some friends and colleagues suggested it might be better to use the term *values realization* in this book to appear fresh and new and to avoid some of the past controversies or misunderstandings about values clarification. Values realization might sell better.

In the end, I decided to stick with values clarification for two reasons. First and most important, values clarification has a long and rich tradition that I am proud of. This book builds on that tradition, and it is fitting and proper to call it what it is. Second, calling something by a new name so that it appears new may be an effective marketing tactic, but in a professional context like this, it strikes me as tacky at best and deceptive at worst. So *values clarification* it is! However, from time to time, I use the phrases "values realization," "realize one's values," and similar constructions when appropriate to convey that aspect of the valuing process.

Value-Clarifying or Values-Clarifying

Some authors and publishers have preferred the term *value clarification* over *values clarification*. Indeed, the publisher of my fourth book on the subject (Kirschenbaum, 1977a) insisted that the title be *Advanced Value Clarification* instead of the plural form, which my coauthors and I had always used previously and have used since. Similarly, when modifying a noun, as in "value-clarifying question," authors sometimes say *value*-clarifying, sometimes say *values*-clarifying, and sometimes leave out the hyphen. I use both the singular and plural forms, with the hyphen, depending on which sounds better to me in that instance. In some cases, I could articulate the reason. For example, when applied to a person's whole values system, "values-clarifying" seems more appropriate. Sometimes I am not sure I could explain my rationale; it just sounds better. In any case, the inconsistency is intentional, but the meaning is virtually the same.

Counselors or Psychotherapists

As the title suggests, this book is about using values clarification in counseling *and* psychotherapy, whether offered by professional counselors, counseling psychologists, clinical psychologists, social workers, pastors, or others. However, it is tedious to keep repeating "counseling and psychotherapy" or "counselors and psychotherapists" every time there is a reference to these fields. I often *do* use both terms, but more often I use just the word *counseling* or *counselor* for short. In most cases, when counseling or counselor is used alone, it is intended to apply to counseling *and* psychotherapy. Exceptions are references to career counseling, pastoral counseling, or other applications where the context suggests that the term *counseling* is intended to stand alone.

He or She

The way I try to avoid repetitive "he or she," "him or her," and similar awkward constructions in my writing—while also avoiding being sexist, while also avoiding wordy circumlocutions around the pronoun problem, and while also avoiding "they" and "them" when I really want the reader to visualize an individual—is to vary the gender assignment in each work. That is, in one book or article, I use the male pronoun for the counselor or therapist and the female pronoun for the client. In the next book or article, I reverse the pattern. Because in the last piece I wrote (Kirschenbaum, 2012), the professional was "he" and the client "she," in this work the pronouns will be female for the counselor and therapist and male for the client or other individual.

3 Implementing Values Clarification

■ **THE OVERALL VALUES CLARIFICATION PROCESS**

Whether in individual counseling or psychotherapy, group counseling or therapy, or psychoeducational groups, implementing values clarification involves the following components.

1. Identify a values issue.
2. Use one or more questions or activities to engage the client or group members in reflecting and working on the issue.
3. Encourage the seven valuing processes.
4. Create an atmosphere of safety, respect, and nonimposition of values.

These are not necessarily sequential steps; rather, they overlap. For example, in individual counseling, one may begin by establishing an atmosphere of safety and respect before identifying a particular values issue to work on, whereas in a psychoeducational group, the values issue the group will focus on may be identified before the group ever meets.

1. Identify a Values Issue

At best, the client identifies the issue or dilemma to work on. This is most consistent with values clarification and with counseling in general.

The *value-rich areas* listed in chapter 2 are among the most frequent *areas of confusion and conflict* that clients may want to work on:

Friendship and relationships	Work
Money and material success	Family
Health	Love and sex
Religion	Personal tastes
Leisure time	Politics and social action
School	Aging and death
Meaning and purpose in life	

These are general areas. More typically, a client has a particular issue or issues within the general area. Under "work," for example, a client may be struggling with figuring out a career direction, finding a job, coping with a difficult boss, overcoming burnout, or achieving balance between work and other life priorities.

Although the client typically takes the lead in identifying the values issue or dilemma to work on, there are occasions when a client is mandated to work on an issue and the client and counselor don't have much choice in the matter. But even when this occurs—for example, when a client is required to work on substance abuse or anger management—values clarification can help the client take some responsibility for the counseling. For example, the counselor could ask the clarifying question, "Is there anything you want to get out of our time together?" "You say you can work on your anger yourself. You've said that in the past and then gotten into trouble. What do you think is different now than when you've tried to go it alone in the past?" Or she could use the Values Continuum strategy (see chapter 6, #4) and ask the client, "On a scale from 1 to 10, where 1 means 'I have absolutely no interest in working on my anger management; it's a total waste of time,' and 10 means 'I know I need to work on my anger management and I'm really looking forward to doing that here,' what number would you put yourself at on that scale?" In other words, values-clarifying questions and strategies can help even resistant clients clarify their goals and feelings about counseling. This is often a helpful beginning.

Counselors also sometimes find themselves in a psycho-educational role, working with a group on a particular topic such as careers, weight management, sexuality, or retirement planning, to name a few. Again, hopefully, the participants have chosen to be in these groups and have shared what they hope to get from the group, and the counselor has responded to their goals. Still, the counselor may choose the particular topic for a given session or exercise.

So whether the topic has been chosen by the client, by the counselor, by both, or by neither, values clarification begins with the identification of the value-rich area to work on.

2. Use One or More Questions or Activities to Engage the Client or Group Members in Reflecting and Working on the Issue

Values clarification has four main delivery modes, illustrated in the figure below. Depending on the setting, counselors and therapists typically use any or all of *three* of them: the clarifying question, the clarifying interview, and values clarification strategies.

The *value-clarifying question* is a single question the counselor asks that engages the client in using one of the seven valuing processes. It is an intervention used in individual or group counseling.

The *clarifying interview* is a series of value-clarifying questions and possibly an occasional values clarification strategy that engage the client in using most or all of the seven valuing processes to work on a value dilemma the client is experiencing. It is the equivalent of a counseling session.

A values clarification *strategy* is a structured activity that has a value-clarifying question at its core and builds on that question with additional questions and exercises. It can be used in individual or group counseling.

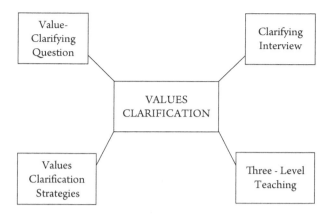

Subsequent chapters of this book are devoted to each of these modes of values clarification. Depending on the situation, clients may respond to the values clarification question, interview, or strategy through reading, writing, thinking, speaking, drawing, or participating in other structured activities.

A fourth delivery mode for values clarification is *three-level teaching*. In this mode, an instructor goes beyond the facts level and beyond the concepts and skills level to work with students on the *values level*. On the values level, the instructor uses value-clarifying questions and strategies to help students relate the study content to their own lives and values, thereby both furthering values clarification and motivating the students to better appreciate the subject matter. Because this book is focused on counseling and not teaching, three-level teaching is not addressed further. However, counselors and therapists who sometimes find themselves in the role of teacher, instructor, or educator in the university or community may want to explore three-level teaching on another occasion (see Harmin, Kirschenbaum, & Simon, 1973). One example of three-level teaching—around counselor/clinical education and supervision—is given in chapter 9.

3. Encourage the Seven Valuing Processes

The clarifying questions and activities the values clarification counselor uses are not random. Each question or activity is intended to engage the client in one or more of the seven valuing processes. The seven processes were introduced briefly in the last chapter. Here they are discussed further.

Prizing

a. Prizing and Cherishing

Clarifying questions and strategies help clients become more aware of what they prize and cherish in life, what their priorities are, what they are for or against, and what is important to them. Figuring out what is important to us goes hand in hand with figuring out what we *want*, which leads to establishing goals. Hence, one aspect of this valuing process is *goal setting*.

b. Affirming and Communicating

This process is broader than simply publicly affirming our values, although that is part of it. The act of sharing, communicating, or affirming our feelings, opinions, beliefs, goals, and other value indicators with others is in itself clarifying. When clients in individual therapy or group counseling state a value indicator out loud—that is, share it with one or more other persons—they often do not stop there. They reflect on it further. Later they muse, "I just said such-and-such to my therapist or to the whole group. Is that right? Is that what I really feel or believe? Did I exaggerate? Did I understate it? Wouldn't it be more accurate to say it this way? And now that I think about it, some new feelings are emerging and new thoughts are occurring to me." Through this ongoing process, they further clarify what they do and do not feel, believe, think, and want. Considering "If others knew..." or "If I were to tell others..." often raises issues of self-concept, including "what's important to me" versus "what's important to others." So sharing is clarifying on many levels, even if no one responds. And when the counselor or group members do respond directly or indirectly to what one says, that can be further clarifying.

Affirming is part of the values realization process in another way. When we affirm our values—whether by sharing them with one other person or by writing a letter to the editor—we help bring those values into the world. Some religious communities would call this "witnessing," "giving witness," or "testifying." Affirming how we feel, believe, and act is a form of acting on our values. It is a step toward creating the world we want for ourselves and others.

Choosing

c. Considering Alternatives

Generating and considering alternatives often means looking at different concrete options for resolving a dilemma or taking action. But examining alternatives also means looking at an issue from different angles, from alternative perspectives. Clarifying questions and strategies do both. They help clients broaden their horizons, use their imaginations, and think outside the box to come up with new and better ideas for the personal, social, or even political dilemmas they may be confronting.

d. Considering Consequences

Again, this is shorthand for a more complex process. Yes, values clarification questions and strategies involve clients in thinking through the possible results or outcomes of different decisions or courses of action. They also involve clients in examining the pros and cons of different alternatives.

As I will repeat in other chapters, considering the possible outcomes of alternative choices does not mean only looking at the consequences for oneself, that is, examining the pros and cons in terms of one's own self-interest. A full or mature valuing process includes examining the pros, cons, and consequences of one's choices and actions for others, for society, and for the planet. Thus values clarification questions or strategies will, when appropriate, ask clients to consider what the choices they are considering might mean for their family, coworkers, congregation, community, country, environment, or other significant relationships.

e. Choosing Freely

Values clarification does not claim to resolve the dilemma of whether humans have some measure of free will or are controlled by fate, prior behavioral reinforcements, social context, God's will, or other determining influences. Rather, choosing freely is a subjective criterion. Clarifying questions and activities ask clients to get in touch with *a felt sense* of the extent to which their attitudes and opinions, the decisions they are making, or the way they are living their lives feels like *their own* choice or whether they have a sense of having been influenced more than they would like by peer, authority, or other pressures. In values clarification, the goal is to help clients ·make choices that feel like their own, that they can take responsibility for.

Surely our choices are not all our own. Social, economic, and political forces exist independently of us and influence our choices to a greater or lesser degree. Part of the valuing process of choosing freely is helping clients examine those forces and influences on them. Yet, in the end, each individual has a choice of how he or she will respond to those forces and influences, and this is what values clarification questions and activities often ask clients to do—to decide, with knowledge of the forces influencing their decisions and of the potential consequences of different choices, "What choice will *I* make in these circumstances?"

Choosing freely involves recognizing not only the various current influences on our choices and decisions but also the importance of prior influences. Therefore, values clarification questions and strategies often ask clients to look back to earlier times in their lives to examine where their value indicators (goals, beliefs, habits, etc.) may have come from. How were their value indicators typically inculcated and instilled in them? Who were their role models? On a particular issue, what did their parents believe, and how did they act? When do they first remember holding a particular belief? There is no presupposition that values inculcated earlier in life are good or bad or that any changes are needed. Rather, the goal is for clients to take charge of their lives by choosing to affirm their beliefs, goals, choices, and actions or to establish new value indicators and values to live by.

As a student of mine from a Cambodian background (Chitaphong, 2004) wrote in a paper on values clarification, "I do not believe anyone can honestly say they make daily decisions free of value-laden or moral influences. No one is free of the influence of others, but within such parameters and influences there exists some liberty to navigate our lives. As limited as the choice(s) may be, having the choice itself is liberating and empowering. Potentially choice increases dignity, self-worth and hope. Limiting choices and alternatives could potentially lead to depression, helplessness, hopelessness and death (physical or spiritual)" (p. 6).

Acting

f. Acting

Values-clarifying questions or strategies ask clients to consider *what they do* and *what they might do* about the issues being focused on. What we do in our lives, how we behave, is one indicator of what we value. But what we do is sometimes merely habit. The values clarification process asks clients to determine whether their behavior is consistent with their beliefs, goals, and priorities and whether they want to continue or change their behavior.

Clarifying questions and strategies also help clients to *take action* on their goals, to close the gap between what they say they believe or they want and how they are actually living their lives. Often clarifying questions and clarifying interviews help clients figure out the *first step* or *next step* toward achieving their goals.

g. Acting Consistently, With a Pattern

Another value-clarifying process is to examine and establish patterns in our behavior, because it is the things we do repeatedly, on a regular basis, that may represent our strongest values. They may also represent our strongest habits or compulsions. So values clarification helps clients look at their behavior patterns and, like single actions, determine whether these are unthoughtful habits and paths of least resistance or conscious choices for how they want to behave and live their lives. Similarly, the values clarification process often helps clients build *more* of the behaviors that represent their goals and ideals into their lives, so that their patterns of action truly help them achieve what they want in the value-rich areas of living and "live a life of value" (Merchey, 2006).

Still another facet of this valuing process is helping clients look at the inconsistencies in the actions they do and don't take in their lives. It can be uncomfortable to face how our actions are not always consistent with one another or with our beliefs and goals. Value-clarifying questions and strategies can invite clients to examine these contradictions and inconsistencies in a safe, relatively nonthreatening way.

4. Create an Atmosphere of Safety, Respect, and Nonimposition of Values

Whether in individual counseling or group settings, the counselor fosters a safe psychological atmosphere characterized by *respect for self* and *respect for others*.

Respect for Self	Respect for Others
Right to participate	No put-downs or intimidation
Right to pass	Good listening
Right to own opinion	Consideration

The client's self-respect is fostered by making it clear that the client has the right to participate, the right to pass, and the right to his own views and values. Clients can choose to participate in an activity or not. When I'm still establishing a trusting relationship with an individual client, I may find myself saying things like "Can I ask you a question about that?" or "If you'd rather not go there, that's okay" or "An activity occurs to me that might help you think about that issue more deeply. It involves making a list. Are you willing to give it a try?" Later, as more trust is established and the client knows he can decline to respond or to do an activity, such explicit requests and reminders may not be necessary.

In group settings, by accepting all answers equally—not praising or rewarding some while ignoring or minimizing others—the counselor conveys to every client or group member: "*Your* contributions are important. I take you seriously." This fosters self-respect and models respect for others. Because peer pressure can easily occur in group settings, it is very important to establish and reiterate their right to say, "I pass." I often remind group members, "If you have something to say, that's fine. And if you'd like to just listen, that's fine, too. Just say, 'I pass,' and we'll go on to the next person" or simply "Remember, you can pass." And when someone does pass, I might say, "Good. I'm glad you felt free to pass. That's everyone's right."

Respect for others in a group setting is fostered by using group methods that give everyone a chance to participate, by communicating the expectation of good listening, by modeling consideration, and by not accepting put-downs or intimidation. Whether this is done by establishing some ground rules at the beginning or by modeling respectful behavior and dealing with exceptions when they occur ("Hey, he's got a right to his opinion. We don't all have to think the same here") is a matter of counselor preference. I often do both.

As discussed in chapter 11, all counseling approaches have values implicit in the counseling process. Beyond that, in an approach like values clarification, which has as its goal supporting clients in clarifying and acting on *their own values*, it is important to do everything possible to avoid or minimize the imposition of values on the client. There are two main ways this is done. First is to *pose clarifying questions and activities that do not have an implied right answer or better answer*. For example, if one asked a marriage counseling group, "When it comes to having the courage to share a difficult feeling with your partner, where would you fall on this continuum? On one end is 'Brave Bob.' On the other end is 'Cowardly Carl.' Where are you on that line?"—that's a pretty loaded question. Most people think it's better to be brave than cowardly. So learning to ask clarifying questions or strategies that don't impose the society's or the counselor's values on clients is one way to both avoid or minimize values imposition *and* to create a safe and respectful atmosphere in which clients feel nondefensive and free to examine the issues more deeply. ("Foolhardy Fred" and "Cowardly Carl" might be a better set of end points. They are equally value-laden.) In the next chapter, more will be said about asking good clarifying questions.

The second important thing counselors and therapists can do to avoid imposing their values on clients is to *respond to clients' statements with nonjudgmental acceptance*. Acceptance does not mean agreement with what the client says. It means recognizing the client's right to his own views, decisions, and actions; acknowledging the client's choices; and not attempting to persuade or steer the client toward other views, decisions, or actions. Some counselors use the phrase, "There are no right answers here." This does not mean that there is no such thing as right or wrong or better or worse, but that in this setting, it is the *client's* job, not the counselor's, to determine what the client's *own best answers* are. If the counselor wants the client to think more deeply about his own goals, choices, and behaviors, this is best accomplished by avoiding any verbal or nonverbal judgment of the content of client's responses, whether positive or negative.

Nonjudgmental acceptance is not the same as taking a laissez-faire approach toward the client. One can accept a client's statement and come back with further clarifying responses or questions. That is how values clarification works. The further clarifying response, question, or strategy is not intended to persuade the client toward a different decision or course of action but to help the client utilize the seven valuing processes to increase the likelihood that his choices and actions will be satisfying for all concerned.

Nonjudgmental acceptance may be difficult to achieve or maintain when the things clients say and do are in conflict with the counselor's own professional judgment or own personal and moral values. The topic of counselor–client value conflicts is the subject of chapter 8.

■ COUNSELOR AND THERAPIST SELF-DISCLOSURE

The counseling profession and different therapeutic approaches have differing views on the subject of counselor self-disclosure. In a recent survey of members of the American Counseling Association, 87% of respondents thought that "self-disclosing to a client" was, in general, an acceptable ethical practice (Neukrug & Milliken, 2011). Although self-disclosure in general may be ethical, just how congruent and self-disclosing should a counselor or therapist be about her own feelings, opinions, values, and life outside the professional relationship? Whatever one's counseling approach, decisions often must be made on the spot when a client asks, "How are you?" or "Are you married?" or "What do you think of me?" or "What would you do in my situation?" or other questions that invite self-disclosure or sharing one's own values.

The general subject of counselor self-disclosure is beyond the scope of this book, but a brief discussion is in order of whether, when, and how it may be appropriate for the counselor using values clarification to share her own values with the client or to answer some of the same values questions she asks her clients. On this subject, I distinguish between individual counseling, group therapy, and psychoeducational groups.

In individual counseling and group therapy, I prefer to avoid disclosing my own responses to the clarifying questions or strategies I might pose to a client or group. I want to keep the focus on the client(s), and particularly in individual counseling, my disclosing my responses to questions I've asked would run the risk of interrupting the client's process or imposing my values on the client. An exception might be if a client doesn't understand a clarifying question I've asked or doesn't understand how to do a clarifying strategy. Then I might give a response of my own as an example. But I would do this only if I thought my limited self-disclosure would be useful as an example or in furthering our counseling relationship. Otherwise, I would give a more impersonal example or rephrase the question.

Another exception might be when offering an additional alternative for the client's consideration, as in Paul's case in the first chapter, where the counselor shared two ideas his friends had tried. If I do think it might be appropriate to share an alternative of my own, I would probably preface it by asking, "Would you be interested in how I handle situations like this?" There is no hard-and-fast rule here, other than trying to do what is in the best interest of the client. Different counselors are comfortable with different levels of self-disclosure and can make that work in their therapeutic relationships.

In psychoeducational groups, by contrast, the counselor or therapist has more latitude to *share her values without imposing them.* Counselors should not feel they must participate in every activity or answer every question they ask a group, but it is often very helpful for counselors to take a turn in sharing their response to a question or participating in a values clarification strategy. For example, a counselor could share where her name would go on a Values Continuum ("about half way between Jack and Ellen"), make an "I Learned Statement" (Strategy 15) of her own at the end of an activity, or volunteer to receive a Group Interview (13) at some point. Good things can result from the counselor taking a turn:

- It helps establish a more trusting relationship between the counselor and group members.
- It models for group members how to respond in an appropriate way—in terms of topic, length of response, voice, degree of self-disclosure, and so on.
- It helps group members feel less stigmatized to know that others, like the counselor, sometimes deal with the same issues in their lives.
- It gives the group members another alternative to think about—and possibly a more mature or healthier alternative than is currently in the group's repertoire. (For example, a counselor in an anger management group can take a turn describing "a time this week when you handled your anger in a way you felt proud of.")
- If the counselor passes, it can model that form of self-respect for the group.
- If the whole group is divided into pairs or trios for an activity and one person needs a partner or two people need a third to complete their trio, the counselor's joining a group helps the numbers work out.

There are a number of ways the counselor can share her values with the group but not impose them.

- *Limit your airtime.* Keep your sharing brief. Don't monopolize. Let the client(s) do most of the talking. Don't turn your comment into a lecture.

- *Keep it personal.* Give your opinion as *your* opinion. Tell your story as *your* story. Don't generalize or give it a moral for everyone.
- *Avoid teaching or preaching.* Clients readily pick up when you are giving them a lesson. This implies to them that you are not sincere about wanting them to think and choose for themselves, but rather you are now teaching them the right way to think or behave.
- *Be strategic about timing.* Occasionally, you may want to go first to give the group an idea of what you are asking them to do. But preferably, go last after all the group members have had the opportunity to think and speak for themselves, or go near the end so it doesn't seem that you always get the last word.

■ INDIVIDUAL AND GROUP FORMATS

Many different individual and group formats can be used for values clarification. In individual counseling, the variety of formats takes the form of different ways of responding. Probably most of the time, the client will respond verbally. But many values clarification questions or activities can invite a written response as well. Thus clients might use paper and pencil or pen to rank choices in order, indicate their position on a continuum, do an inventory and coding, complete unfinished sentences, or draw a picture that reflects their response.

In group counseling and psychoeducational groups, clients can utilize the same variety of response modes, verbally or in writing. But there are also many ways to vary the group dynamic. These include the following.

- *Individual reflection.* In the whole group, individuals respond to a value-clarifying question or strategy by reflecting silently or in writing.
- *Whole group random response.* In the whole group, members respond aloud randomly, in no particular order, each member having the opportunity for one turn.
- *Whole group discussion.* In the whole group, members respond randomly, in no particular order, each member having the opportunity to respond more than once.
- *Whole group whip.* In the whole group, members respond in order, whipping around the circle, each member taking a very brief turn or passing. For example, they might simply read or say their completed Unfinished Sentence (14) or state their Rank Order (2) without explanation or elaboration.
- *Whole group circle.* In the whole group, members respond in order, going around the circle, each member taking a turn or passing. However, unlike a whip, members can elaborate on or explain their response. For example, they might say their completed sentence or their rank order and also expand on their sentence or explain the thought process behind their ranking.
- *Whole group interview focus.* In the whole group, the focus remains on one member who receives an extended interview from the counselor or the group.

- *Small groups.* The whole group can be subdivided into pairs, trios, quartets, or other sizes for discussions or activities. Some activities work better in pairs, others in trios, and so on. If it does not matter otherwise, I like to vary the small-group sizes for variety.
- *Small-group random.* Each member of the small group randomly gets a chance to share their response to a value-clarifying question or strategy.
- *Small-group circle.* Each member of the small group, in any order they or you decide upon, gets a chance to share his response to a value-clarifying question or strategy.
- *Small-group discussion.* The small group talks freely among themselves on the topic or sharing their response to a values clarification strategy.
- *Small-group interview focus.* In each small group, the focus is on one member, who receives an extended interview from the other group members. One or more members might take a turn receiving an interview, that is, receiving the group's focus and questions for a period of time.
- *Physical movement.* Group members move to a place in the room to indicate their response to a question, for example, placing themselves along a Values Continuum (4), moving to one side or another for an Either-Or Forced Choice (5), or moving to one of four locations to indicate their top choice of four alternatives.
- *Combination.* Many of these group formats can be combined, for example, (a) beginning with a circle in which each member gets one turn and then having an open discussion or (b) moving to one side of the room or the other and then pairing with someone from the other side.

One of the major contributions of the early values clarification movement in the late 1960s and 1970s was that it helped popularize the use of individual, small-group, and large-group experiential exercises to create high levels of participation and motivation in educational and personal growth settings. Values clarification did not invent these group formats, but values clarification questions and strategies readily lend themselves to the varying formats. When counselors utilize a variety of clarifying strategies along with a variety of individual and group formats, it increases the likelihood of creating and sustaining a high level of client interest and engagement.

4 The Value-Clarifying Question

A counselor in Colorado likes to ask her clients a simple value-clarifying question: "What are your goals?" or "What are your goals for yourself?" She (Shinbaum, 2009) describes the many benefits that often follow:

- It helps them set goals.
- It helps them expand their goals.
- It helps them refocus on their goals.
- It creates positive energy.
- It raises self-concept issues ("Who am I to have goals? Am I entitled?").
- It helps them explore whether they are trying to achieve their own goals or other people's goals.
- It raises resistance to change ("Do I really want to achieve these goals or stay as I am?").
- It raises other counseling issues to work on.

All this from a simple value-clarifying question.

The value-clarifying question or values-clarifying question—the terms are used interchangeably—is the foundation for values clarification in counseling and other settings. Values-clarifying questions grow out of the seven valuing processes. They help clients better identify what they prize and cherish. They help clients make decisions and examine their choices in greater depth. They help clients take action to accomplish their goals and close the gap between their feelings, beliefs, and actual behavior.

▪ HOW CLARIFYING QUESTIONS WORK

How is this so? How can simply asking someone a thought-provoking question cause him to narrow the gap between his beliefs and behaviors? One answer is that human beings have an inherent need to resolve cognitive dissonance (Festinger, 1957). When we have two or more ideas that appear to contradict one another— the world is flat; the world is round—we need to resolve the conundrum. We can do this by choosing one idea over the other (the world can't be round because it looks flat and because people would fall off the sides and bottom of a round earth; the world can't be flat because ships sailing a long distance never fall off the edge) or by gaining more information that provides another way of understanding the competing ideas.

Using the theory of cognitive dissonance, psychologist Milton Rokeach (1961, 1973) did some important early work on values that helps us understand how the values clarification process works. He developed his values survey in which he had subjects rank in order their terminal values and instrumental values. Terminal values were ultimate or universal values like truth, beauty, faith, love, and freedom. Instrumental values were those that presumably led to the terminal values, for example, money, material possessions, good looks, recreation, and a nice home. Subjects ranked 18 terminal and 18 instrumental values on "How important are these values to *you?*" He also gathered data on how they spent their time and money and otherwise lived their lives. Then Rokeach and his students showed the subjects how their behavior often contradicted their stated values. He pointed out, for example, "You say you value freedom, but you haven't given any of your money to support the civil rights movement." "You say you value family, but you also say you spend little time with them." After creating this level of cognitive dissonance in his clients, Rokeach tracked changes in their behavior, if any. He found that, indeed, there was a statistically significant tendency for the subjects to alter their behavior to narrow the gap between their values and behavior and that most of the change was in altering the behavior to fit the values rather than altering the values to fit the behavior. In short, a good, well-timed value-clarifying question or activity can lead to growth and change.

I have another theory for why values-clarifying questions and activities work. I'll introduce it with a story. Years ago, in a weeklong summer workshop for teachers and counselors, we asked some of the participants to invite their own children to come in the next morning so we could demonstrate values clarification strategies with actual young people. On the panel of eight or so youth from elementary to high school age was a towheaded, mischievous fourth grader named Timmy. To illustrate the Values Continuum strategy (4), we asked them, "Where would you put yourself on this line representing *how you typically keep your room?*" On one end was Washing Willie, who was so neat and clean that he kept a footbath outside his room and washed his feet before he entered. He had a tracing of a comb and brush on his dresser and always lined up the comb spoke-for-spoke on the tracing, so it would be exactly where it belonged. And so on. On the other end of the continuum was Cyclone Sam. Sam hated neatness so much that after his parent put the newly laundered clothes in his drawers, he would remove the laundry and throw each item around the room until every surface was covered. He would sprinkle a little garden soil around the room so he could feel the good earth underfoot. And so on. (Note: This is an example of a relatively *not-loaded* values question. Compared to, say, Tidy Tina and Messy Mary, which would imply good and bad end points, this one makes both ends equally absurd, so the young people could think freely and nondefensively about their own position.)

When it was Timmy's turn to respond to this continuum, he proudly told me to put his name about as close as he could get to Cyclone Sam. His mother, from her place in the audience, wryly affirmed, "Yes, that's Timmy!" to the chuckles of the other workshop participants. I simply thanked the lad for responding, as I did with the other young people whose names were arrayed in a fairly broad range across the continuum. We did not discuss that particular issue any further. We went on to other strategies and other issues. This was a Tuesday.

On Thursday morning of the workshop, the mother said she wanted to share something with the group before we began. With a tone of awe and wonder, she reported how when she drove Timmy and a couple of his friends home from the workshop that day, they had not discussed the continuum, nor had the subject of room tidiness come up that night or the next day. Yet, the night before, on his own, without anyone raising the topic, Timmy, for the first time she could ever remember, cleaned up his room—not just a token tidying up, but a thorough reorganization. She could hardly believe it.

I relate this anecdote with some trepidation, because the last moral I would want anyone to draw from the story is that if we just come up with the right clarifying question or strategy, our children will turn out just the way we want them to and our clients will live happily ever after. Actually, this story could also have gone the other way. A Washing Willie type might have decided to experiment with a messier room. There are no guarantees accompanying values clarification. Rather, to me the story illustrates *the power of the values clarification process.* Timmy was asked where he stood on an issue, not the most important issue in the world, but an issue in *his* world. He publicly affirmed his position. He recognized, graphically, that others had alternative positions. Implicitly, he realized, "I don't have to be where I am on this line. I could choose to be different." And he did. He chose to try out a new behavior. He took action. And the fascinating thing to me is that he did this all on his own. A simple activity got him thinking about how he wanted to be, and once he started thinking, he decided to try a new behavior in his life.

So here's my theory for why a good clarifying question works, that is, how it can actually contribute to changes in thinking and behavior. I believe that virtually all of us, to varying degrees, are continually on the lookout for alternative value indicators (goals, beliefs, behaviors, etc.) that will make our lives better, richer, more satisfying, and meaningful. To some degree, whatever our age, *we are all trying to figure out who we want to be when we grow up.* Even when clients—an adult, a teenager, a student—seem resistant or uninterested, their radar is operating, scanning the horizon for ideas, role models, alternative solutions to their problems, new ways to make their lives richer. That is why people of all ages are usually very receptive to being asked clarifying questions in a supportive, nonjudgmental atmosphere. Aside from enjoying the focused, accepting attention of another person or group, which is gratifying and often therapeutic in its own right, people like to think and talk about themselves. They like to work on who they are and who they might become. Good clarifying questions harness clients' intrinsic motivation and help them along their own lifelong clarifying journey.

■ THOUGHT-PROVOKING QUESTIONS

Ever since Socrates began upsetting his fellow Athenians by asking them thought-provoking questions—"What is truth?" "But if this is so, dear Meno, would not the following be so?" "To what end do we live?"—many cultures have valued the use of questions to further the search for wisdom (Duane, 2004; Marinoff, 2003). More recently in history, we have come to value the process of introspection for moral and personal development. As individuals, if we don't feel defensive, when someone asks us a thought-provoking question and is interested in our response, it's enjoyable to think about and share our response. For example, Gregory Stock (1985) wrote a little book called *The Book of Questions.* It contained 200 value-clarifying questions, such as: "How many of your friendships have lasted more than 10 years? Which of your current friends do you think will still be important to you 10 years from now?" "Would you be willing to eat a bowl of live crickets for $40,000?" "Is there something you've dreamed of doing for a long time? Why haven't you done it?" The book became a popular best seller. People sat around at parties and at dinner tables asking one another the questions.

Of course, there are classic value-clarifying questions. We have all heard them in one form or another:

- If you won the lottery (or if you had a million dollars), how would you spend it?
- If you had one year left to live, how would you spend that year?
- If you were marooned on a desert island and could have only one (or two or three) companions, whom would you choose?
- If there was a fire in your home and you had time to grab one armful of things to take out with you, what would you take?
- If you were in prison for a year and could have only one book to read the whole time, what would that book be?
- And so many more.

■ CLARIFYING QUESTIONS

A good value-clarifying question in a social occasion can be fun, can help us get to know one another better, and when the answers are respected and not ridiculed, can build closer, more trusting relationships. These results can occur in a counseling setting as well, but the main difference between the two settings is that, in counseling and psychotherapy, a values-clarifying question should be as relevant as possible to the topic at hand, not just used to generate random interesting reflections. In other words, clarifying questions should serve a counseling purpose. To achieve a counseling purpose, clarifying questions always operate on two levels:

1. *They help clients explore more deeply the issue under consideration* by helping them clarify their goals and purposes, make choices and decisions, implement those decisions in their lives, and thereby contribute toward the development of a workable values system.

2. *They help clients learn to use the clarifying process,* so that considering what they prize and cherish, choosing from alternatives, considering consequences, trying to close the gap between their goals and their behaviors and using the other value-clarifying processes become second nature for them in their lives. *Eventually, they*

use the valuing processes themselves, even when there is no one else asking them clarifying questions.

Because clients are so different and the topics they may explore are so many, there are an infinite number of values-clarifying questions that counselors can ask in individual and group counseling. Following are some examples that suggest the wide range of questions to help clients clarify their goals, priorities, and action steps to realize their values.

One other useful distinction is that clarifying questions can be categorized as either *clarifying responses* or *clarifying questions*. Both are clarifying, in that they engage one or more of the seven clarifying processes. The clarifying response is always a response to the client's previous statement, and it takes a generic form; that is, virtually the same wording can be used for many different topics. For example, "Have you considered any alternatives?" is a clarifying response in that it only makes sense in response to the client's previous statement, and it might be an appropriate question whether the client was talking about a choice of job, religion, place to live, or any number of other values issues. A clarifying question is not generic or formulaic; it is appropriate only to the specific topic at hand. It may be asked in response to a client's statement or when initiating a new topic or direction. For example, "What is the most satisfying work you have ever done?" and "What does faith mean to you?" are not generic questions; they apply specifically to the topics of work and faith.

The second part of this chapter presents many examples of clarifying responses and clarifying questions that engage each of the seven valuing processes.

■ GOOD CLARIFYING QUESTIONS

There are a number of standards for a good clarifying question. Some overlap with others. Seeing them all at once might seem intimidating, but keep in mind that questions don't have to be perfect. If clients find the question interesting and they trust your motives, they will readily excuse an awkwardly worded question and willingly engage with it.

1. *The question strikes the client as interesting or relevant.* People generally do like to talk about themselves. Ask a question that captures their interest and seems inherently connected to them or their concerns, and off they go.

2. *The question elicits clarification rather than information.* A client says, "I grew up in a large family." An informational question in response might be "How many children were there?" A clarifying question might be "Did you value growing up in a large family?" or "What did you appreciate or find problematic about growing up in a large family?" There's nothing inherently wrong with a counselor asking for some information if she, the counselor, would find that helpful. A clarifying question, however, is intended to engage one of the seven valuing processes. It may also produce a good deal of information, but that is not its purpose. Another way of saying this is that a clarifying question is intended to provide data primarily for the client, rather than the counselor.

3. *The question is usually open-ended.* Rather than eliciting a single word or short answer, it invites extended reflection. "How long have you felt that way?" is a closed-end question. It solicits a brief or abrupt answer. "How do you think you came to feel that way?" is open-ended. It invites more reflection.

Although usually more of the valuing processes are elicited with open-ended rather than closed-end questions, that is not always the case. Sometimes a yes-no or short-answer question can be very clarifying, as when a counselor asks a resistant client, "I understand that you don't want to be here, but is there *anything* you might want to get out of talking with me?" A good deal of thinking and feeling might precede a yes or no answer in this case, which the client could then elaborate on or be invited to do so. Similarly, one might ask a vacillating client, "If you had to make a choice today, which would it be?" This might elicit a short answer, but only after some serious reflection.

4. *The question is invitational, not cross-examinational.* If the counselor seems genuinely curious or interested in the answer, rather than accusatory or judgmental, the question is more likely to engender reflection.

5. *The question is personal, not general.* Clarifying questions are you questions. They are intended to be personal, not philosophical. For example, a counselor is talking to an older client about the client's need for independence. She could ask a similar question three ways:

- "Is there such a thing as being too independent?"
- "Do you think a person can be too independent?"
- "Do you see any risks in your becoming more independent or too independent?"

The questions represent a continuum from more general to more personal. The third example is the best clarifying question. It elicits all the thinking required of the first two questions and also invites the client to apply the issue to himself. Similarly, working on human sexuality, a counselor might ask an individual or group:

- "How important is sexual ecstasy versus physical and emotional intimacy in sex?"
- "How important to you is sexual ecstasy versus physical and emotional intimacy in sex?

The second is the better value-clarifying question. (In some settings, however, the first one might feel a little safer and might therefore be preferable.) Socrates was a great philosopher, but if we were to teach him to ask value-clarifying questions, we would show him how to move from

- "What is truth?" to
- "What does truth mean to you?" to
- "How important is truth to you?" to
- "How truthful have you been today?"

All are good questions, but the latter two move from the philosophical level to that of personal values.

6. *The question doesn't make the client feel defensive.* Partly this is a matter of timing. If the question is too personal, too deep, or too soon in the relationship, the client might not feel safe enough to explore it. Partly it is a matter of the counselor's tone, that is, invitational, not cross-examinational. Partly it is a matter of wording. "Why did you do that?" could strike the client as accusatory, as if he did something wrong or should not have done that. Or it could imply that he should know why he did it, but maybe he doesn't know why, so again he'll feel defensive. "Could you share with me what was going through your mind when you made that choice?" is a gentler way of asking the question and less likely to create defensiveness. In general, it's best to avoid "Why?" questions, although there are always exceptions.

7. *The question has no implied right or better answer.* "Would you like someone to do that to you?" "Are you more like Selfish Sam or Altruistic Al?" "Do you think a son should do more than you are doing for his parents?" "Are you a good girl?" "Do you really think that's a good idea?" In some circumstances, these might be good clarifying questions, but in many or most circumstances, clients would sense that there is a correct or better or preferred answer to the question. If the client senses that the counselor is looking for a particular answer, the client is less likely to engage in the valuing process and instead will try to second-guess the counselor.

Assuming the counselor really does not have a correct or preferred answer in mind, it is still important to word the question in a way that the client does not think there's a preferred answer. So rather than ask, "What's the smart thing to do in this situation?" (which implies there's one smart choice here and the counselor probably knows what it is), the counselor might ask, "What do you think a smart choice would be in this situation?" or better yet "What do you think a smart choice *might be* in this situation?" (*Might* is a frequent word in clarifying questions. Its tentativeness allows clients to think more freely without having to come to premature answers or decisions.)

8. *The question is sensitive and unbiased with respect to gender, class, culture, and other diversities.* In wording questions, don't assume that all clients or group members are heterosexual ("How would your husbands feel about that?") or Christian ("What might Jesus do in your situation?"). Avoid male-female stereotypes ("Is that a feminine thing to do?" "Would a real man conduct himself that way?" "Are you more like Ditsy Daisy or Rational Ralph?"). Because all couples are not married, it may be more sensitive to use *partner* instead of *spouse*. Questions that seem to reflect racial and ethnic characteristics (e.g., which groups value education, family, etc.) can easily be biased because, even when they reflect a statistically valid generalization, the generalization may not fit a large number of group members and may fit a large number of members of other groups. So questions and activities should be worded to be inclusive of all, especially in working with new clients or groups. Of course, once you get to know a

client or group, in context, some questions that would be insensitive in a new group (like the ones about husbands and Jesus) might be very appropriate to the particular group.

Further discussion of how to avoid reflecting cultural stereotypes and biases in values clarification questions and strategies can be found among some of the values clarification strategies in chapter 6 and the discussion of multicultural issues in chapter 11.

■ WHERE DO CLARIFYING QUESTIONS COME FROM?

When I'm working with a client or group, clarifying questions sometimes just occur to me without much or any conscious thought. In those cases, I'll make a quick judgment as to whether it seems appropriate—Does it seem relevant? Might it be helpful? Will it engage a valuing process? Is the timing good?—and if it does, I'll probably go ahead and ask it.

Sometimes the clarifying question doesn't come spontaneously to me; rather, I'll do a very quick search for a question to ask. While I'm listening and absorbing what the client or group member is saying, while I'm getting a feel for it, I may also think to myself: *prizing, affirming, alternatives, consequences, free choice, action, pattern*. I can do this little mantra in a split second. In effect, I'm asking myself, "Might it be useful to ask the client if this is important to him? Might it be useful if I ask if he's considered any alternatives or if I posed the alternative that just came to my mind? Might it be interesting to ask him what he does about this?"

This all happens in split-second timing. It is not the same as full, empathic listening in which I would be so attuned to understanding the client's inner experience that there simply would be no room for me to think about a question that might be useful to the client. Rather, I am splitting my attention. Part goes to listening carefully to the client, to achieving a significant level of empathy. (And as shown in the next chapter, I may very well listen actively and reflectively to see if I understand what the client is trying to communicate.) But part goes toward making a professional decision about what to say or ask and then doing so skillfully. I find I can do this—maintain an empathic attunement with the client *and* ask good clarifying questions that the client himself feels are sufficiently attuned to his inner experience that he is willing to continue the clarifying process.

This skill does not come all at once. Having taught values clarification to thousands of students and workshop participants, I have observed them going through the stages of mastery common to most new endeavors. At first, it feels artificial, contrived, awkward. Then the counselor begins to feel more skillful. It feels a bit less artificial, contrived, and awkward, but one is still self-conscious that she is employing a technique. Eventually, the method begins to be internalized. It feels natural, like this is a normal way to communicate. Value-clarifying questions start to come more spontaneously and "feel right" to the counselor and the client.

▪ EXAMPLES OF CLARIFYING QUESTIONS

Examples of clarifying responses and clarifying questions are provided here for each of the seven valuing processes. Again, *clarifying responses* might be used to respond to a client's statement on many different topics. *Clarifying questions* are pertinent only to the particular topic under consideration. Rather than present random examples of clarifying questions, I have selected four types of counseling and chosen an issue that might come up in each of those counseling settings.

> *Marriage and Family Counseling*: A couple is trying to find a balance between time together and time apart. (Heading: *Couples*)
> *Substance Abuse Counseling*: A young adult is ready to leave his residential substance abuse program and live independently in the community. (Heading: *Recovery*)
> *Geriatric Counseling*: An elder is finding it difficult to live at home by himself and is considering moving. (Heading: *Elder Living*)
> *Pastoral Counseling*: A member of one's congregation is experiencing a crisis of faith. (Heading: *Faith*)

For other applications of values clarification to religion and faith, see Larson and Larson (1976) and Elkins (1977).

For each of these counseling situations, examples are given of clarifying questions a counselor might ask at appropriate points in a counseling session. A counselor might ask some of the same questions in a psychoeducational group on that topic.

Examples of clarifying responses and questions are given for each of the seven valuing processes. Sometimes a clarifying question engages more than one valuing process.

1. **Prizing and Cherishing**. We prize and cherish our values. Clarifying questions help people better understand what is important to them, what they prize and cherish, and set goals accordingly.

Clarifying Responses

- How important is this to you?
- What do you want to happen?
- Are you proud of (or do you feel good about) how you are handling this?
- What do you most like about … ?
- Would you be proud or ashamed or have some other feeling if people knew about this?
- What would be the best outcome?
- What do you value most about this?
- Would you like more of this?
- Are you glad about that?
- How do you feel about that?
- Have you thought much about that? [Implies: Is this important to you?]
- Is that a personal preference, or do you think everyone should believe or do that?

Clarifying Questions

Couples:

- What are the one or two activities you most enjoy doing together—just the two of you?
- What are the one or two things you most enjoy doing together with your friends?
- What are the one or two activities you most like doing alone—by yourself?
- What are the one or two things you most like doing yourself with your friend(s)?
- Is there anything you're proud of about how you organize your time, separately or together?
- Was there a time in your lives when the balance of together and alone felt just about right?

Recovery:

- Are you proud of the work you've done in rehab? Why do you feel good about it?
- What are you most looking forward to about being out in the community again?
- What, if anything, will you miss about living at the rehab facility?
- What are your strengths that will help you succeed out in the community?

Elder Living:

- On a scale from 1 to 10, how important is independence to you?
- Do you think independence will always be important to you?
- Do you think you could be too proud of being independent?
- What do you most prize about living at home? Are any of these things transferable to another living situation?

Faith:

- What about your faith do you prize?
- What have been your most meaningful, important experiences in your church, temple, or mosque?
- Do you have any role models you cherish when it comes to religion or faith?
- When did you first begin to value your religion or faith?

2. **Affirmation, Communication**. We are willing and likely to affirm our values in appropriate circumstances. Clarifying questions give clients opportunities to affirm their values and help clients consider whether they would share or do share their values with others.

Clarifying Responses

- Have you told anyone about this?
- Would you be willing to let others know your viewpoint?
- Who would you feel comfortable sharing this with?
- Would you like to tell others (me, us) about your view?
- Would you like to tell others (me, us) what you do about this?
- Would you write a letter to the editor about it?
- Would you do the same thing again? [That is, would the client affirm a prior choice?]
- Who could you talk to about this?
- Are you saying you _____? [Invites affirmation or clarification]
- Is there a reason you haven't told _____ about this?

Clarifying Questions

Couples:

- Is it hard to tell your partner that you want more time by yourself?
- What do you need to tell your partner about this if you're going to achieve your goal?
- Could you talk about this with your friends? Would you be embarrassed for them to know you're struggling with this?
- Who else could you talk to about this?

Recovery:

- Who do you want to know that you're sober?
- Who do you want to tell that you're back in the community?
- Is there anyone you want to describe your recovery experience to in depth?
- How do you think it would feel to tell people you're proud of what you've accomplished?
- Is there someone you'll feel safe talking to about how you're doing?

Elder Living:

- When you picture your friends learning that you are giving up your home and moving to assisted living, how does that make you feel?
- How would you feel if you learned your friend had moved to assisted living?
- Picture writing a holiday card telling your friends and family that you had moved in with your daughter. What would you tell them? How does that feel? Could you do it proudly, happily?
- How would it feel to talk about this issue with a friend or relative?

Faith:

- Would you be willing to share your doubts with others?
- Is there anything about the church that you would still be willing to give witness about (anything about your religion that you would publicly affirm)?

- Is it hard to talk about your doubts with me?
- How have you affirmed your faith in the past? Did you feel it then or were you just going through the motions?

3. **Alternatives**. Values are chosen after considering alternatives. Clarifying questions help clients consider alternative viewpoints and courses of action.

Clarifying Responses

- Have you considered any alternatives?
- What else did you consider?
- What might you do differently?
- If you couldn't do that (or if that didn't work), what would the next best choice be?
- How would you answer people who say _____ (a different idea or viewpoint than the client expressed)?
- Some people do this _____. Do you think that might work for you?
- What's another way to look at this situation?
- What other possibilities are there?
- Can you give me an example of that? What do you mean by that? [Asking clients to go more deeply often gives them a new perspective on what they are saying.]

Clarifying Questions

Couples:

- What are some activities you like to do together? [They visualize the alternatives.]
- What activities would you have no problem with your partner doing alone or with friends?
- What activities would make you feel uncomfortable or threatened if your partner did them alone or with friends?
- Would you consider doing a joint activity that your spouse loves but you don't, if he did one that you love but he doesn't?
- Would you consider developing a new pastime, sport, or hobby to do together?
- Would you consider taking a class together?

Recovery:

- What are three activities that would be good for you to engage in when you get out?
- What are three activities that would not be good for you?
- Could you name three people you think it would be healthy for you to hang out with?
- How about two or three people you think could lead to problems?
- If you start to feel like you might start using again, what are your options?
- What are some things you could do at home alone instead of drink?

Elder Living:

- What housing options have you considered?
- You've mentioned assisted living and moving in with your daughter. Would you consider inviting a friend to live with you at your home … or getting a new place together?
- If you decided to keep living at home, is there anything you might do to get some help to make it easier to live here?
- If you had a friend in a similar position as you, what would you advise her? [This isn't so much an alternative choice but an alternative way of looking at the situation.]

Faith:

- Can you think of some people you might talk to who might have insights about your questions?
- If you were a pastor (rabbi, imam, etc.), what would you say to someone who came to you with the questions you're asking?
- Are there any historical or biblical figures in church history or in your religious tradition you can think of who have had doubts similar to your own?
- Would you like to hear how I have come to think about this question?
- Would you consider giving yourself a holiday from these questions, for example, go a month without dwelling on them and seeing what thoughts and feelings emerge on their own?
- Do you think it would help to learn how other religions think about or answer these questions?

4. **Consequences**. Values are chosen after considering the consequences, both positive and negative. Clarifying questions help clients choose more thoughtfully and reflectively by considering the pros and cons, consequences, and other dimensions of their decisions, choices, and actions.

Clarifying Responses

- What are the pros or benefits of that approach?
- What are the cons, the downside?
- Where would that lead?
- Do you think you'll feel the same way a year from now?
- How will doing that affect the other people in your life?
- What's the best (worst) thing about that idea?
- How would this decision or action affect _____ (partner, children, etc.)?
- What would your life be like if that happened?
- Have you given this enough thought?
- Have you thought about _____?
- Is what you just said consistent with what you said before?
- What's the likelihood of that working?

Clarifying Questions

Couples:

- Will that option give you each the space you were talking about?
- How do you think you'd feel if John [Jane] took a vacation with a friend?
- Would you resent it if she was out of the house more than you were?
- If you did have at least that one date each week, do you think you'd look forward to it? Dread it? Or what?

Recovery:

- What would be the best thing for you about staying clean?
- What might be the likely result if you engaged in that activity you said would not be good for you?
- What are the possible consequences if you skip your support group meetings?
- What would the pros and cons of moving into that neighborhood be for your recovery?

Elder Living:

- What are the benefits of living at home by yourself? What are the drawbacks?
- What are the benefits and drawbacks of the next option you're considering?
- If you stay where you are, what's the worst thing that could happen?
- If you moved to assisted living and it didn't work out, what would the consequences be?

Faith:

- What might be the consequences if your doubts persist? Where might it lead?
- Is there anything good that is coming out of this soul searching?
- What's the worst result that could come out of this?
- When biblical figures experienced doubt (e.g., Jacob, Job, Thomas), what happened? How did it turn out?
- If you gave up your faith (or if you left the church), what would stay the same in your life and what would be different?

5. **Free Choice**. Values are freely chosen, that is, chosen without undue authority or peer pressure. Clarifying questions help clients consider the sources of their choices and take responsibility for their choices.

Clarifying Responses

- Is that what you want to do?
- How did you develop this belief?
- Have you felt this way a long time?
- Do you believe this is the best choice?
- If it were totally up to you, what would you do?
- Is this your choice?

- Are you feeling pressured about this?
- How committed are you to doing this?
- What did your parents do about this? [Asking about parents often allows clients to consider whether they are just following their role models or whether they are choosing for themselves. Of course, it's their choice, but an aware choice is better.]
- Was that something you chose?
- On a scale from 1 to 10, how much is this *your* choice?

Clarifying Questions

Couples:

- Is the date idea one you think you'd like to do?
- Do you feel pressured toward it because she seems to be excited about it? Do you feel you can say no?
- What would *you* like to do about this dilemma?
- Are you following the same or a different path than your parents in terms of how you spend your time?

Recovery:

- Why do you want to stay sober?
- When you say you're going to gravitate toward these friends and avoid those friends, are you saying that because you think that's what I want to hear, or do you really believe this will be better for you?
- You could make a lot more money dealing drugs than taking this entry-level job. Why are you choosing the entry-level job?
- How committed are you to staying clean?

Elder Living:

- What do your children want you to do?
- What do *you* want to do?
- Do you feel pressured to make a decision?
- What did your parents do at this time of their lives? Do you want to do as they did?

Faith:

- Are those around you supportive of or resistant to your questioning?
- Will your husband (parents) accept your choice?
- Do you feel you have free will to make these decisions?
- Would Christ (Muhammad, Buddha, etc.) want you to continue asking these questions or to cease the questioning and accept his or the church's teachings?
- Do you think you are free to interpret the Bible (Quran, Bhagavad Gita, etc.) in your own way?

6. **Action**. People act on their values. Values show up in people's behavior. Clarifying questions help clients consider what they are doing or might do about their beliefs, goals, and values. Clarifying questions help them take action toward their goals.

<u>Clarifying Responses</u>

- Are you doing anything about it?
- Have you done anything about that?
- What might you do to achieve your goal?
- What would the first step be?
- When was the last time you _____?
- What do you plan to do about _____?
- Now what?
- Are you willing to commit to this?
- What help might you need to do this?
- Are you willing to spend money (time) on this?
- How far are you willing to go?

<u>Clarifying Questions</u>

Couples:

- Which of your current activities will you continue doing together?
- Which will you keep doing alone?
- Is there anything new you think you'd like to do together?
- So you've decided to have a once-a-week "date." Are you ready to set the date now? When will you make the date?
- What help will you need? A babysitter? Reservations?
- Is there any thing else you want to act on?

Recovery:

- What are the first things you can do back home to get off to a good start?
- If someone offers you a drink, what will you say or do?
- When you see your old group of friends—the ones you say you need to avoid—and they say, "Hey, we're having a party. Come with us," what will you say or do?
- You said in the past you had trouble being alone at home. What do you plan on doing about that now? [Note: An earlier question, "What are some things you <u>could</u> do alone at home?" fits in the *considering alternatives* category. "What <u>will</u> you do?" or "What do you <u>plan on</u> doing?" fits in the *acting* category. Sometimes the distinction is blurry, and the category can be discerned only in context, or the question spans two valuing processes. It doesn't really matter as long as it's a useful question.]

Elder Living:

- So you decided you need more information about assisted living options. What might you do to find this information? [Alternatives.] What will you do? [Action.]
- Are you ready to act on this, or would you like to think about it some more? When do you think you might be ready?
- Whenever you begin talking about all you'd have to do to sell the house and pack and move, you seem to feel overwhelmed. Would you like to explore alternatives for making such a move easier? [Then it's back to exploring alternatives, in the service of taking action.]
- Do you plan on calling your daughter, like you talked about before?
- What else do you need to do?

Faith:

- Is there any action you could take that might help you figure this out?
- What's something you could do that might give you a more genuine religious experience?
- What is your next step?
- Would you like us to pray together over this?

7. **Patterns**. People act repeatedly and with consistent patterns on their values. Clarifying questions help clients examine their patterns of action, consider new ones, and confront the inconsistencies in their value indicators (goals, beliefs, and actions).

Clarifying Responses

- Do you do this often?
- Is there a pattern here?
- How do you typically handle this issue in your life?
- Would you like to do more of it? Will you do it again?
- Are you consistent in this?
- Is what you said about this consistent with what you're doing about that?
- Would people who know you well say you were … ?
- Are you willing to work hard to achieve that?
- What's worked before?
- Are there other things you can do like this?

Clarifying Questions

Couples:

- Which one of you typically makes the social plans?
- Is that a pattern you want to continue?
- Will a weekly or monthly or other routine help you get the time alone you want?
- You say you enjoy this together. Would you want to do more of it?
- Would you like to do this regularly?

Recovery:

- In the past, when you got into trouble, what were the first warning signs?
- Are there any daily routines that might help you stick to your recovery plan?
- How hard has it been in the past for you to ask for help? Is it going to be different now?
- Will you keep attending your weekly support group?
- You said you get in trouble when you're alone, yet you're choosing to move away from your family. Are you worried about that?

Elder Living:

- How do you normally handle change? Is this typical?
- You've described yourself as stubborn. Is that operating here?
- Have there been other times in your life when you've moved or contemplated moving? How did you handle those occasions? How did they work out?
- What have you learned from other transition times in your life? Can you apply any of those learnings to this turning point?

Faith:

- Are there any rituals you typically practice that have meaning to you?
- Considering how you are living your life now, how might an outside observer describe the place religion or faith has in your life?
- What other times and ways have you experienced doubt in your life, whether on matters of faith or other issues?
- Is how you live your life consistent with your faith? If you gave up your faith, would those patterns of living change?

These relatively few examples only begin to suggest the hundreds and thousands of clarifying questions a counselor can ask clients to help them think more deeply about their feelings, beliefs, actions, goals, and values. Whether by using generic clarifying responses to a client's statement or by framing situation-specific clarifying questions to further clients' exploration, clarifying questions engage clients and group members in the seven valuing processes. Even when used alone, a single, good clarifying question can begin a process of reflection that can lead to insight, goal setting, decision, and action.

But clarifying questions are not just used alone. The next two chapters expand on the clarifying question. Chapter 5 shows how clarifying questions can be applied in a sequential way in the *clarifying interview*, that is, a particular type of counseling session. Chapter 6 shows how clarifying questions can be adapted into *values clarification strategies*, that is, more elaborate activities and structures for asking clarifying questions.

5   The Clarifying Interview

The clarifying interview is the basic model for using values clarification in an individual counseling setting. The word *interview* is a term used historically to describe a counseling session. In practice, a clarifying interview can take place over 10 minutes, over an entire session, or over many sessions.

The clarifying interview uses values-clarifying questions (chapter 4) and may use values-clarifying strategies (chapter 6) to help the client go through the value-clarifying process that leads to values realization.

■ STEPS IN THE CLARIFYING INTERVIEW

THE CLARIFYING INTERVIEW

Clarifying
Clarifying the Dilemma
Acknowledging Feelings
Goal Setting
Establishing Goals and Priorities
Alternatives
Generating Alternatives
Consequences
Considering the Pros and Cons
Choosing
Making a Free Choice or Decision
Planning
Determining the Next Steps
Committing or Resolving to Act

The steps of the clarifying interview are listed sequentially because there is a self-evident logic to following this sequence. One should identify a problem before solving it, one should consider the pros and cons of alternatives before making an important choice, and so on. However, in practice, the steps do not always take place sequentially. For example, generating alternatives (step 3) can remind a client of some feelings that were not adequately expressed in step 1, so the focus shifts back to exploring those feelings. Or exploring the consequences of the various alternatives (step 4) may help the client realize that none of the alternatives so far is acceptable, which may return the discussion to the previous stage, generating additional alternatives. Nevertheless the interview—sometimes gradually, sometimes quickly—moves forward in the following order.

1. Clarifying

a. *Clarifying the Dilemma*

Many problem-solving models begin with identifying *the problem*. In values clarification counseling, we prefer to use the term *dilemma*, because dilemma usually
implies a choice between or among alternatives and that is where values clarification
is most appropriate. If a client's problem is a huge lack of self-confidence, feelings
of hopelessness, psychosomatic symptoms, or a myriad of other psychological and
emotional difficulties, values clarification is not an appropriate counseling method
for working on the core problem(s). But if a client is ready to set goals or make a
choice where competing priorities are involved, or the choices seem limited or con-
fusing, or strategic thinking or action planning is required, then values clarification
is a useful method for moving forward. Indeed, at a later stage in the counseling or
therapy process, when the client lacking self-confidence, feeling hopeless, or working on emotional problems is now ready to make some new choices in pursuit of his
goals, values clarification may be a useful part of the therapy as well.

So the first step in the values-clarifying interview is to help the client identify and
clarify the dilemma, the values conflict, or the values problem, if one prefers. This may
be a quick and easy task if the client is quite clear about his dilemma, or it may take a
while to unpack the quandary and isolate one or more issues and decisions to work on.
If it takes more than one or two sessions, however, this is probably an indication that
the values dilemma may be complicated by emotional conflicts or unaware feelings
that might better be explored further with another or additional counseling methods.

Good listening is an essential behavior on the part of the counselor at this stage
and in every stage of the clarifying interview. The goal is to identify the issues and
dilemmas that are important to *the client*, not the issues or choices the counselor
thinks are important. Ideally, the dilemma should be able to be summarized by the
counselor or client, to the client's satisfaction, in a single sentence, such as, "So you
feel stuck in your job and don't know what to do." "I don't have the resources I once
had, and I'm trying to figure out how to live within my means." "This relationship
is not working out; I'd like to save it but don't know if that's possible." "You can't
manage the house yourself anymore, and you're trying to decide on what other
living options make sense for you."

"Clarifying the dilemma" means more than simply identifying it. It also means
exploring it to appreciate it more fully. A wide variety of clarifying questions can be
asked at this stage to help the client view his dilemma from other perspectives or gain
further insight about his situation. "When did you start experiencing the frustration
at work?" "Do you feel alone in your situation, or do you know others who are going
through what you are?" "On a scale from 1 to 10, how fed up with the current situation are you?" "Have you talked with anyone else about this, and was that helpful?"
The counselor's desire to better understand and her curiosity, intuition, and tentative insight are all useful guides to clarifying questions that can help the client and
counselor explore and more fully understand the dilemma from many angles.

b. Acknowledging Feelings

Almost every values dilemma or problem, no matter how cognitive and objective the considerations may be, has emotional elements. As already stated, if the major problem the client is facing is of an emotional nature, then values clarification is not the core counseling approach for him. But it is only natural for a client at the verge of making important life decisions to feel fear, anxiety, confusion, anger, grief, or other emotions associated with change, including positive ones like excitement, exhilaration, and determination. Again, the counselor needs to be listening carefully to hear such emotions. And when clients do express these feelings, it is appropriate and desirable for the values-clarifying counselor to empathically acknowledge them, so the client feels understood and accepted and can continue to go through the valuing process. Again, if clients seem unable to move beyond this stage, if it appears that the emotional issues need a good deal of further exploration and attention, then other counseling and therapeutic modalities are probably needed.

2. Establishing Goals and Priorities

The main goal in this step of the value-clarifying process is to help the client identify and articulate what he wants, what is important to him, what he prizes and cherishes in terms of the values and choices inherent in the dilemma. For example, there could be a conflict in important values here—between family and career, between health and money. Or on a more mundane level, a person deciding what kind of car to purchase might have a conflict between status and functionality, between wanting to look sporty and cool versus wanting a vehicle that is practical and versatile, between carrying capacity (utility) and gas mileage (environmental stewardship), or even between blue and green. The key question to explore at this stage is "What is important to you?" "What are your goals and priorities?" And if there is a conflict between values, "Are some values more important to you than others?" As the clarifying process moves forward, it may become apparent that there is no way to realize all of one's goals or values fully. That is why it is important to set priorities—now, if possible, but also later in the interview process.

3. Generating Alternatives

At this stage, the client and counselor begin considering alternative solutions to the dilemma. What are the client's possible choices? Consistent with the valuing process, it is most helpful when the client can choose from alternatives. Thus the goal at this point is not to try to immediately zero in on the right choice or the best choice, but to assume a brainstorming attitude and attempt to generate several possible choices. The alternatives may simply be stated verbally as the conversation proceeds, or the counselor or client may write them down on a pad visible to one or on a surface visible to both.

Sometimes this stage begins with a gentle invitation to the client, such as "Do you feel ready to begin looking at possible solutions to your situation?" or "Well, I feel like you've pretty clearly described your dilemma and identified what you want to achieve in a solution. Do you agree? Do you think you'd like to begin working on ideas for moving forward?" Other times, the client or counselor senses a readiness to enter this phase, and they just begin, without an invitation or preamble. Once the process begins, here are some guidelines for proceeding.

a. Begin With the Client's Alternatives

Always start with the ideas or solutions generated by the client. The goal is not just to find an answer to the current dilemma, but to help the client learn a problem-solving, value-clarifying process that can be used in his life on an ongoing basis. The more active the client is, the better he learns the process.

The counselor may begin by asking something like "So what choices have you considered?" or, more generally, because maybe the client hasn't actually considered any choices yet, "Have you been thinking about any choices you might make in this situation?" Then again, the client may have already identified some of the choices in the conversation so far. In that case, the counselor may say, for example, "So I've heard you mention two choices so far—stay in your present job or quit. Is that right? [Client confirms this or reminds counselor of another option previously mentioned.] Okay, are there any other choices you might consider?" Or "Are there any other options that someone in your situation might consider?"

Notice the subtle difference between the two ways of asking the last question. The first way—"Are there any other choices *you* might consider?"—could steer the client to look for choices he would really like. In other words, it might lead less toward brainstorming or thinking creatively and more toward a limited or even desperate "What's-the-right-choice-for-me?" query. The second version—"Are there any other options that someone in your situation *might* consider?"—takes the pressure off the client to come up with an immediate solution for himself and think more broadly about alternative choices. It's not that one way is necessarily better than the other. Each has its advantages, and the counselor who is adept at phrasing a comparable question in multiple ways will be more likely to find the words to best facilitate the client's progress.

b. The Choices Are Not Judged, Particularly by the Counselor

The goal is for the counselor to accept all the client's ideas with equal respect, to avoid judging some choices as better than others. In fact, the counselor may think some of the client's potential choices are excellent, for example, the career client who says, "I think I need more information about what jobs are out there" or the elder who says, "Maybe I'm going to have to learn to ask for help more." Similarly, the counselor may think some of the client's alternatives are awful, such as the disabled elder client who says one of his choices is to stay at home without any caregivers available or the struggling client on welfare who says one way to get out of poverty is to bet his available funds on the lottery. There may be times for the counselor to share her validation or her concern or additional information with the client, but this is not one of them. At this point, the goal is to get all the ideas on the list (actual or figurative)—both the initial and more obvious alternatives the client generated and the additional ideas the client thought of in response to the counselor's invitation to consider other alternatives.

c. The Counselor May Offer Additional Alternatives

All of our lives, inside or outside of counseling, are potentially enriched—and potentially complicated—when we are exposed to new ideas or choices we were not aware of. In values clarification counseling, the counselor has a legitimate role in broadening the client's awareness of possibly useful alternatives—job training resources, elder care options, or debt counseling, to use the previous examples. The key is to *offer* such alternatives and not *impose* them.

One way to offer and not impose is to ask the client whether he would like to hear about these alternatives. After showing that she has accepted and respected the different alternatives the client has generated (and unless the client feels this acceptance, anything the counselor subsequently offers will *feel* like an imposition), the counselor might ask, "Another alternative occurs to me. Would you like to hear it?" Or "A friend [or another client] of mine was in a somewhat similar situation. Would you like to hear what he tried?" Or "Let's see; you've come up with three things you might do. Would you like to hear a couple of more ideas that I've heard of?"

Granted that in the unequal power relationship that often (some would say always) exists in counseling and psychotherapy, or just to be polite, most clients will say they want to hear the counselor's or therapist's alternatives. But I think of the situation a bit differently. If the counselor has up until now listened well to the client, has accepted and respected the client *as he is*, has avoided judging the client's past behaviors, and has accepted the alternatives the client has already generated, then *of course* the client will want to hear what the counselor has to say. In this respect, counseling is no different than other human relationships: when we listen to and respect someone else, it is more likely that person will listen to and respect us. (It's not guaranteed; it's just a lot more likely.) So I have no problem that the client is now open to hearing alternative ideas or actions I may have to offer based on my personal or professional experience.

But again, the counselor's goal is to *offer* the alternatives, not *impose* them. This is done by the words and tone of the counselor. If, by the particular words used or the number of words used or the energy the counselor puts into her statements, the counselor implies, "Those other alternatives were okay, but now *here's* an idea you really should think seriously about," then the counselor is imposing her alternative. At this stage, you are still brainstorming. The alternatives suggested by the counselor should be stated or summarized briefly (perhaps with the implication that further details can follow if of interest to the client) and not turned into a lecture. The words and tone should convey "This has been useful to others" or "This might work," not "This *will* work."

The client may be tempted to immediately react to the counselor's alternative. If possible, ask the client to defer evaluation to the next stage, or use the opportunity to move to the next stage. But if the client immediately rejects the counselor's alternative, she should willingly drop the idea, at least for now.

4. Explore the Consequences, Pros, and Cons

This is the time for evaluating the alternatives that have been generated. The counselor's role is to help the client spend some time thinking about the pros and cons of the various alternatives and thinking ahead to the consequences of choosing one or another. It may be tempting for the client to scan "the list" and immediately select the most or the only promising choice, but here the counselor tries to forestall a too-immediate choice by the client. The process of thinking about each, or at least many of the alternatives, gives the client the opportunity to further clarify what his goals are, because each alternative may do better or worse at accomplishing particular goals. A first choice may indeed achieve some of the client's goals. But on closer examination, other goals may not be achieved by that choice. Hence spending additional time exploring the consequences of all or many of the alternatives generates more data for the client to consider than his initial intuitive reaction.

There are many value-clarifying questions the counselor can ask to engage the client in considering the pros, cons, and consequences of the different choices. For example:

- What's good about that choice? What's bad about it?
- Which choices achieve your first goal? Which choices achieve the second goal you identified?
- If you did that choice, how do you think it would turn out for you? How do you think it would affect your spouse? Your children?
- What would be the short-term consequences? How about a year or 5 years from now?
- You've talked before about how your religion (or politics) is important to you. How do you think your pastor (or your political mentor) would view the pros and cons of these alternatives?
- Could you rank-order all the choices from the one that meets the most of your goals to the one that meets the fewest?
- Would you be willing to do a Consequences Search (values clarification strategy 14 described in chapter 6) to explore the pros and cons of these alternatives?

These are but a few of the ways the counselor can ask the client to explore his potential choices and solutions more deeply. The questions are not asked to subtly guide the client to the choice or choices the counselor thinks are best for the client. Rather, they are based on the belief that people make better choices, for themselves and others, when they have more information. A more thorough, accurate picture of the pros and cons and consequences provides such information. So do educated guesses or projections on the likely outcomes of various alternatives.

5. Making a Choice, Freely

This part of the process has two aspects: making a choice and making *one's own* choice.

Making a choice means the client selects one or more of the alternatives to implement in order to resolve or make progress with the dilemma. Maybe it's just one choice—the winner—after exploring the pros and cons of the different alternatives. Or maybe it's two or more choices, each of which might be part of the solution. If the client is inclined to choose *many* alternatives for working on his issue, the counselor may want to ask the client to think about the pros and cons of selecting a more limited number of choices or changes at this point.

The other part of decision making at this stage involves the counselor helping the client take responsibility for his decision by examining whether it is indeed *the client's* choice. "Do *you* think this the best choice for you?" "Do you feel pressured to make this choice?" "This was an idea I suggested for your list of alternatives. Are you selecting this choice in part because you think *I'm* in favor of it?" The goal is for clients to separate the part of them that may just be following along with the flow of counseling but not really taking responsibility for it from the part of them that is taking ownership of the process and actively making their own decisions. The decision may be the same, but when clients take ownership—even when they say, "Okay, I don't really want to do this, to make this change, but damn it, I'm going to do it"—they begin acting on *their* values, and that is more likely to produce a successful outcome than if they do the same thing because someone "made them do it."

What if a client says he *does* feel pressured? For example, he feels pressured by his parents to make this choice. It is still important for the client to take responsibility for the choice. The counselor might say, "Okay, you feel pressured. So that's one of the cons of this choice. You said when you feel pressured, you resent it. We explored that one of the negative consequences of this choice was the possibility of your resenting your parents. So let's pause to ask, 'Do you *still* want to choose this alternative, knowing you're going to feel some resentment and will have to deal with that?'" If people feel like someone else—parents, authorities, therapists—made them do something, they may have less of an investment in making it work. So both for ethical reasons (counselors shouldn't impose values on clients) and practical reasons (free choices are more likely to be implemented well), it is helpful to work with clients to make their own choices to the extent possible.

One more thought about free choice. In some instances, clients (and therapists) simply do not have free choice. A client may be ordered by the court to undergo drug treatment or anger management. A therapist may have to write a treatment plan for the client that will satisfy the court's mandate. Even in such situations, one of the most powerful aspects of values clarification is how it helps the client take responsibility. When the counselor, as part of establishing a "contract" with the client, says, "I know the court ordered you to be here and you resent it, so I want to ask you, are you determined to sit through these required sessions and do as little as possible, or is there something, *anything*, that *you* want to get from our time together?" the counselor is asking a crucial clarifying question involving free choice that could be the beginning of their productive work together.

6. Planning for Action

Clients often have insights or make decisions in counseling sessions but do not necessarily follow up on them. This step in the value-clarifying process moves the interview from goal setting and decision making to acting. The counselor remains the facilitator, not the director of the process. She doesn't tell the client that it is now time for him to act or how to implement his choice; she invites him to consider what the next step or steps would be, if he were to move forward with his decision.

The "*if* he were to move forward" is important at this stage. The question for the client is not "Now that you made a choice, how are you going to implement it?" but "Now that you've made a choice, how *might* you implement it?" The goal is to have the client think in terms of "I could" or "I would do thus and so," rather than "I will do thus and so." (That's part b.)

The distinction is important because it may be difficult for a client to know right away what action he wants to take. No one wants to commit to a course of action and then not follow through with it or not carry it off successfully. A client can think more clearly and creatively about next steps if he doesn't feel "If I say it, I have to do it." Thus it is helpful to separate action planning into two stages—first thinking about what action is desirable and then making the decision to actually do it.

a. Determining Next Steps

At this stage, the counselor's clarifying questions are couched as hypotheticals. "Now that you've decided you want some money, how could you act on this decision?" "You've decided that job training is the choice you'd like to pursue to get yourself back on track economically. Can you think of any ways you could begin a job training program?" "You've chosen assisted living as the best alternative for this stage of your life. What are some ways you might move ahead with this choice?"

Sometimes, like the little Russian dolls that hold even smaller dolls inside, there are next steps embedded in next steps. Thus, when the client says one way to move ahead with his choice to move into assisted living is to visit some assisted living facilities, the counselor might ask, "And what would you have to do to visit some facilities?" If the client then said, "I'd have to call my daughter to drive me," the counselor might say, "Okay, one possible next step would be to call your daughter. Would there be anything else you'd have to do to carry off these visits?" To which the client might say, "Well, we'll have to figure out where we're going and make appointments."

Or if the client did not think of that himself, the counselor could ask, "Do you know what facilities you'd like to visit, or will you have to figure that out?"

In other words, the counselor's clarifying questions help the client visualize one or more of the steps that might be taken to implement the client's choice or decision. Hopefully, the client will think of some of the possible action steps himself, but as with the stage of generating alternatives, the counselor can invite the client to consider other action steps. For example, if the client doesn't say anything about making an appointment with the assisted living facilities, the counselor could ask, "Do you think you need to make an appointment?" or could even say, "In my experience, some facilities welcome drop-ins, whereas others require appointments. What is your thinking about whether to call for an appointment?" Then again, the counselor might sense that enough next steps have been identified and details like calling for an appointment might best be left to the client to think of himself. As in any human communication, sensitivity about when one has said or done enough, when it's time to move on, is always a helpful asset. If in doubt, one can always ask the client, "Have we done enough planning for now, or would you like to explore possible further details?"

b. Committing to Act

At this stage, the counselor invites the client to take a deep breath (figuratively or literally) and commit to a course of action—or not. The "or not" is important. This is the ultimate clarifying question in the clarifying interview: "Are you going to do it?" In the previous step (6a), the client worked out what it would take to implement his decision to achieve his goal. At this stage, the question is whether he is ready to walk the walk.

As always, there are many different words the counselor can use to ask this basic clarifying question: "Are you ready?" "Are you ready to commit yourself to calling the job center?" "Will you call your daughter to drive you?" "Are you really going to put aside $20 a week?" "How serious a commitment is this?"

As always, there is no right answer to these questions from the counselor's viewpoint. Sure, we're human. We've been working with this person for some time. We hope they are ready to take this step and act to achieve their goals. But at the same time, maybe they don't feel ready, *and we've got to accept that*. Clients should feel that whether they commit themselves to act or not, we will continue to accept and support them. Our goal is for them to develop *their own* values. If they are not ready to take responsibility for acting on their own volition, we do not want to pressure or guilt them into it. If they are not ready to act, or if they say they are going to act but then don't act, we want them to feel accepted enough that they will feel free to come back and work on the issue some more.

At the same time, their statement of commitment—"I'm going to call my daughter," "I'm going to save $20 a week"—may be subject to further clarification and action planning. The counselor might ask, "When are you going to call her?" or "By when are you going to call her?" "When are you going to save the first $20?" "Are you going to do it the same day every week?" "Would it help if you made an arrangement with a friend to tell her each time you saved the $20? Would that kind of structure make it more likely you'll follow through?"

This stage has been described exclusively as a verbal process, and it usually is. The client asserts aloud that he is going to act on his decision. The commitment can also be written down. There is a values clarification strategy called the Self Contract (see chapter 6, 24) in which a person makes a written commitment to himself to follow through with a course of action. It ups the ante when a client reads his contract, "Within one week from today, I will call the job training center and make an appointment," and the counselor then asks, "Are you ready to sign your name to this contract with yourself?"

As these examples above indicate, the clarifying interview process has a logical sequence but not a rigid one. It keeps turning back on itself as new iterations of prioritizing, generating alternatives, and action planning take place. It cannot be done by a formula. Only the client and counselor can know at the particular moment whether it seems more useful to continue exploring alternatives or to move on to evaluating them, whether it seems more useful to stay with next steps and action planning or move on to commitment—or go back to acknowledging feelings churned up by the prospect of a commitment. As always, counseling is both art and science.

■ ANALYZING A CLARIFYING INTERVIEW—PAUL'S CASE REVISITED

Chapter 1 contained an example of a brief clarifying interview. Let us replay that interview here, analyzing it from the perspective of values clarification counseling. First, a little more background about the client.

When the counselor first met Paul, then a ninth grader, Paul was coming out of his Nazi period. A very intelligent, very angry young man, Paul worked hard at maintaining his attitude of superiority toward others. He had briefly been enamored with the skinhead movement that promised a sense of superiority at the expense of non-whites, Jews, and other minorities. Paul had backed off from this extreme, but he still seemed to relish his own nonconformity—grungy clothes, long hair, work boots— all signs of his scorn for conventional middle-class values. Thus it was natural for him to be attracted to the new male teacher-counselor in the school who sometimes came to work on a motorcycle, became faculty advisor to the student peace group, and offered an optional, noncredit course on the poetry of Bob Dylan. Ironically, the counselor was Jewish. No matter. Paul was searching for an identity, and the counselor was a potential role model.

The counselor recognized that Paul had some significant, unresolved emotional issues, not the least of which was his estrangement from a father who failed to meet Paul's unrealistic expectations, and Paul's shaky sense of self-esteem that was as likely to manifest itself in broad condemnation of others as in self-deprecation and self-doubt. On the other hand, what teenager who sought independence and saw beyond the conformist, material culture around him *didn't* suffer from the angst of adolescence? Rather than viewing Paul as a candidate for mental health counseling per se, the counselor chose to regard Paul as a young man in the painful process of growing up. So on this particular day when Paul swept into his office unannounced, the counselor responded to Paul's presenting problem as it was presented—a practical dilemma in navigating the shoals of adolescence, balancing the need for self- and social acceptance, establishing an identity, developing a set of values.

PAUL: I've really had it with those guys! They hassle me all the time about my hair being long. What do they know, the creeps? I just want to get the hell out of here. I'm tired of being hit on by those jerks.

COUNSELOR: Sounds like you're really fed up with those guys, to the point that you'd really like to leave.

This is pure empathic listening—the foundation and a major component in any counseling relationship. Through his total attention, facial expressions, guttural expressions (which don't necessarily appear in the transcript), and overall demeanor, the counselor is demonstrating that he genuinely cares about what Paul is saying and is concerned for Paul's well-being. By his empathic response, he demonstrates he understands Paul, or at least that he wants to understand him. He doesn't try to talk Paul out of or minimize his frustration (as in, "Oh, surely you wouldn't want to quit school over such a trivial incident") but rather accepts that this is how Paul feels at this moment. By his complete acceptance of Paul's feelings, he shows a respect for Paul, *as he is*, which enables Paul to feel safe in the relationship and be open to the counselor's subsequent invitations to move beyond his upset feelings.

PAUL: Yeah. My hair is my business. I don't want to look like them... they all look like carbon copies of each other. This is a free country, and a person has a right to wear his hair any way he wants to.

COUNSELOR: So your hair is an important statement of who you are? You really believe that it's your right to wear it any way you want to.

Again, the counselor demonstrates his desire to understand Paul's feelings, to understand the situation, and to show his trust and acceptance of Paul and his concern for him. Yet embedded in the counselor's empathic response is a values clarification concept—a focus on *what is important to Paul*.

PAUL: Yeah... but I'm getting really tired of those guys bugging me.

COUNSELOR: I hear how fed up you are. [Pause.] Tell me, is your long hair primarily a social statement for you, or do you really like wearing it long... the look and feel of it for you? If, for example, all the guys in the school were to let their hair grow, would you keep yours the way it is because you really like it... or would you cut it short to make your statement about wanting to be different?

After another expression of empathy and a pause that communicated that the counselor was letting what Paul said sink in, the counselor asked a clarifying question that asked Paul to consider what it was that he valued here, what he actually prized and cherished. Was it the hairstyle itself or was it being different from others? The counselor didn't have a correct answer in mind to this question. He would accept whatever response Paul might give. He was simply asking Paul to examine in greater depth what was important to him.

Where did that question come from? Out of all the possible, helpful, clarifying questions the counselor might have asked, why did he ask how Paul would feel if all the other kids grew their hair long? Short answer: it just occurred to him. Longer answer: when one is working in a values clarification framework, asking clients to examine their situation from another point of view, including how they came to adopt particular value indicators (likes, dislikes, opinions, etc.), is a frequent behavior. This is based on the premise that reflecting on our value indicators increases the likelihood of our developing more mature values. So the counselor, half intuitively, half consciously, was scanning the horizon for such a question that would invite Paul to look more deeply at his attitudes about hair, and this question popped into his mind. Other questions might have accomplished the same goal: "How did your hair come to be important to you?" "Has your hair always been important to you?" "Do you think most ninth graders care a lot about their hair, or is this something that's special to you?" And so on. There's no one right question. If it engages the client in the valuing process, it's probably helpful.

PAUL: Hmm, I never thought of that. I guess I grew it at first to spite my dad. It was the first thing I ever did that went against his orders... that he couldn't make me change. Then after a while I got to really like it. Maybe someday I'll get bored with it, but right now I'd keep it long even if everybody else grew theirs.

COUNSELOR: So, more important than trying to make a point by wearing your hair long is the fact that you really *like* it that way.

Again, an empathic listening response. It is useful to remember that in addition to conveying understanding and acceptance, empathic listening is clarifying in itself, emotionally and cognitively. By reflecting back to Paul what he understood Paul to say, the counselor holds a mirror up for Paul, enabling him to clarify "Is that what I said? Is that what I believe? Does that really capture my meaning or do I mean something else? Did the counselor state my feelings more strongly, less strongly, or just how I feel them?"

PAUL: Yeah.

COUNSELOR: Have you thought about how you might be able to lessen their hassling?

At this point, the counselor thinks the problem is sufficiently defined and Paul's most immediate feelings have been expressed and understood, that he thinks it may be acceptable to Paul to begin exploring alternatives. Hence he asks Paul a clarifying question that invites him to begin the process of exploring alternative solutions to his dilemma. It is phrased in a gentle way, so that Paul won't feel defensive if he hasn't thought about any solutions yet. If Paul seems unready to start thinking about alternatives, or there's another problem that's more pressing for Paul than this one, they can return to the previous stages of the interview.

PAUL: Yeah, I want to leave. I just can't take it. I mean, it was really bad today.
COUNSELOR: So the first thing that comes to mind is wanting to quit school. [Paul: Yeah.] Can you think of any others?

(Paul's comment that "it was really bad today" is a potential red flag. Paul may have been deeply humiliated and hurt, emotionally or physically. He might benefit from deeper empathy, a chance to cry, or further psychotherapeutic exploration of his situation. In this instance, the counselor chooses to remain on the level of problem solving and values clarification. Likewise, this incident alerts the counselor to a bullying situation in the school that may warrant an intervention. He will come back to this on another occasion than the current interview.)

Here the counselor recognizes that Paul's initial flight impulse is, indeed, one alternative solution and validates it by acknowledging it explicitly. Obviously, the counselor would not like to see Paul quit school over this incident—after all, counselors are human, with feelings, opinions, and values of our own—but he does not want to impose that value judgment on Paul. He wants to help Paul think through the issues himself and make *his own* best choice. The counselor also wants Paul to learn *how to* make thoughtful decisions, beyond this particular problem. So Paul's first alternative is accepted as just that—the first alternative. But the counselor doesn't stop there. Following the values clarification process, the counselor asks Paul if he can think of any other alternatives.

In fact, even if Paul's first alternative had been a mature and realistic suggestion, one that the counselor thought was a positive choice, the counselor would *still* have asked Paul if he had any other alternatives to suggest. This is a very important point. This is not an exercise to get Paul to do something the counselor thinks is wise or good, but to help Paul find his own best choice. The counselor must really believe that, given a safe and supportive setting to think through an issue, the client really is capable of making good or better choices. A counselor who does not have that basic trust in her clients should not use values clarification.

PAUL: I could cut my hair... but I won't!
COUNSELOR: So cutting your hair is another alternative... [At this point, the counselor reached for a marker he kept handy and wrote on a board behind him "Quit" and, below that, "Cut hair."]

The counselor had no initial plan to start listing alternatives, but there it was. He had asked Paul the alternatives question, Paul had mentioned a second alternative, and the counselor suddenly visualized a list of alternatives in the making. So he wrote them down. He could have written them on a piece of paper that he and Paul could see, or he could have just repeated them aloud—creating a virtual list—but he happened to have a marker board behind him and decided at the spur of the moment to use it. By actually listing the alternatives, the counselor focused the dialogue and demonstrated respect for Paul's ideas.

PAUL: I won't do it!
COUNSELOR: You feel pretty certain of that.... Might there be any other alternatives?

Paul's feelings of anger and injustice reemerge here, so the counselor shifts to empathic listening again. It is important for the counselor to maintain that empathy and acceptance throughout the values clarification process. It helps keep the process focused on the client and enables the client to trust the counselor and be willing to continue the values clarification process because he knows the counselor is not trying to impose his own solutions. By having his feelings understood and accepted, Paul settles down and is ready to continue the consideration of other alternatives.

There is no correct number of alternatives to shoot for. Every situation is different. Here the counselor sensed that Paul was thinking about the situation and was capable of taking it further on his own. By asking the client to continue considering other alternatives, the counselor is not only facilitating more alternatives onto the table but also teaching the client the process of searching for alternatives, of not necessarily choosing the first or second idea to come along.

PAUL: Well, maybe I could cut it a little—get one of those haircuts that are done by someone who knows what they're doing. I cut it now. Maybe if it was cut better, it would look better.
COUNSELOR: Okay, cutting your hair just a little and well is another alternative. [He added "Professional cut" to the list.]

In just moments, Paul went from insisting he wouldn't cut his hair to entertaining that he might cut it a little. This is the power of values clarification's nonjudgmental acceptance. Paul does not have to feel defensive about what he says or thinks. He can think creatively and be open to new alternatives.

Again, the counselor does not place a value judgment on Paul's latest alternative ("Now you're talking!"). Some of Paul's ideas may seem better from the counselor's viewpoint, but it's not his job to praise or criticize the different alternatives, not even subtly.

PAUL: But I haven't got the bucks to do it....
COUNSELOR: Uh-huh.... I can think of one or two other ideas. Would you like to hear them?

Again, the counselor's "Uh-huh" (which could just as well have been an "I see" or a nod of the head or the like) conveys acceptance and empathy, which is very important at this point, because the counselor is about to ask Paul whether he'd like to hear some of the counselor's ideas. The last thing the counselor wants to convey is "Okay, we've gone through the obligatory steps of getting your ideas on the table; now we'll get to the really *good* ideas—mine." On the contrary, although the counselor may or may not prefer some of his own ideas to Paul's, he knows that Paul is the one who has to make this decision and live with the consequences, so he makes every effort not to privilege any ideas over any others. That's not always possible; sometimes our own biases as counselors—or in this case, as adults—creep in even though we try to hide them. That's all right occasionally. As long as clients trust our sincerity about wanting them to find their own best solutions, they will be able to ignore our occasional lapses.

Perhaps the counselor should have asked Paul, "Any other options?" and only when Paul said, "No" would the counselor begin to introduce his own alternatives. But rightly or wrongly the counselor sensed that Paul had exhausted his ideas, the counselor had accepted them nonjudgmentally, and the timing was right to offer Paul an alternative of his own. Thus Paul is not left to his own limited resources, information, or imagination. There is a role for the counselor's experience, knowledge, or creativity here to support Paul's values clarification. However, the counselor first asks Paul if he would like to hear the new alternatives. He does not want to impose them on Paul.

PAUL: Yeah.
COUNSELOR: Well, I had a friend with long hair who wore it tied back... and another who wore a headband to kind of keep it neat.
PAUL: Huh. I have a headband that a friend of mine once gave me. I wonder where I stashed it.

Paul immediately seemed to respond positively to one of the counselor's ideas. I say "ideas" rather than "suggestions." The counselor is not suggesting Paul *should* wear a headband; he's merely contributing the alternative to the list of ideas. Once it's on the list, Paul can evaluate it more objectively on its merits, rather than perceive it as the counselor's idea that the counselor might have a stake in. This is one of the most important points I can make about the values clarification process, which is especially dramatic when working with young people. If the counselor is truly respectful of the client's perspective, the client will be more likely to be open to hearing the counselor's perspective.

This is one of the great ironies of using values clarification with children and youth. Many adults are worried that to the extent we allow or encourage young people to make their own choices, they will ignore their parents' and society's wisdom. Paradoxically, I have found the opposite to be true. The more we respect their choosing process, when it's a thoughtful process, the more they will be interested in what alternatives we have to offer. *The more we listen to them, the more they'll listen to us.*

COUNSELOR: [After adding "tie back" and "headband" to the list.] Well, let's take a look at these ideas. How do you respond to each of them? And do you think they'd help to lessen the guys' hassling of you?

Here the counselor moves to the next step of considering the pros and cons and consequences of the different alternatives. But he does this in a natural sort of way. He doesn't say, "Now let's consider the consequences of these alternatives. Let's look at the pros and cons of each of them." In some situations, those words might be fine, but in this instance they would have felt too formal and formulaic. Not that the counselor thought it through in these terms. He just hit on what seemed to him a natural and comfortable question, one that asked Paul to begin evaluating the choices.

PAUL: I don't know. I still feel like quitting, but I think that I'd be giving in to them if I did. I think I'd feel a little funny wearing the headband—like I was playing hippie or something. I kind of like the idea of tying my hair back or getting a professional haircut...
COUNSELOR: So those two seem the best ideas to you, huh?

The counselor's response is both an empathic reflection of Paul's last comments and a value-clarifying question that helps Paul narrow down the alternatives.

PAUL: Yeah. I guess that if I got it cut by someone, it would look better. It wouldn't look so homegrown.... Until I get some cash, though, I think I'll try tying it back. I have a friend who used to wear his hair that way.

Paul seems to have made a tentative decision. Sometimes the counselor has to ask one or more questions to help the client move from a short list of alternatives to a decision, then to a choice that can be acted upon, and then to a commitment to act. Sometimes it just happens on its own, as in this instance.

COUNSELOR: So you're going to tie it back while you're figuring out a way to raise the money to get a good cut.... When do you think you'll begin tying it back— today... next week... ?

The counselor summarizes what he understands to be Paul's choice. Although peer pressure brought about the necessity for a decision, the counselor has no sense that Paul is bowing to undue pressure from peers or from authority (himself) in making *this* decision, so he does not ask Paul questions like "Are you comfortable with this decision?" or "Do you feel this is your decision... that no one, including me, is pressuring you to choose the tie-it-back choice over the others?" Instead, he proceeds to the next stage of exploring next steps. That is, he asks Paul to begin considering the action implementation of his decision.

PAUL: Well,... maybe tomorrow morning.
COUNSELOR: Okay, then. Stop by and let me know how things turn out, all right?
PAUL: Yeah, thanks.

Sometimes a client's proposed actions are unrealistic. For example, a client who wants to start saving money may say that he is going to save every penny from now on. In a case like that, one may ask clarifying questions about whether this is a realistic goal or even cycle back to considering alternative paces or methods for saving money. But in this case, Paul's strategy for tying his hair back the very next morning seemed entirely realistic to Paul and to the counselor. So the counselor acknowledges Paul's plan with a simple "Okay, then."

The counselor also communicates that he is interested in the outcome. In effect, he shows his genuine interest in Paul's well-being, and he leaves the door open for continuing the clarifying process—evaluating Paul's decision and action in light of the actual results. In fact, many problem-solving models include *evaluation* as a final step. In the values clarification process, some level of evaluation is inevitable as, in this case, Paul experiences whether he implemented the new behavior and whether it achieved the desired goals. Further evaluation can take place in another counseling session, if Paul so chooses.

As it turned out, the headband approach worked for Paul. He thought it was cool, and if it didn't entirely eliminate the bullying, it reduced it to a tolerable level for him. But if the solution hadn't worked, the counselor had made it safe for Paul to come back and work on the problem some more.

Did this brief episode of values clarification counseling settle all of Paul's emotional issues—for example, his troubled relationship with his father or his vulnerable self-esteem? Of course not. Those are longer, possibly lifelong tasks. Did it result in a little bit more clarity about how to achieve his own goals and sense of identity in an environment of bullying and peer pressure? Yes—and that certainly can't hurt one's self-esteem.

Paul's case reminds us of the distinction made at the beginning of the book between values clarification counseling and mental health counseling. Let's say a man in his late 20s has lost his job and is confused about his goals and career direction. He's anxious. His self-esteem is falling. He's worried he's letting his parents down. His relationship with his partner is suffering. He feels like a wreck. He comes to a counselor who is skilled in both mental health and career counseling. What does this client need? Do they work on his anxiety, his low self-esteem, his relationship with his parents, his relationship with his partner, or his career confusion? Which is more appropriate—mental health counseling or values clarification and career counseling? If both, where does one start?

In general, I would follow the client's lead, working on what the client perceives the most pressing issue or issues to be. In the context of a clarifying interview, our first step would be to clarify what the most pressing issue(s) or dilemma is. Having said that, when in doubt, I work on the pressing value dilemmas first. Working on the client's career confusion using values clarification may work out very well for the present and for years to come. If it leads toward great value clarity and landing a decent job, the other issues may fade into the background. However, if the other issues of anxiety, low self-esteem, and relationships are large enough, they will resurface, sooner or later. Similarly, with other clients, solving a problem at work, getting organized, or making some good choices about diet, exercise, and health can do wonders for self-esteem, mood, and relationships. If underlying emotional or mental health issues still need attention, they will surface soon enough.

6 Values Clarification Strategies

■ INTRODUCTION

Values clarification strategies are values-clarifying questions combined with a structured format for responding. A client may write his response in a journal, rank a series of alternatives in preferred order, place himself along a continuum of responses, compile an inventory, complete sentence stems, indicate agreement or disagreement by a hand signal (in a group setting), and on and on.

Let's say, for example, the counselor is working with a recovering substance abuser in a residential rehabilitation program around the challenges the client will experience when he returns to his home community. Let's say the specific issue is how the client will be able to say no when offered a drink or drugs by his old buddies. Possible values-clarifying questions might include the following.

- What would a good response be when your friend offers you a drink?
- What are different ways you might respond when a friend offers you a drink?
- How comfortable would you be telling your friend, "I'm taking a break from booze. You have a drink if you want; I'll have a soda (or whatever)"?
- What do you wish your friend would understand about you and drinking?

The same questions can be turned into values clarification strategies by combining them in a structured format for responding. For example:

Rank Order

Which would be the best response when a friend offers you a drink? Rank all the choices from best to worst.

- Say no thank you.
- Take the drink, but only have an occasional tiny sip.
- Say you don't feel well and leave.
- Explain why you can't accept and ask for his or her support.

Continuum

How comfortable would you be telling your friend, "No thanks. I'm taking a break from booze. You have a drink if you want; I'll have a soda (or whatever)"? Put your initials on the line between these two end points:

Completely   Incredibly
Comfortable _____ Uncomfortable

Inventorying

Make a list of all the possible responses you could give when your friend offers you a drink. Put a P for "possible" next to all the responses you might consider doing. Put an N for "No" next to any of the responses on your list that seem totally unrealistic or you'd never do them. Put a question mark (?) next to any of the ideas on your list you're not sure about. Next, of the options you considered possible, rank them in order from the most feasible for you to the least feasible.

Sentence Stems

How would you complete the following sentence? (Choose one) OR

On your paper, choose three of the following incomplete sentences and complete each of them for yourself.

- If a friend offered me a drink, I would _____.
- If a friend offered me a drink, I would not _____.
- I wish my friend would understand that _____.
- I'd like to tell my friend _____.
- No friend of mine would _____.

Each of these strategies can be done with individual clients or in group counseling, group therapy, and psychoeducational groups. Whether in individual or group settings, the strategies are not meant to be ends in themselves. *Each of them can and probably should be followed by further exploration of the topic.*

In a group situation, clients can respond aloud randomly, respond in turn around the circle, share their responses in a pair or trio, discuss them in the whole group, or use a variety of other group formats, as described in chapter 3. Values clarification strategies are structured to make it relatively easy for clients to respond and to maximize participation in a group setting. One of the real benefits of values clarification strategies in groups is they give everyone a chance to participate, feel successful, and feel a part of the group.

The counselor can also participate in these activities from time to time. Guidelines for the counselor's participation are discussed in chapter 3.

Forty-one values clarification strategies are described here. The following table lists the strategies and indicates whether they are appropriate for individual counseling and/or group settings. Most strategies work in both individual and group settings, although the format for responding may be different. The table also indicates whether the strategy is a "basic" values clarification strategy. A basic strategy might also be called a repeatable or bread-and-butter strategy. Just as bread and butter is a staple in a traditional American diet (for better or worse), a bread-and-butter or basic strategy can be used again and again. For example, one can ask a client or group many different Continuum questions (#4) on different topics over the course of counseling or the life of the group. In contrast, Values Name Tags (#26) and What's in Your Wallet? (#27) are strategies that would probably be used only once with a particular group.

#	STRATEGY	INDIV	GROUP	BASIC (repeatable)
1	Inventories	X	X	X
2	Prioritizing—Rank Order	X	X	X
3	Forced Choice Ladder	X	X	
4	Continuum	X	X	X
5	Either-Or Forced Choice		X	
6	Strongly Agree/Strongly Disagree		X	
7	Values Voting		X	X
8	Proud Questions	X	X	X
9	Magic Questions	X	X	X
10	Percentage Questions	X	X	X
11	Pie of Life	X	X	
12	Public Interview		X	X
13	Group Interview		X	X
14	Unfinished Sentences	X	X	X
15	I Learned Statements		X	X
16	I Wonder Statements		X	X
17	Alternative Search	X	X	X
18	Consequences Search	X	X	X
19	Pattern Search	X	X	
20	Alternative Action Search	X	X	X
21	Force Field Analysis	X	X	X
22	Removing Barriers to Action	X	X	
23	Getting Started or Next Steps	X	X	X
24	Self-Contract	X	X	X
25	What We Know & Want to Know		X	X
26	Values Name Tags		X	
27	What's in Your Wallet		X	
28	One-Minute Autobiography		X	
29	Pages for an Autobiography	X	X	
30	Role Model Analysis	X	X	
31	Board of Directors	X	X	
32	Chairs or Dialogue with Self	X	X	X
33	Life Line	X	X	
34	Who Are You?	X	X	
35	Epitaph	X	X	
36	Self-Obituary		X	
37	Self-Eulogy		X	
38	Life Inventory	X	X	
39	Values Cards		X	X
40	Values Diary	X	X	X
41	Values Journal	X	X	X

Rather than presenting random examples of these many values clarification strategies across a myriad of counseling topics, I have selected 10 counseling topics—recovery, careers, work, couples, money, sex, health, religion/spirituality, loss, and aging—and illustrated how different strategies can be used to explore these topics—or any topics. This approach is meant to demonstrate how values clarification strategies are not meant to be formulaic activities that one takes out of a book. Rather, they are created or adapted by the counselor to engage a particular client or group around a topic of relevance to them.

■ 1. INVENTORIES

One day many years ago, John, a precocious 11th-grade student, walked into my office looking totally defeated and informed me that life had no meaning. It seemed he had just read an essay by Albert Camus and was staring existential despair in the face for the first time. After listening and chatting a bit, I gave him a piece of paper and a pen and asked him to make a list of 10 or 15 things in life that he really loved to do. Looking a little puzzled but willing, he set to work and quickly came up with a list of a dozen or so things that fit the bill. When his inventory had run its course, he looked up at me. "So what do you think?" I asked. "Thanks," he said. "That was good." And with a totally different and more upbeat energy, he sauntered out of my office. Clearly, this would not be the last time that John would grapple with existential anguish, but this time, anyway, this simple values-clarifying strategy helped him through another day.

With apologies to Murray Burns, the lovable if immature protagonist in the movie *A Thousand Clowns*, who bemoaned that his nephew Nick might be adopted by "a family of list makers," the inventory is a wonderful strategy for helping clients look more closely at the choices in their lives.

Twenty Things You Love to Do is possibly the most famous values clarification strategy. It is useful in individual and group settings. Clients or group members draw a grid on their paper that looks like this:

Things You Love To Do	Alone(A) People(P)	$	Father(F) Mother(M)	Last Did It
1				
2				
etc.				

The counselor or leader asks them to make a list of *20 things in life that they love to do*—big things, small things; it doesn't matter. They should do this in any order that things come to mind. No one will see their lists unless they want to share them, so they can feel free to be honest about their lists. When they are done, the counselor asks various coding questions, such as the following, to enable them to examine what they prize and cherish even more closely.

1. Put an *A* next to those items you prefer to do *alone*, put a *P* next to those things you prefer to do with other *people*, and put an *AP* next to those you love to do equally alone or with others.
2. Put a dollar sign ($) next to any of the items that requires money for you to do. (If it doesn't take money or takes only a negligible amount for you, leave it blank.)
3. Use an *F* for *father* and/or *M* for *mother* to indicate which of these things your father and mother (or grandmother or guardian, etc.) liked to do. [This gets at the free choice valuing process.]
4. When did you last *do* this thing? Put a day, or date, or word in the column to indicate when you last did it. [This question gets at the action step in the valuing process.]

5. Put an asterisk next to the five things in life on your list that you love to do the most. Finally, use the numbers 1 to 5 to rank-order those five from the thing you love the most (it's the last thing in the world you'd give up if you had to), second most, third, fourth, and fifth.

An inventory like this is a prefabricated strategy that can be brought into any number of group situations. Other inventories can be prepared ahead of time or made up on the spot. In my interview with Paul in the opening chapter, it just occurred to me in the moment to ask him to give me a list of all the possible responses he could think of to being hassled about his long hair. He came up with the list; I wrote each of them down.

Recovery: Make a list of all the possible responses you could give when your friend offers you a drink.

Careers: Make a list of 20 different careers that you know someone who works in them.

Work: Make a list of 10 to 20 different tasks you perform in your work. On a scale from 1 to 5, indicate how satisfying each is.

Couples: Make a list of 10 things you love or like to do by yourself, 10 things you love or like to do together, and 10 things you like to do with your own friends.

Money: Make a list of expenditures that almost always bring you pleasure and you don't later regret. Make a list of expenditures that often are disappointing or you later regret.

Sex: Make a list of all the things you do that give sexual pleasure to your partner.

Health: Write down 5 to 10 things you do that are good for your health. Now write 5 to 10 things you do that are probably not good for your health.

Religion, Spirituality: Try to remember all the times you felt connected to God or a wider force in the universe. Code them *C* if they took place in church or other religious structure, *N* if they took place in nature, *R* if they had to do with religion, and *W* if you've ever given witness or made a public affirmation of your experience.

Loss, Bereavement: Make a list of 20 things you love to do. Which have you done less of since your loss (use a minus sign)? Which have you done more of (+)? Which have you done about as often as before your loss (=)? Which do you hope to do more of in the future (++)? For the things you hope to do more of in the future— and no one will hold you to this—when do you think you might be ready to start doing a bit more of them? Write a day or month or date for each of them.

Aging: Make a list of 20 things you love to do. Put a 5 next to those things you hope and expect to be doing 5 years from now. Put a 10 next to those you hope and expect to be doing 10 years from now. Put a *D* next to those you hope and expect to be doing until you die. Add 1 to 5 new items to your list to indicate things you might like to learn to do in the coming years.

■ **2. RANK ORDER (PRIORITIZING)**

Prioritizing is an important values clarification strategy that helps clients clarify what they prize and cherish, evaluate better to worse choices, and rank preferred action steps. Value-clarifying questions (chapter 4) can elicit the process of prioritizing, as in "What is the best thing about that?" or "What is your favorite _____?" However, other values clarification strategies, like the Rank Order and Forced-Choice Ladder (3), enable clients to prioritize in a more structured way.

The Rank Order typically presents three or four choices for clients to put in order of preference or in an order based on how the question is phrased. For example:

Recovery: Which of the following groups do you think will be most helpful to you in staying sober?

_____ Family
_____ Friends
_____ Professional Helpers
_____ Religious, Spiritual Contacts

The idea is for the client or group members to put *all* the choices in order—in this case, the most helpful, second most helpful, and so on, to the least helpful.

The choices can come from alternatives the client has mentioned himself or from the group, or they can be provided by the counselor.

Such an exercise is a forced choice in the sense that there is limited information provided and the client's ranking might change, depending on the circumstances. That's okay. The goal is not to get a ranking that perfectly reflects all the client's feelings and opinions, but to help the client get in touch with many feelings, attitudes, thoughts, issues, and questions about the topic. Less important than the order is the reflection that the client engages in as a result of being asked to rank the items. The client typically has quite a lot to say after doing a rank order, providing lots of good material for further exploration in the counseling session or group discussion.

If a client resists a Rank Order, don't argue about it. Ask, "What's another choice that expresses your first choice better than the ones I gave you?" Or "Okay, let's forget the rank order. What thoughts and feelings went through your mind or body when you started to think about the issues the rank order raised?"

Here are some other examples of Rank Orders on different topics. But as with all values clarification strategies, they often are best when made up on the spot out of choices the client is discussing. When I hear a client mention two or three options around an issue, a potential Rank Order often occurs to me. Whether I present the Rank Order to the client is a choice based on many factors, including whether it seems relevant, whether it fits the flow of the conversation or might interrupt the client's process, whether I sense it might be helpful, and whether we've done a similar structured exercise recently and this might seem too repetitious.

Careers: How do you generally like most to work?

_____ Individually
_____ With one other person
_____ With a small group

Work: When your boss overloads you with work, which are you most likely to tell him or her? (Then: What would you most like to tell him or her? Which would be the most professional response?)

_____ "Do it yourself."
_____ "I don't have time."
_____ "Yes, sir."
_____ "Given limited time, would you rather I do this before that other task I'm working on?"

Couples: If you had a Saturday afternoon that you were going to spend together, how would you rank these choices in order of preference?

_____ Go for a walk.
_____ Go to a play, concert, or cultural event.
_____ Play a sport.
_____ Make love.

Money: Who are you most like when it comes to how you handle money?

_____ Your mother
_____ Your father
_____ Your best friend
_____ Your spouse or partner

Sex: When do you most enjoy lovemaking?

_____ Morning
_____ Afternoon
_____ Evening
_____ Variety of times

Health: Which do you think you're most likely to die from?

_____ Heart attack
_____ Lung cancer
_____ Old age
_____ An accident

Religion, Spirituality: If you think of God (Allah, the Tao, etc.), which comes closest to your conception of God?

_____ A humanlike figure
_____ An abstract concept
_____ A form of energy
_____ I have no conception of God

Loss: What do you most fear about (or what has been hardest about) losing your partner?

_____ Finances
_____ Being alone
_____ Loss of intimacy
_____ Managing daily life

Aging: What do you most look forward to about getting older?

_____ Being more at peace with myself
_____ Being wiser
_____ Being financially independent
_____ Having grandchildren
_____ Being retired

There is nothing magical about three or four choices. More options are possible. When there are many more choices, the Forced-Choice Ladder strategy is often a useful structure for handling the larger number of options.

■ 3. FORCED-CHOICE LADDER

There are other strategies that use prioritizing. For example, the Forced-Choice Ladder uses a diagram of a ladder or staircase. Clients are given a larger number of choices to rank in order. They can be given the choices all at once and asked to rank them, putting a key word for each choice onto one rung of the ladder or one step of the staircase, or they can be given one choice at a time, so that with each new option, they are required to rethink the issues and rearrange their ranking.

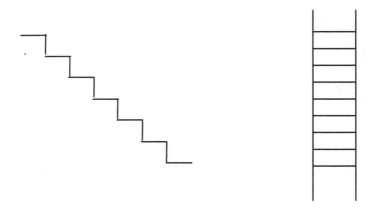

For example, a counselor working with a group in recovery might distribute a page with a blank staircase with 12 steps on it to each member, along with 12 small blank slips of paper, and say,

Here's the situation. You're out of alcohol treatment. You're back home. You've been sober for three weeks. You and three friends are at one of their houses, playing poker. The host brings out a small keg and glasses. Your three friends eagerly fill their glasses. One offers to pour one for you. You say, "No thanks." One of your friends says, "Whatsamatter? Did they turn you into a teetotaler?" Another says, "You're not turning into a wimp, are you?"

Now I'm about to give you 12 different responses to this situation, one at a time. I'll give you a key word or two for each response. Then I'd like you to put that response on one of the steps on the staircase, somewhere between the top, which is what you think would be the best choice in the situation, and the bottom, which is what you think would be the worst choice in the situation. Okay, here goes:

- "Shut up and deal the cards." [Key words: Shut Up]
- "If you guys were my friends, you'd know I have a drinking problem and would support me in trying to quit." [Key words: If Friends]
- "Sure, fill it up"—and you wouldn't drink it. [Fill, Don't Drink]
- "Just pour me a little"—and you wouldn't drink it. [Little, Don't Drink]
- "Lay off; I can't afford to go off the wagon." [I Can't]
- "Sure, fill it up"—and you'd sip it very, very slowly and make it last the whole night. [Fill and Sip]
- "I don't feel well; I need to leave." [Leave]
- "I've been sober for three weeks. I don't want to blow it." [Don't Blow It]
- "I've got a problem with alcohol. I'll just have a Coke, thanks." [Problem–Coke]
- "I don't feel like alcohol tonight." [Don't Feel Like It]
- "My stomach's a little off; I'd better not." [Stomach Hurts]
- "My car has a Breathalyzer in the ignition system. I can't." [Breathalyzer Lie]

Similar examples can be created for other topics.

Careers/Work: Think of 12 jobs that teenagers do in the summer. Arrange them on the ladder from the most interesting to you to the least interesting.

Couples: Here are 12 things some couples are good at (playing together, making decisions, fighting, having sex, traveling, etc.). Arrange them on the ladder from those you and your partner are best at to those you are worst at.

Money: Which of these 10 things are you most likely to spend money on? Arrange them from most likely to least likely. Now rearrange them in an order showing which of these expenditures is most likely to least likely to give you the satisfaction you hoped for from the expenditure.

Sex: Here are 12 things that some people find pleasurable in sex. Arrange them from those you find most pleasurable to least pleasurable.

Health: Here are 15 foods. Arrange them on the staircase from healthiest to least healthy. Rearrange them from those you eat most often to those you eat least often.

Religion/Spirituality: Here are 15 stories from the Bible (or other religious text). Arrange them from most meaningful to you to least meaningful.

Aging: Here are 10 things that sometimes occur as people age (they become wiser, depressed, peaceful, anxious, mellow, etc.). Arrange them from those you think you are most likely to be like as you get older to those you are least likely to be like.

Loss: Now that you are on your own, arrange these 12 leisure activities on the staircase from ones you are most likely to do to those you are least likely to do.

Planning Board

Sid Simon, one of the founders of values clarification and a creator of many of its strategies, as of this writing is 85 years old and still leading workshops. His favorite values clarification strategy these days is a variation of the Forced-Choice Ladder that he calls a "Planning Board".

It begins with the same ladder or staircase, but instead of writing the key words directly on the ladder or staircase, group members are given a number of sticky notes or Post-Its on which they write the key words. The counselor or group leader explains three key words to begin with. Participants write the key words on their sticky notes and rank them in order by placing them on three rungs or steps on their diagram. Then they sit with a partner or a trio to discuss their rankings.

The counselor then gives the group three more choices; they write the key words on sticky-notes, and they rank these along with the first three choices on their ladder or staircase. The nice thing about the sticky notes is that they can be moved and moved again around the diagram as new choices are added until the person is satisfied with his ranking. (Nonsticky slips of paper can also be used, but they can easily move out of place or get blown away.) Again, participants discuss their rankings with another person or in a small group. The process is repeated until all the choices have been presented, ranked, and discussed.

A final variation that Sid likes to use is to give group members a "wild card" in their last set of choices. A wild card is a choice they make up themselves—for example, an option they would prefer over all the other choices that have been presented to them.

▪ 4. CONTINUUM

The continuum graphically demonstrates that many issues and dilemmas in life do not have either-or answers, but that there are many positions between the extremes that one can choose. The Continuum helps clients better recognize the alternative choices that are available to them. And seeing the choices clearly arrayed before them reinforces the idea that *they have a choice*, that they do not have to remain where they have been in the past on this continuum of possibilities.

A Continuum is a straight line bordered by an extreme opposite position on each end and many—perhaps an infinite number of—positions between the two extremes. Continuums can be created for almost any values, counseling, or therapy issue. The idea is for clients to place themselves on the line at a position that best represents where they fall on this continuum of possible positions.

There are three ways to construct a continuum—with numbers, with extreme words, and with symbolic words and examples. For example, one might ask an elderly client considering a housing move, "How independent are you?"—an appropriate *value-clarifying question* that the client thinks about and responds to. However, one can ask the same question in the form of a *continuum*. Here are five continuums based on the same clarifying question: How independent are you?

Numbers:

1 _____ 10

Here, 1 means not at all independent, and 10 means completely independent. What number represents how independent you are?

Extreme Words:

How independent are you? Where do you fit on this continuum?

Not at all _____ Completely

Completely Dependent _____ Completely Independent

Symbolic Names and Descriptions:

Dependent Donna _____ Independent Irma

Help Me Henry _____ Keep Away Carlos

Dependent Donna (or Help Me Henry) is so *not* independent that when she (he) drops a tissue on her lap, she'll ask someone to hand it to her. Independent Irma (or Keep Away Carlos) is so independent that if you offered to help her (him) lift the other end of a 20-foot log into her truck, she'd say she'd rather do it herself.

One form of continuum is not necessarily better than another. Each is versatile and can work for an infinite number of topics and settings. I find I tend to use symbolic names and descriptions in group settings and numbers or extreme words in individual counseling, although there are many exceptions. Using a person's name for the end points makes it livelier and less abstract. Describing the end points with extreme, sometimes amusing examples makes the exercise more fun and enables someone who is far down the continuum to not feel judged. Instead, they react, "I'm not *that* extreme."

Staying with these examples, I also prefer Help Me Henry and Keep Away Carlos to Dependent Donna and Independent Irma. I would also prefer Not at All and Completely to Completely Dependent and Completely Independent. The reason is that *dependent* and *independent* are value-laden words. In many western cultures, particularly in the United States, independence is a prized value, and dependence is considered weak and undesirable. (In other cultures, and in some U.S. subcultures, the value judgment might be reversed, with independence seen as an undesirable character trait.) By putting these words on opposite ends of the continuum, it gives clients a choice between more desirable and less desirable positions. In other words, it stacks the deck and creates subtle pressure toward putting themselves on the independent side. The two amusing extremes, by contrast, make *both* ends of the continuum equally absurd and therefore allow participants to make a freer choice to put themselves where they really think they belong.

For a similar reason, I prefer to use the same gender on both ends of the continuum. For example, Dependent Donna and Independent Irwin run the risk of reinforcing gender stereotypes. Even when stereotypes or cultural biases are not operative, there may be an unconscious bias for male clients to identify with the male name on the continuum and for female clients to identify the female name. This is especially true with younger clients or groups.

Similarly, try to avoid always putting the conservative extreme on the right and the liberal extreme on the left, if such labels apply. It stimulates more thinking if such expectations are not reinforced. The same goes with always putting the negative side on one end and the positive on the other.

Here are examples of the values continuum for our sample topics:

Recovery: How much do you really want to be sober (or drug-free)?

I'm happy just as I am.		I'd give/do anything to be sober (drug-free).

Work: How much or little do you look forward to going to work in the morning (or whenever you go to work)? (Or What would be an acceptable place on this continuum for you?)

Dread It Dan someone has to pull the covers off him and dump him out of bed		Excited Ernie gets there two hours early, and janitor has to kick him out at night

Couples: How much of your free, discretionary time would you like to spend doing things together or doing things alone or with others?

100% Together		100% Alone or With Others

Money: How important is money to you?

Maria the Monk		Midas Mary

Sex: How much variety would you like in sex with your partner?

Always _____ Always
different   the same

Health: If someone looked at how you lived your life, how important would they
say good health was to you?

Not at all   Extremely
Important _____ Important

Religion: Which aspect of what your religion teaches or offers you is the most
important to you?

Relationship   Relationship
to God or the _____ to Other People
Universe   or Morality

Loss: Which are you most likely to be like?

Mourn   Recover
Forever _____ Tomorrow
Fred   Tom

Variations on any given continuum could ask clients to indicate the place on
the line

- where they are now
- where they would like to be
- where they used to be
- where their parents, partner, or religion would like them to be
- where people who know them a little would put them
- where people who know them well would put them
- where their parent, partner, or role model would be

In individual counseling or therapy, the counselor may present the continuum verbally ("If you can imagine a line, and on one end of the line are the words 'Not
at All Independent' and on the other end of the line are the words 'Completely
Independent,' where would you be on that line?"), and the client can answer verbally
("I guess I'd be about halfway between the middle and the independent end"). Or
the counselor can draw the continuum on a piece of paper, write in the end points,
and ask the client to indicate where he falls on the continuum. While the client is
speaking, he can point to the place on the line to make it vivid, or the counselor
could point to the line and ask, "About here?" as a way of testing her understanding
of the client's response.

In group situations, it works best when all group members can actually place
their names or initials on a continuum. The three most common ways this happens
are (a) the counselor asks group members to draw the continuum on their own

paper, write in the end points, and place their name or initials where they think they belong; (b) the counselor draws a continuum on the board or on newsprint and asks some or all members to come up and place their names on the continuum; or (c) the counselor draws an imaginary continuum across the room (or uses masking tape to create a real line), indicates and explains the two end points on the line, and asks everyone to physically move themselves to the place on the continuum that best describes their position on the issue. This can be followed by small-group conversations with people who are near them on the continuum or who are at different positions on the continuum.

When people place their names on a continuum, they usually welcome the opportunity to explain what their placement means to them. This is not a mathematically precise exercise. One person's 7 on a 1-to-10 continuum can be another person's 5. The important thing is the internal valuing process that is engaged when clients are asked to consider their feelings, thoughts, and behavior patterns elicited by the continuum and, if it's a group setting, sharing their responses and seeing and hearing other people's responses.

You know you are getting the hang of creating good continuums when your clients or group members don't all put themselves on the same place on the continuum. That means you have asked a question with some complexity and you have not inadvertently imposed a "more correct" answer.

■ 5. EITHER-OR FORCED CHOICE

The Values Continuum strategy (4) asks clients to consider where they belong on a myriad of possible positions between two extremes. The Either-or Forced-Choice strategy asks them, if they had to choose one of the extremes, which extreme is more like them or more preferable. Like the Rank Order strategy (2), which also elicits a forced choice, it requires clients or group members to process many attitudes, opinions, and issues to make their choices. The value of the activity is not in the final ranking or either-or choice they make, but in the valuing processes they utilize in making the decision and sharing their process with others.

In individual counseling, a client may be asked an either-or clarifying question, such as "If you had to choose this or that, which would you choose?" "Are you more like this or more like that?" or "Would someone who knows you describe you this way or that way?" But as an elaborated strategy, the Either-or Forced Choice is typically done in a group setting to help participants clarify and affirm their own attitudes, choices, behaviors, and other value indicators and learn from others.

The counselor first identifies an issue or question and two opposite stances or answers for that issue or question. For example, in a career development group, a counselor might say, "Are you more like a team member or an independent?" In a recovery group, she might give the choice between drunk or sober. In a financial counseling setting, the either-or choice might be spendthrift or tightwad.

Here are a couple of examples for each of our sample topics. A myriad more could be created for each topic. The two extreme ends of a Values Continuum (4) often make good opposing choices for the Either-or strategy.

Recovery:

Are you... ?	Sober OR Drunk
Are you... ?	Reluctant OR Motivated

Careers:

Are you a/an... ?	Team Member OR Independent
Are you an... ?	Employee OR Entrepreneur

Work:

Are you a... ?	Workaholic OR Lazy Bum
Is work for you a... ?	Nightmare OR Joy

Couples:

With your partner are you more like your... ?	Mother OR Father
With your partner are you a... ?	Leader OR Follower

Money:

Are you a... ?	Tightwad OR Spendthrift
Are you... ?	Casual OR Concerned

Sex:

Are you an/a... ?	Addict OR Monk
Are you... ?	Inhibited OR Uninhibited

Health:

Are you more like a... ?	Junk Food Junkie OR Health Nut
Are you a... ?	Wreck OR Role Model

Religion/Spirituality:

Are you... ?	Religious OR Secular
Are you a... ?	Saint OR Sinner

Aging:

Are you a... ?	Couch Potato OR Live Wire
How do you regard your aging?	Bummer OR Opportunity

Loss:

At what stage are you?	Grieving OR Recovered
Are you into... ?	Wallowing OR Denial

A set of either-or choices related to the topic under consideration can be given to group members on a piece of paper, where they circle the choice closest to their own viewpoint or self-concept. A more interesting and energetic approach to the activity is to post the either-or choices at opposite ends of the room and ask group members to go stand at one end of the room or the other. You can be sympathetic with them, acknowledging that they may really be a combination of both choices, but remind them that sometimes life presents us with choices that aren't perfect for us and we have to choose, so you are asking them if they *had to* choose one or the other, which side of the room would they go to? You can reassure them that they will soon get to explain themselves in all their complexity if they wish, but for now, they should please choose one side or the other.

One could turn this activity into a Values Continuum exercise by giving group members the opportunity to stand anywhere along the line that represents their own position. But as an Either-or Forced Choice, most people are willing to live within the narrow parameters, and there is good energy in the room when they move to their position on either end. If any group members, in the end, can't or won't make a choice, that should be completely accepted as in any values clarification activity. Whether they remain seated (the equivalent of "I pass") or stand in the middle in protest, that's fine. They have still been thinking about the issue or question, possibly even more than some who quickly chose a side.

Once group members have circled their either-or choice(s) on paper or moved to either side of the room to indicate their position, (a) they can be asked to talk to the person next to them or in trios about why they made the forced choice they did; (b) they can be grouped with one or two people from the opposite position to, again, discuss why they made the choice they did; and/or (c) they can discuss their choices in the whole group. In any of these group formats, they are free to discuss the complexity of their thinking and feeling and all the issues and conflicting forces that pushed them in either direction.

■ 6. STRONGLY AGREE/STRONGLY DISAGREE

In this activity, group members are presented with a series of declarative statements on the topic under consideration, and for each statement they indicate whether they *strongly agree, agree somewhat,* are *neutral* or *undecided, disagree somewhat,* or *strongly disagree.* This familiar tool of social science research can also be used as a values clarification strategy. It clearly elicits individuals' attitudes, feelings, beliefs, and opinions and the strength of those value indicators. It is particularly useful in psychoeducational groups in which the counselor uses the activity to help participants identify their attitudes and opinions and begin thinking about issues they may not have explicitly considered. Having identified some of their views on the issues and gotten in touch with the strength of their attitudes, group members are more motivated to share or affirm these views in the whole group and listen to others' views and opinions, which extend the values-clarifying process.

When Strongly Agree/Strongly Disagree employs a list of *many statements,* it is typically used as a group strategy. It can also be used with individual clients as a diagnostic tool or as a way to involve a client who seems reluctant to initiate or respond to conversation, but for values clarification purposes, it is primarily a group strategy. However, when focusing on a *single statement,* Strongly Agree/Strongly Disagree can be used in individual counseling, as when a counselor might ask a client at a relevant moment, "When you hear someone say _____, do you strongly agree,

agree somewhat, disagree somewhat, or strongly disagree?" Or "How strongly do you agree or disagree with the idea that _____?"

The remaining part of this section is meant for group work settings. Before the group session, the counselor prepares a series of declarative statements on the topic. The declarative statements go on the left side of the page, with the SA, AS, NU, DS, and SD response options to the right of each statement, as shown in the sample activities. The statements should not all be ones that the counselor or conventional wisdom agrees with. Otherwise, group members will soon get the idea that there are right answers to these items and that one is supposed to agree with them. Ideally, some or many of the statements will elicit a variety of positive and negative responses from the group members, demonstrating that the statements were complex enough not to have obvious responses.

During the session, the counselor gives a copy of the activity to each member of the group. Group members individually go down the items and circle their response to each statement. Alternatively, the counselor can explain the activity to the group, post the response options (SA, AS, etc.) on the wall or board for all to see, read each numbered statement to the group, and have members write their responses next to the corresponding number on their papers. The first approach is better because the group members continue to have the statements before them throughout the activity and subsequent discussion.

Once group members have responded to each of the statements, depending on where the counselor or group wants to take it, group members can discuss their responses to all the statements or discuss their responses to one or two selected statements; discuss their responses in pairs, trios, small groups, or the whole group; or discuss their responses in random groups or groups consisting of those who both agreed and disagreed with the statement to be discussed.

Here are examples of strongly agree/strongly disagree statements for our 10 sample topics. For additional ideas for strongly agree/strongly disagree statements, see the Values Voting strategy (7).

Recovery:

1. I can drink in moderation.	SA AS NU DS SD
2. 12-step groups are for wimps.	SA AS NU DS SD
3. I couldn't quit abusing without God in my corner.	SA AS NU DS SD
4. Marijuana should be legalized.	SA AS NU DS SD
5. If I could live my life over again, I'd be smart enough not to use drugs.	SA AS NU DS SD

Careers:

1. It's not what you know that determines success, but who you know.	SA AS NU DS SD
2. I expect to have one career all my life.	SA AS NU DS SD
3. I want a career that will make me wealthy.	SA AS NU DS SD
4. I've found my career.	SA AS NU DS SD

5. I have a role model for my (desired) career.   SA AS NU DS SD

Work:

1. No matter the type of work, it can be done
   with dignity and pride.   SA AS NU DS SD
2. Most people hate going to their jobs.   SA AS NU DS SD
3. It's unfortunate that union membership is falling.   SA AS NU DS SD
4. I often enjoy working.   SA AS NU DS SD
5. I don't care if I work alone or with others.   SA AS NU DS SD
6. If I were unemployed, I could not hold my
   head up high.   SA AS NU DS SD

Couples:

1. It's unrealistic to expect two people to be completely
   faithful to each other over a long marriage.   SA AS NU DS SD
2. Many couples' love for one another grows
   deeper over time.   SA AS NU DS SD
3. I don't have a problem with commitment.   SA AS NU DS SD
4. Being in a gay or lesbian relationship is no more
   difficult than being in a straight relationship.   SA AS NU DS SD
5. Taking some separate vacations would be healthy
   for our relationship.   SA AS NU DS SD

Money:

1. Money is the root of all evil.   SA AS NU DS SD
2. I have healthy attitudes about money.   SA AS NU DS SD
3. I'm addicted to shopping.   SA AS NU DS SD
4. If I had tons of money, I'd be a happier person.   SA AS NU DS SD
5. I don't give enough to charities and causes.   SA AS NU DS SD

Sex:

1. Good sex is necessary for a successful marriage.   SA AS NU DS SD
2. Intimacy is more important than orgasm.   SA AS NU DS SD
3. Variety is important for sustaining a good sex life. SA AS NU DS SD
4. Premarital teenage sex usually is a bad idea.   SA AS NU DS SD
5. Sex is overrated.   SA AS NU DS SD

Health:

1. Exercise is more important than diet.   SA AS NU DS SD
2. I'll do almost anything to avoid going to the hospital. SA AS NU DS SD
3. If there was bad news about my health,
   I'd rather not know it.   SA AS NU DS SD
4. The dangers of high cholesterol are grossly exaggerated. SA AS NU DS SD
5. It's mostly genetics, so why bother?   SA AS NU DS SD

Religion, Spirituality:

1. There is life after death.	SA AS NU DS SD
2. God is dead.	SA AS NU DS SD
3. I wish I were more spiritual.	SA AS NU DS SD
4. I really respect my minister (or priest, rabbi, imam, etc.).	SA AS NU DS SD
5. We'd be better off if everyone had the same religion.	SA AS NU DS SD

Loss:

1. I wish I had died first.	SA AS NU DS SD
2. My loved one wouldn't want me to still be mourning.	SA AS NU DS SD
3. My religious or cultural rituals around death and mourning were of no help to me.	SA AS NU DS SD
4. I have one or more friends or family members who really understand how I feel.	SA AS NU DS SD
5. If I could legally and without suffering pain join him (her) now, I would.	SA AS NU DS SD
6. It's a great life.	SA AS NU DS SD

Aging:

1. I like being my age.	SA AS NU DS SD
2. I wish I were a young adult again, knowing what I now know.	SA AS NU DS SD
3. I'm scared of dying.	SA AS NU DS SD
4. I feel lucky to be alive and living my current life.	SA AS NU DS SD
5. Our society does pretty well by its senior citizens.	SA AS NU DS SD

■ (7) VALUES VOTING

How many of you like _____?
How many of you believe that _____?
How many of you would choose to _____?
How many of you do _____?
How many of you would never _____?

Values Voting is a popular values clarification strategy that can be used in groups from a few members to audiences of over a thousand. I rarely begin a public presentation without starting with a few voting questions related to the topic at hand. It immediately gets people thinking about the topic—what they are for or against, what they believe or don't believe, what they do or don't do in relation to the topic, and how they are similar to or different from other members of the group or audience around them. It raises the energy level in the room. It creates what in pedagogy is called an *anticipatory set*, a focus on and motivation to engage in the topic.

Group members vote with their hands. Either three or five hand-signal options may be presented, with instructions like these:

- If I ask about something you like, or are in favor of, or agree with, or you do in your life—in other words, if you have a favorable or positive response to the question, raise your hand. [I demonstrate.]
- If I ask about something you *dislike*, or are *not* in favor of, or *don't* agree with, or you *don't* do in your life—in other words, if you have a negative response to the question, put your thumb down, like this. [I demonstrate]
- And if you can't decide whether you like it or not, or you're not sure about it, or you don't want to tell anyone, fold your arms, like this [I demonstrate], as a way of saying, "I pass."
- Now you can't just leave your hands on your lap; you've got to do something active—whether raising your hand, putting your thumb down, or passing.

Optional

- Now sometimes in life, we not only agree with something, we *strongly agree*. We not only do something, we *do it all the time*. So if I ask you about something that you have a *very positive* response to, then you can wave your hand. [Again, I demonstrate.]
- And if I ask about something that you not only disagree with but you *strongly disagree*, or not only don't you do it, you *hate the idea* of doing it—in other words you have a *very negative* response—then you do this [I move my thumb and arm up and down or around], like you're stirring your coffee with your thumb.

Okay, let's practice the hand signals now. If I ask about something that you have a favorable response to, what do you do... ? Right. And if I ask about something you have a negative response to, what would you do... ? Good. And if you don't want to tell anyone... ? Excellent. You pass. Okay, now here are some questions for you to vote on....

The questions relate to the topic at hand. I'll usually ask about 6 to 10 Values Voting questions. My questions are a combination of prizing, choosing, and acting questions, that is, value-clarifying questions that elicit the different value-clarifying processes. Here are a few examples for each of our sample topics. For additional ideas for Values Voting questions, see the Strongly Agree/Strongly Disagree strategy (6).

Recovery: How many of you...

- came to this group voluntarily?
- are finding staying sober harder than you thought?
- have a sponsor or confidant you can talk to if you need to?
- have a family that doesn't understand what you're going through?
- feel hopeful about your future?
- know what to do when you're feeling temptation?
- really believe you'll be recovering all your life?

- have anyone you want to apologize to or make amends for hurting them?
- feel proud of how far you've come in the last few weeks [or whatever time frame applies]?
- have a good line or response you use when someone offers you a drink or a drug?

Careers: How many of you...

- think of yourself as actually having a career, as opposed to a job?
- think the world needs your career?
- are sometimes embarrassed when people learn what career you do?
- experienced pressure from your parents regarding your career choice?
- would say you drifted into your career rather than chose it?
- would choose a different career if you could do it all over again?
- sometimes consider changing careers?
- think you will change careers—not just jobs, but your career—before you retire?
- would recommend your career to a young person?
- would go to a school for "career day" to talk about your career?

Work: How many of you...

- take some pride in the work you do?
- have someone you admire at work for their skills or talents?
- think anyone at work admires you for your skills or talents?
- hate going to work in the morning (or whenever you go)?
- would like to become better about some aspects of your work?
- would choose to get additional job training or education if money were not an issue?
- have a pattern of switching jobs regularly?
- will probably remain at your current job until you retire?
- would like to remain at your current job until you retire?
- have an up-to-date resume?

Couples: How many of you...

- think your communication with your partner is better than your parents' communication with each other?
- know another couple you admire for their relationship?
- look down on couples who go for couples or family therapy?
- would go to a couples' counselor if you were having serious difficulties in your relationship?
- wish you received more compliments or appreciation from your partner?
- compliment or appreciate your partner on a regular basis?
- are spending just the right amount of free time with your partner?
- often have a good laugh together?
- have one activity you really enjoy doing together?
- spend some good time every day talking or connecting with your partner?

Money: How many of you...

- have a personal or family budget?
- think you spend too much time thinking about money?
- would describe yourself as an impulse buyer?
- think your parents were good role models for handling money?
- often regret a purchase you made?
- donate to charities and causes?
- sometimes help friends out financially?
- would ask a friend for a loan if you needed it?
- would like to save a higher proportion of your income?
- think other people who know you would say you are too materialistic?

Sex: How many of you...

- think our society has healthy attitudes about sex?
- think *you* have a healthy attitude about sex?
- feel sexuality is important for your current happiness?
- think sexuality will always be important for your happiness?
- have sexual fantasies?
- would share your sexual fantasies with your partner if he or she asked?
- would ask your partner to do something or do more of something if you had the courage?
- can go to sleep happily after you made love with your partner even if you didn't have an orgasm?
- enjoying looking at the Victoria Secrets catalog?
- like the pattern of your sexual relationship, in terms of timing, frequency, variety, and the like?

Health: How many of you...

- think about health issues a good deal?
- are worried about your health?
- would describe yourself as healthy?
- think you follow a healthy diet?
- think that our culture's focus on health is overdone?
- are similar to your mother (if you're a woman) or father (if you're a man) in terms of health issues and practices?
- have a form of exercise that works for you?
- get enough sleep?
- agree with my grandmother, who said, "Your health is the most important thing"?
- regularly read at least one magazine dealing with health?

Religion/Spirituality: How many of you...

- feel religion or spirituality is important in your life?
- think of yourself as more religious than spiritual?
- think of yourself as more spiritual than religious?

- have experienced God's presence personally?
- think that religion is responsible for a great number of the world's problems?
- practice the same religion as your parents practiced?
- could consider changing religions?
- attend religious services regularly?
- would prefer a pastoral counselor to a secular one?
- would like to read the Bible (or Quran or other religious text) more frequently?

Loss: How many of you...

- are still grieving?
- feel embarrassed that you are still grieving?
- would judge negatively someone who began dating six months after their spouse or life partner died?
- follow your religious or cultural practices around mourning?
- have read a book about grief and bereavement?
- find yourself sometimes talking to the person you lost?
- sometimes go 2 hours or more without thinking about the person you lost?
- believe it's okay these days to laugh and have a good time?
- have someone you can talk to about your feelings of loss?
- think that someday you'll be ready to date or have another intimate relationship?

Aging: How many of you...

- think you are wiser than you ever have been?
- think we live in an ageist society?
- assuming your current state of health remains the same, would like to live another 20 years?
- think you will live another 20 years?
- believe your "self" will remain in some form after you die?
- have a role model for aging well?
- have made a will?
- if you were suffering greatly, would consider assisted suicide, if it were available?
- would like to get out more?
- feel pretty good at this time of your life?

As with the Strongly Agree/Strongly Disagree strategy (6), the voting questions should not always elicit positive responses or always elicit negative responses. Ideally, some or many of the questions will elicit a variety of positive and negative responses from the group members. This demonstrates that the questions were complex enough not to have obvious responses and that the questions were not subtly imposing the counselor's viewpoint or preferences on the group, leading them to vote the way the counselor would.

■ 8. PROUD QUESTIONS

Proud Questions engage clients in the valuing processes of considering what they prize and cherish and sharing and affirming this with others. Of course, the pride elicited in values clarification is not meant to be the false pride of feeling better than others, but the pride that results from accomplishing one's goal, living up to one's ideals, or achieving what one prizes. Proud Questions help clients become more aware of the degree to which they are proud of their beliefs and actions, which encourages them to do more things for which they can take pride. In group settings, clients also hear new alternatives from the lives of other participants.

In its basic form, a Proud Question can be a simple value-clarifying response that can follow something an individual client or group member has said.

- Are you proud of that?
- Do you prize this?
- Is this very important to you?

In its more structured form, in group settings, the proud circle or proud whip (as in whip quickly around the circle) gives each participant the chance to share something he or she is proud of about the topic under consideration. For example, if a counselor is working with a group of seniors in an assisted living facility on issues of aging, she can say, "Let's go around the circle and give each person who wants to take a turn the chance to share something you're proud of in relation to being independent, in doing something for yourself."

Similarly, a counselor might ask a group to do a proud circle on our other sample topics, for example, "Something you are proud of...":

- about you and alcohol this week (*recovery*)
- doing at work since we last met (*work*)
- in terms of communicating with you partner (*couples*)
- doing to save money (*money*)
- regarding meeting your partner's needs (or your own) (*sex*)
- doing for your health (*health*)
- having done for your spiritual life (*religion/spirituality*)
- having done to honor your grief (*loss*)

Proud circles can be done on the same topic in relationship to

- something you did
- something you did not do
- something you learned
- something new you tried
- something you did to take care of yourself
- something you did to help someone else
- something you did to ask for or accept help
- something you did that involved creativity
- something you persevered at

and so on.

The counselor may write the sentence stems "I'm proud of _____" and/or "I'm proud that I _____" on the board or newsprint as she is explaining the activity.

A proud circle can be used in counseling and therapy with groups with any particular focus or with a general focus. For example, the counselor could start off a group session by saying,

> Let's begin this week with a proud circle. Can you think of anything you're proud of doing this week, that is, anything you feel good about having done this last week in relation to the issue(s) you're working on [or in relation to anything else in your life]? We'll go around the circle, and if you take a turn, you'll begin by saying, "I'm proud that I _____," and you'll finish the sentence by telling something that you feel good about yourself for having done. Of course, you can pass by simply saying "I pass," and we'll go on to the next person.

The reason it is often a good idea to make the sentence stem say "I'm proud *that I _____*," rather than simply "I'm proud _____" or "I'm proud of _____," is that "I'm proud that I _____" focuses clients' attention on what they have done. It emphasizes their responsibility. In many cases, it is easier to say, "I'm proud of my son" or "I'm proud of the Yankees" than to deal with the riskier question of how we are living our lives. Experience has demonstrated that the extra words "I'm proud *that I _____*" usually elicit a more fruitful level of personal exploration.

However, there are other times when the focus is broader, a wider range of responses is appropriate, and there is no need to limit the sentence stem to "I'm proud that I _____." For example, for a counselor working with geriatric clients whose self-esteem may be challenged by their diminishing abilities, it is often very helpful for them to recall the many things in their lives they have reason to be proud of. Asking an individual client, "I'd love to hear some of the things that you are proud of in your long life. Would you be willing to share some of these with me?" In a group setting, the counselor might post a variety of sentence stems up front—

- I'm proud_____
- I'm proud of_____
- I'm proud that_____
- I'm proud that I_____

—and ask participants to go around the circle and complete any of the sentence stems in relation to "something you are proud of regarding…"

- your family
- your country
- work you've done
- accomplishment
- religion or faith
- relationships
- aging
- sports
- hobbies
- anything else

■ 9. MAGIC QUESTIONS

A classic values clarification strategy is the "magic box," which can grow or shrink in size and contain any three things the holder wishes. Like Aladdin's wonderful lamp, in effect, the Magic Box grants the holder three wishes. Basically, the strategy asks what your three wishes would be, concrete or abstract, for yourself, your family, the world, or anything or anybody else.

The Magic Box can be adapted for particular counseling settings and issues, such as:

Work: In your box, your employer has written on each of three slips of paper a change in your working conditions. What would you like the three pieces of paper to say?

Couples: You open your Magic Box, and your partner has given you three changes he or she is ready to make. What are the changes?

Sex: The Magic Box has three drawings, each showing a sexual position or activity you would like to engage in or engage in more frequently. What are they?

More broadly, *Magic Questions* are a type of clarifying question that allows us to suspend disbelief and imagine a somewhat altered reality that helps reveal our hopes, desires, wants, priorities, and other value indicators. Like any "what if?" questions, magic questions allow us to temporarily view our situation from an alternative perspective and thereby gain insight that may be helpful in our development and decision making.

General Magic Questions might include the following.

- What three things would be in your Magic Box?
- If you had a lamp that could grant you three wishes, what would you wish for?
- If you could live anywhere you wanted to, where would it be?
- If you had the wealth of Bill and Melinda Gates, how would your life be different?
- If you knew you would live to be 200 and would be healthy the whole time, how would you live your life from now on?

Magic Questions can also be tailored for particular counseling situations.

- If you could change three mistakes you made in the past, including people you hurt, what mistakes or hurts would you erase? (*Recovery*)
- If your employer let you run the company, how would you rewrite your job description? (*Work*)
- If you could start your relationship over again (or start the last month over again), what might you do differently? (*Couples*)
- If money were not an issue, how would this affect your decision? (*Money*)
- What is a sexual fantasy you have? (Would you be willing to share this with your partner?) (*Sex*)

- If you did not have this health problem, what three things in your life would be different? (*Health*)
- If you could talk to God (Allah, etc.) and God answered you, what would you say or ask? (*Religion/Spirituality*)
- If your loved one was watching you now, what would he or she want you to do? (*Loss*)
- If you could live another 50 years, what would you want to do? Where would you want to go? What would you like to learn? (*Aging*)

Magic Questions can be asked in the course of individual counseling or in group settings. In groups, responses can be kept private, shared with a partner or small group, or shared in the whole group, respecting the right to pass, as always.

■ 10. PERCENTAGE QUESTIONS

One might ask a client or group, "Do you find your work satisfying?" or "How satisfying do you find your work?" Both are fair questions, but the first asks for an either-or response, while the second asks for more complex thinking. One can take it a step further by asking a *Percentage Question*: "About what percentage of the time do you find your work satisfying?" This requires the person answering to think even more specifically and thoroughly about the question.

Percentage Questions tend to focus on life patterns. They are useful to help clients examine how they are actually living their lives and how they would like to live them.

Recovery: What percentage of the day are you thinking about using?

Work: What percentage of days do you leave work feeling "I did good work today"?

Couples: What percentage of household tasks do each of you do?

Money: What percentage of your income do you donate to charities or causes?

Sex: On what percentage of sexual occasions do you reach orgasm?

Health: What percentage of your calories are fat? Sugar? Etc.

Religion/Spirituality: What percentage of times in church (temple, the mosque, etc.) do you feel a spiritual connection to God?

Loss: When your spouse was alive, what percentage of your activities did you do with her? What percentage did you do with others or by yourself? What percentage of the latter group are you doing now?

Aging: What percentage of days do you leave your apartment? Ideally, what percentage of days would you like to leave your apartment?

■ 11. PIE OF LIFE

This strategy is an elaboration on the Percentage Question strategy (10). It divides an area of life into many categories and asks clients to estimate the percentage of time, money, or other criteria that they devote to each of these categories. In so doing, clients examine more deeply the patterns of behavior in their lives and consider the possibility of alternative ways to live.

The counselor may create a Pie of Life activity spontaneously, based on issues a client or group may be exploring, or prepare one beforehand and bring it to the counseling session. For example, a couple may be discussing how one or both of them are not satisfied with the quality of their life together. At some point, the counselor might ask them to enumerate the different activities they *do together*. They list the following.

- Family occasions
- Attending movies, plays, concerts
- Lovemaking, sex, physical affection
- Talking
- Physical activity—walking, sports
- Hobbies—gardening
- Chores
- Travel
- Other

This could lead to an Inventorying activity (1), a Percentage Question (10), or a Pie of Life activity, in which the counselor draws a circle and asks each of them, working separately or together, to indicate the approximate portion of their together time that they devote to each of the activities. Let's say they decide to leave travel aside and just focus on what they do together when they are living at home. Their pie looks something like this:

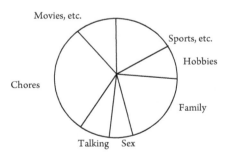

Just discussing their sometimes differing perceptions of how they spend their together time may prove useful. But once they have a pie divided in a way they agree is more or less representative of their lives, they can explore further how they feel about this pattern and what they may want to do differently. They have moved from the level of generalities ("We don't do enough together" or "We spend all our free time with your family") to carefully looking at how they want to spend their time together.

One Pie of Life can sometimes lead to another. For example, it may turn out that the spectator events they attend together are a source of friction or dissatisfaction to one or both of the couple. The counselor might suggest doing a Pie of Life on that activity, with separate slices for movies, concerts, theater, and sporting events.

Of course, these divisions are not meant to be mathematically precise. Clients may need to be reminded that these are estimates and approximations. That is sufficient for generating all the values issues and other issues associated with the subject. It is not the pie itself that is important but the feelings, thoughts, and insights it raises. These can then be explored further by the client or group.

Here are a few more examples for Pies of Life on some of our sample topics.

Money: Aside from housing, utilities, groceries, medical needs, transportation to work, and other areas you have little or no discretion over, how would you divide your discretionary spending? Divide a pie into the following categories: Entertainment, Eating and Drinking Out, Clothing, Beauty, Cigarettes and Drugs, Travel, Gifts, Other.

Health: Divide the pie into slices for how your typical day or week looks in terms of the following levels and types of physical activity: Sleeping, Sedentary—inactive, Sedentary—active, Mild activity, Moderate activity, Vigorous activity.

Aging: Thinking about living in this assisted living facility, divide the pie into slices to indicate how much time you spend on the following activities. The key words to put in the slices are italicized: *Sleeping*; Dressing and Getting Ready for Bed (*Preparing*); *Eating*; Attending *Programs*; Passive activities in the apartment, such as watching TV, listening to music (*Passive-apt.*); Active activities in the apartment, such as paying bills, being on the computer (*Active-apt.*); *Going Out*.

See Percentage Questions (10) for other examples that lend themselves to the Pie of Life strategy on our other sample counseling topics.

■ 12. PUBLIC INTERVIEW

A Public Interview provides an opportunity for a group to focus on an issue of relevance to the group as a whole and/or to the individual being interviewed. It gives the individual an opportunity to explore his value indicators (feelings, beliefs, choices, etc.) and utilize the valuing process of sharing and affirmation. Later on, inevitably, the client who was interviewed reviews the questions and answers in his mind and continues to think about what he said, what he wished he had said, and the feelings and thoughts that the experience raised. The Public Interview gives the group an opportunity to further consider the issues being discussed, reflect on how they would respond to the same questions, and get to know one member of the group in greater depth.

The counselor explains to the group what a Public Interview is. It's very much like a TV talk show in which the interviewer asks the guest a series of questions. It lasts 5 to 10 minutes (the counselor should set and announce the time limit), and the interviewee can pass on any and all questions he does not wish to respond to at this time. The counselor then asks for volunteers from the group to receive a Public Interview. She chooses one volunteer. If it is an ongoing group, the counselor can say there will be more occasions in the future for others, or everyone who wants to, to receive a Public Interview.

The counselor and interviewee then move to appropriate places for the interview—each in adjacent chairs, both behind a table, interviewee in the front of the room and counselor standing in the back of the room, or seated across from one another in the group circle—however the counselor's sense of drama or the client's comfort level may dictate. The counselor proceeds to ask the interviewee questions on the topic under consideration.

For example, let's say this is a group working on anger management. The counselor might ask questions like the following.

- When in the past have you been most likely to lose control of your anger?
- Can you describe one incident in particular that, if you could replay the scene, you wished you had dealt with your anger differently?
- With the benefit of hindsight, how do you wish you had handled it?
- Can you tell about a time that you are proud of how you controlled your anger?
- What are one or two things you've learned in the group so far, if any, that you have found useful about dealing with your anger?
- Can you describe one situation in your life now where you are likely to have to exercise good anger management?
- Can you think of three different things you might do in that situation (not necessarily all at once) that might help produce a good outcome?
- Which is the one you would most likely try?
- Is there anything more you'd like to know about anger in general or your anger in particular?

If the topic is known ahead of time, the counselor can prepare a list of questions beforehand, although always being ready to depart from the prepared list with clarifying responses to what the client has just said. Once a counselor becomes more skilled and experienced in asking clarifying questions, she may no longer feel the need to prepare questions ahead of time.

When the time is up or the counselor senses it's time to stop, she thanks the volunteer, and they resume their original seating. Some counselors like to offer volunteers at the end of the interview the opportunity to ask them, the counselor, any question or two that the counselor just asked. It has a nice reciprocity to it and gives the counselor an opportunity to share some of her values and insights in a nonimposing way. In any case, once the interview is concluded, the counselor may ask the rest of the group, "Would anyone else like to respond to one of the questions I asked [the interviewee]?" or she may invite a discussion on any of the issues that were raised in the interview.

The subject for the interview can be any topic relevant to the counseling group, therapy group, or psychoeducational group focus—how one group member handles his illness, how one group member has learned to live without her deceased spouse, how one group member manages time alone versus time with his partner, and so on. If one is doing values clarification counseling, it is important to keep in mind that the purpose is engaging one or more of the seven valuing processes in a more or less random, nonsequential fashion. If one begins to ask clarifying questions in a sequential manner (clarifying, generating alternatives, exploring consequences, deciding, exploring action, next steps, etc.), then it is no longer a Public Interview but a clarifying interview (chapter 5) conducted before a group. If one begins to use other counseling approaches to achieve a therapeutic outcome, then it is no longer a clarifying interview but group therapy.

■ 13. GROUP INTERVIEW

The Group Interview has the same purposes as the public interview, but it gives more opportunity for active participation by all the group members.

Again, the counselor explains to the group what a Group Interview is. It is very much like a press conference, in which the audience of reporters asks the politician or expert or celebrity a series of questions. It lasts 5 or 10 minutes (the counselor should set and announce the time limit), and the interviewee can pass on any and all questions he does not wish to respond to at this time. Also, as in a press conference, the interviewee can end the interview at any time by saying, "Thank you for your questions."

After explaining the structure of the activity, the counselor asks for volunteers from the group to receive a Group Interview. She chooses one volunteer. If it is an ongoing group and she would like to make this a regular feature of the group, she can tell them that there will be more occasions in the future for others, or everyone who wants to, to receive a group interview.

The seating is rearranged as in a press conference, with the interviewee up front or otherwise the center of attention and the rest of the group members facing the interviewee. The counselor reminds everyone of the rules—and adds one, that each member is limited to one question until everyone else who has a question has had the opportunity to ask it. In that way, no group member can monopolize or turn the interview into an inquisition.

When the time is up, or the interviewee brings it to a halt, or the counselor senses it's time to stop, she thanks the volunteer, and the group resumes its original seating. The Group Interview can then be followed by further discussion on the topic.

In a large group, it can be very productive to break into smaller groups with five or six members in each small group. Then one member of each group volunteers to be interviewed, and the other four or five group members conduct the interview.

Or every small-group member can receive a Group Interview. For example, in a half hour, in groups of six, each person who wants to can receive a 5-minute group interview. The counselor can move from group to group, listening in and contributing a question from time to time if that seems like it would be helpful to get things moving or to model good questioning. In a workshop setting, I have used this format very successfully with groups as large as 200.

In any size group, it has often proved useful to begin with a Public Interview (12) to demonstrate appropriate questions and then move into a Group Interview format where all the participants get to be the interviewers.

■ 14. UNFINISHED SENTENCES

Although Unfinished Sentences can be used with individuals for counseling ("How would you complete the following unfinished sentence?") and diagnostic purposes, it is most typically used as a values clarification strategy in group settings.

Asking someone to complete an Unfinished Sentence makes it relatively easy for the person to respond. There is a free association aspect to the task; it does not typically require a great deal of thought. Yet a person's response usually reveals a good deal about their value indicators (feelings, goals, beliefs, actions, etc.). This provides much data for further reflection and discussion.

For example, in a group working on careers, the counselor might pass out a sheet of paper with the following sentence stems, or she might post them in the front of the room.

- The main thing I want from a career is_____
- I respect workers who_____
- I want to earn enough money to_____
- I expect to work for _____ years.
- My parent's job is_____
- The thing I look forward to about working is_____
- The hardest part about looking for work is_____
- Prospective employers should like my_____
- When I go for an interview, I have to remember to_____
- Work is_____
- If I were to consider a different career, I might like to_____

There are many different ways to work with Unfinished Sentences. The counselor could ask the group members to complete all the sentence stems or choose, say, five of them to complete. Group members could then pair off and share and talk about their completed sentences with each other. Or they could go around the circle, giving each person the chance to read and/or talk about one of his or her sentences. Further discussion could follow on any issues that particular sentences or the activity as a whole seemed to raise.

Here are a few examples of Unfinished Sentences for our other sample topics.

Recovery:

- My biggest challenge in staying sober will be_____
- When I feel the urge to drink, I will_____
- The best thing about being clean is_____
- The person it would be hardest to disappoint is_____
- A good thing for me to do instead of drink is_____

Couples:

- My two favorite things to do together are_____
- One thing I appreciate about my partner is_____
- One thing I wish my partner would do more often is_____
- One thing I need to do differently or more of is_____
- I love it when he (she)_____

Money:

- Money is_____
- If someone gave me $100 that I had to spend today, I'd_____
- One thing I have to be careful about money is_____
- What I do about donating to charities and causes is_____
- Regarding money, I'm proud that_____

Sex:

- Sex is_____
- My attitudes about sex came from_____
- One thing I'd like to know about sex is_____
- If I were completely comfortable with my sexuality, I would_____
- The problem with sex is_____

Health:

- Regarding health, I'm proud that I_____
- Regarding health, I need to_____
- The healthiest thing I do for myself is_____
- The least healthy thing I do for myself is_____
- I admire _____ because she (he) stays healthy by_____

Religion/Spirituality:

- A memorable religious experience I had was_____
- The most spiritual person I know is_____
- To me, spirituality means being_____
- God is_____
- My attitude toward other religions is_____
- I think the role of women in my faith is_____

Loss:

- One of my fondest memories of _____ is_____
- What people don't understand about my loss is_____
- What scares me about being alone is_____

- Now that _____ is gone, I have an opportunity to_____
- I need to_____

Aging:

- When I hear the phrase "older but wiser," I think_____
- The best thing about being old is_____
- The worst thing about being old is_____
- I admire _____, who handled aging by_____
- Something I'd still like to learn is_____

■ 15. I LEARNED STATEMENTS

I Learned Statements are a follow-up to any values clarification activity or, for that matter, any group experiential learning activity. Examples of I Learned Statements follow.

- I learned that I_____
- I relearned that I_____
- I noticed that I_____
- I was surprised that I_____
- I was pleased that I_____
- I was displeased that I_____
- I was proud that I_____
- I see that I need to_____

Not only is it good teaching or facilitating to ask participants to pause and reflect at the end of a learning experience, I Learned Statements also personalize the reflection by adding "that I_____" to each of the statements. There is nothing wrong with the shorter sentence stem "I learned _____," but adding "I learned *that I___*" increases the likelihood that clients will engage in the values clarification process and decreases the likelihood that they will soar into tangential, intellectual realms.

One can certainly ask an individual client, "Did you learn anything about yourself from that activity?" but it would probably be awkward to ask an individual client to finish the sentence "I learned that I _____," let alone a list of such unfinished sentences. Therefore, I Learned Statements are more appropriate for group settings.

I Learned Statements, like Unfinished Sentences, can be done in many ways. One way is for the counselor to post a list of I Learned Statements where they are visible to all, or the counselor could give each person a handout with the I Learned Statements on them. The counselor asks the group members to think about the previous activity they just did and complete as many of the unfinished statements as they can. It's best if they actually write out their answers. When people have pretty much completed their writing, the counselor asks for volunteers to share one of their completed I Learned Statements aloud. I like to tell my groups, "We won't discuss them right now. We'll just let them hang in the air for a few moments, and then someone else who wants to can say one of their I Learned Statements."

Participants typically want to share one or more of their statements. As in all group activities, I sometimes serve as gatekeeper, facilitating the process by saying things like "Is there anyone else who would like to share one of his or her I Learneds?" or "You can take another turn, but let's be sure that everyone who wants to has had a turn first," or I may also contribute an I Learned Statement of my own, as one more learner in the process of growing and developing his values. It is often a very satisfying experience for me as a group leader to hear participants voluntarily share their learnings and insights and to have these heard and accepted by the group. At times like this, it feels like we are a community of people growing and learning together.

I Learned Statements can be used several or many times over the course of a typical group's life. There are other ways to do I learned statements.

- Instead of asking members to complete all the statements, ask them to complete one, two, or three.
- Go around the circle and give each person the opportunity to share one of their completed statements. Remind them of their right to pass.
- Give them the opportunity to expand on their statement.
- Once the group has gotten the hang of I Learned Statements, skip the list. Just say after an activity, "Let's go around the group and give each person a chance to say an I Learned Statement—I learned that I, I relearned that I, I was surprised, pleased, displeased that I, and so on. Of course, you can pass. Okay, who wants to start?"

■ 16. I WONDER STATEMENTS

Still another variation on Unfinished Sentences (14), I Wonder Statements reinforce that we are all on a continuing journey to learn about ourselves and our world and to clarify and realize our values.

- I wonder _____   I wonder about_____
- I wonder if_____   I wonder if I_____
- I wonder how_____   I wonder how I_____
- I wonder why_____   I wonder why I_____
- I wonder when_____   I wonder when I_____
- I wonder whether_____   I wonder whether I_____

I have found, unlike with I Learned Statements (15), that it does not matter much if I include the second I in I Wonder Statements. People often reflect along personal lines anyway, and, even if they do wonder about things outside themselves, the wonders tend to be quite thoughtful and related to the experience at hand.

I Wonder Statements are done in the same way as I Learned Statements, except I Wonder Statements work well *before* a learning experience, as well as after it. If we're about to explore a particular counseling or therapy topic (recovery, careers, sex, loss, etc.), asking clients to think about something they wonder about the topic generates a host of issues for the group's further consideration. Similarly, one can ask at the very beginning of individual counseling, group counseling, or group therapy what clients are wondering as they commence this experience. In individual counseling, the question would be asked more informally, as in "Is there anything you're wondering about as you begin counseling? Anything about the process and how it works? About yourself? About me?" In a group setting, the counselor might post the whole list or just "I Wonder _____" in a visible place and say,

> As we begin our group together, I wonder what each of you is wondering at this time. How would you complete this sentence: I wonder, I wonder what, I wonder how, I wonder how I, I wonder whether, I wonder whether I, and so on? What are you wondering about? Let's go around the circle and give each person a chance to say what you're wondering about right now. If you're not wondering about anything, or if you'd rather not share it at this point, that's fine. Just say "I pass," and we'll go on to the next person. But I'd be really interested to know what at least some of you are thinking or feeling at this point. I'll share my "I wonder statement," too. So, Latisha, here on my right, will you start it off?

Ending a session or a group with I Wonder Statements also works well. It both provides individuals with the opportunity for further reflection and gives a realistic sense of ending to the group experience. Implied is: "Our session on this topic or our group may be ending, but our personal growth and values clarification will continue."

■ 17. ALTERNATIVES SEARCH

Considering alternatives is a basic value-clarifying process. A value-clarifying question like "Have you considered any alternatives?" typically generates one, two, or maybe three ideas. The Alternatives Search is a more structured activity that invites clients to spend more time considering a larger number of alternatives. It can lead to generating alternatives that they might not otherwise have considered.

Using a prepared grid or creating one on the spot on a piece of paper, ask clients to generate as long a list as possible of alternatives for the issue under consideration. For example, if the individual or group is working on recovery planning, one might say, "Make a list of as many ideas as possible for things you might do with one or more friends that don't involve drinking." Remind the client(s) of the rules of brainstorming:

- as many ideas as possible
- be creative
- don't censor or evaluate any ideas at this point
- piggyback or build on others' ideas

Once clients have generated all the alternatives they can think of, or during the brainstorming, the counselor can add ideas of her own, making clear these are *possible* ideas in the spirit of brainstorming, not recommendations the counselor is trying to impose.

Alternatives	I'll try it	I'll consider trying it	I won't try it
1			
2			
etc.			

Once the list of alternatives is generated, ask clients or group members to go down the list and, for each alternative, put a check mark next to each alternative, depending on whether they plan on trying or implementing it (first column), are pretty sure they won't do it (third column), or will consider doing it (second column). The activity can be followed by general discussion or by further clarifying questions or strategies, such as "Let's go around the circle and give each person the chance to talk about one of the alternatives you really liked or didn't like."

Myriad topics can be plugged into the activity. Here are some alternative searches for the sample topics we are using in this chapter.

Make a list of as many possibilities you can think of for:

- ways people earn a living (*Careers/Work*)
- things you might do together to have fun as a couple (*Couples*)
- ways to save money (*Money*)
- ways to eat more healthily (*Health*)
- sexual activities and positions (*Sex*)
- ways to bring more spirituality into your life (*Religion/spirituality*)
- things that belonged to your deceased spouse that a friend or relative might cherish owning (*Loss*). Adapt the headings: I'll give it to ____, I'll consider giving it to ____, I'll keep it, I'll dispose of it.
- Ways you don't want to act as you get older (*Aging*). Adapt the headings: I won't be that way, I might be that way, I will be that way.

■ 18. CONSEQUENCES SEARCH

This strategy can be a good follow-up to an Alternatives Search (17) or an Alternative Action Search (20) but can also be used by itself. For an example of the latter, a client may be going around in circles about two or three choices he's considering. This could be a good time for the counselor to suggest a consequences search.

In this strategy, the two or three (or more) top choices the client or group is considering are written at the top of the columns. Below these, the client or group lists all the possible consequences they can think of for each alternative, that is, all the possible results or outcomes, benefits or downsides, that are likely to result from choosing or doing that alternative. After the client or group has generated a good number of possible consequences, the counselor can offer one or more additional possibilities. One good way to do this is to say something like "Another possible consequence that occurs to me is _____. Shall I add that to the list?" In that way, the locus of control remains with the client or group.

Alternative #1	Alternative #2	Alternative #3
Possible Consequences	Possible Consequences	Possible Consequences

A variation is to divide the list into two sections, with the top part of the page devoted to *positive* consequences and the bottom part of the page to *negative* consequences. This has the advantage of encouraging clients to look at both types of consequences, not just the ones that fit their hopeful (positive) or skeptical (negative) mind frame. Alternatively, the consequences can come randomly, positive or negative, and then the counselor can ask clients to classify the consequences as positive (P or +) or negative (N or –), depending on how they view each consequence. After all, one person's negative ("He might leave me," sob) could be another person's positive ("He might leave me," smile).

■ 19. PATTERNS SEARCH

One way to help clients reflect more deeply on the issues they are exploring is to ask them to consider the nature of their current behavior patterns around the issue. Is what they are doing now a compulsion, a habit, or a free choice?

- Compulsion—they feel they must do this because of some inner compulsion or outside pressure.
- Habit—they do this because... well... they've always done it.
- Free choice—they feel they have made the choice to do this themselves; it feels like *their* choice.

For example, a therapist is working with an individual or couple around the tensions and conflicts associated with family gatherings. Using the patterns grid below, the therapist says, "List all the times and ways you get together with your extended family." The list might include "Thanksgiving at Grandma's," "the twins' birthday," "July 4 barbecue," and so forth. The list might also include another level of specificity, such as who does the cooking at Thanksgiving, how presents are handled at the twins' birthday, or watching the fireworks on July 4.

What do you do about this?	Is this a pattern?		Do you do it out of			Are you proud of your answers?		
	Yes	No	Compulsion	Habit	Free Choice	Yes	No	?

The strategy engages at least three of the valuing processes—examining the action patterns in our lives, considering whether we have made free choices about how we live our lives, and considering whether we prize and cherish (whether we value) how we are living our lives. When a couple engages in such an activity (or any values clarification activity, for that matter), it is not uncommon that their responses differ. One partner's free choice may feel like a compulsion to the other partner. Such discrepancies in perception and feeling can provide fruitful data for further exploration.

Pattern Searches on our sample topics might include the following.

- How you spend your leisure time (*Recovery*)
- Routines at work (*Work*)
- How you spend money (*Money*)
- How and when you have sex (*Sex*)
- All the ways you get exercise (*Health*)
- Your religious and spiritual practices (*Religion*)
- What happens when someone dies in your family (*Loss*)
- All the changes in your life in the past 10 (5) years (*Aging*)

■ 20. ALTERNATIVE ACTION SEARCH

A variation on the alternative search (17) is the Alternative Action Search. If an individual or group is considering a particular dilemma where some action is required by the client or a group member, the counselor can suggest, "Let's try an Alternative Action Search on this dilemma. What are all the possible ways you (we) can think of to deal with this situation?"

- Your probation officer tells you she doesn't believe you have the strength to stay clean (*Recovery*)
- Your coworker insults you in front of others (*Work*)
- Your partner walks out of the room in the middle of a discussion or argument (*Couples*)
- Your friend who borrowed $25 from you always has an excuse for not paying you back (*Money*)
- Your partner seems to be losing interest in sex (*Sex*)
- You're gaining more weight than you want to (*Health*)
- You'd like more spirituality in your life (*Religion/Spirituality*)
- You'd like to get out on your own more but are nervous about doing so (*Loss*)
- Your son tells you to give him your car keys and stop driving (*Aging*)

The client or group then explores the pros and cons of these alternative courses of action. In a group setting, smaller groups of three or four could discuss which possible actions would be most or least desirable, followed by further discussion in the whole group. The counselor could also suggest role-playing one or more of the alternatives, which not only produces further insight but also offers an excellent coaching opportunity, teaching or helping clients learn useful skills in communication and problem solving.

■ 21. FORCE FIELD ANALYSIS

This strategy, created by pioneering social psychologist Kurt Lewin (1943), teaches clients and group members an important set of skills for analyzing alternative courses of action. Although it can be used in any planning exercise, it is a particularly useful values clarification activity when applied to life choices and value dilemmas. It highlights the valuing processes of considering pros and cons (consequences) and action planning.

Decision, Choice, or Action Step:	
Pros or Helping Forces	Cons or Restraining Forces

In its simplest form, the Force Field Analysis helps any decision maker examine more thoughtfully the pros and cons, the potential benefits or problems, of any decision. For example, an individual client who is considering taking a new job would write the name of the new job or position in the top row of the table and then list all the pros or benefits or good aspects of taking the job in the left column and all the cons or possible negative outcomes of taking the job in the right column. An elderly client considering a move from home into an assisted living facility would do the same; that is, he would write "Move to assisted living" at the top and list all the possible good things about such a move in the left column and all the negatives or possible downsides in the right column.

The counselor can ask clarifying questions to see if the client would consider adding other items to the list of pros and cons; for example, "How about your ability to go to your church, which you've said is important to you? Would the move to assisted living be a pro or a con on that dimension?" The Force Field Analysis can also be done in group settings, with all the group members (as a whole group or in pairs, trios, etc.) filling in the force field grid. Like other Inventories (1), further clarifying questions can be asked to examine the pro and con lists more deeply, such as:

- Which are the three most significant pros and three most significant cons? Indicate these with a 1, 2, and 3.
- Which pros and cons are short-term versus long-term issues? Indicate these with ST or LT.
- Which pros and cons involve financial considerations? Indicate these with a $.

Another way to approach the Force Field Analysis (which explains the name of the activity) is to consider that any goal or course of action has forces in the environment (the "field") that are encouraging or hindering forces. These forces may be in the external world or the client's internal world. Encouraging forces may be support-ive people in the client's life, skills the client has, rules that allow the contemplated action, financial resources available, and the like. Hindering forces may be unsup-portive people, skills the client lacks, rules that possibly block the contemplated action, lack of financial resources, and so on. This form of Force Field Analysis is more strategic than a general listing of pros and cons. It is focused on how to get to a goal. When the hindering forces in a particular situation are relatively equal to or greater than the encouraging or helping forces, the individual is blocked from mov-ing forward. But by strengthening the helping forces and/or weakening or removing the hindering forces, the individual can move toward the goal.

Force Field Analysis experts maintain that we get more bang for the buck, so to speak, more likelihood of success, by lessening or eliminating the hindering forces. Either way, the Force Field Analysis allows clients, as individuals or in groups think-ing together, to carefully assess the forces in their lives that are helping or hindering their goal attainment and plan strategies for strengthening or weakening those forces so they can achieve their goals.

The next values clarification activity, Removing Barriers to Action (22), takes part of the Force Field Analysis and uses it to plan action strategies to achieve one's goal.

▩ 22. REMOVING BARRIERS TO ACTION

As described in the Force Field Analysis strategy (21), one major way to achieve our goals is to understand the forces in our environment and within ourselves that are hindering our moving forward and then taking action to reduce or eliminate the strength of those hindering forces. Removing barriers to action helps clients do exactly that.

Goal, Outcome:	
Barriers or Hindering Forces	Actions to Lessen or Remove Those Forces

This activity can work well when the goal is quite general, such as a recovering addict with the goal of staying clean. It also can work well when the goal is quite specific, such as an elderly client who can no longer drive and has a goal of "getting out to see friends more often," as opposed to "enjoying life more," which is rather general. As the latter example illustrates, the activity works best when the goal is a *behavioral* outcome, that is, something the client will *do*. Rather than a goal of feeling better, having more self-confidence, or becoming wealthy (which is an end state, not a behavior, like getting a higher paying job or investing successfully in the stock market), it is preferable for the goal to be an action or activity the client would like to undertake. That goal is then written in the top row of the table.

In the left column, the client or group members list all the barriers or forces that are impeding the client from taking the desired action—or that might emerge if the client tries to achieve this goal. Then, in the right column, for each barrier, the client writes all the ideas that occur for things that he might do to lessen or alleviate or remove that barrier. After the client has done as much thinking for himself as possible, the counselor can help the client consider additional barriers or solutions with clarifying questions: "Would you like to hear a couple of other ideas that occur to me?" "Would you consider this a possible solution?" "Would you like to add this to your list of barrier-removing strategies?" And so on.

Removing barriers to action can be followed with further discussion and action planning based on the richer array of action steps that the strategy generated. It can also be followed by the Self-Contract strategy (24).

Removing Barriers to Action can be done with individual clients or groups. For example, in a group focusing on health issues, the goal of "Eat less food" could be an outcome they work on together. Collectively, they would list the barriers or obstacles to achieving that goal—for example, a parent who continues to offer more and more food, the easy access to food all around, the desire to be social with friends, or the feeling of hunger that demands to be satisfied. Then, one at a time, they would work on practical steps that could be taken to lessen the strength of or eliminate these barriers to achieving their goal of eating less food.

■ 23. GETTING STARTED OR NEXT STEPS

Clients—indeed, all of us—often know what we want and even make vague plans to act on our goals. But we don't always take the concrete actions required to achieve those desires or goals. We never quite get started. This activity engages clients in the acting process of values clarification by inviting them to consider possible *Next Steps* they might take to achieve their goals or implement their decisions.

This strategy has as its core three value-clarifying questions that might often be asked in counseling settings.

- What would you like to do?
- What might the next step be?
- When might you begin?

Getting Started uses the following table to make a more structured activity for individuals or groups.

What I Would Like to Do	Next Step(s)	Date
1.		
2.		
3.		
Etc.		

The counselor asks the individual or group members to list some of their goals or things they would like to do regarding the topic under consideration. The list can range from a few to a dozen or so items. (More than that can get tedious.) For example, a client in career counseling might list "find out what jobs are available, update my resume, network with a few former coworkers, and work on my portfolio." Group members in a weight-loss group might list things they would like to do to improve their health. A couple who has been talking about wanting to do more things that they enjoy doing together might list those things in the left column.

The counselor then asks them to use the second column to indicate one or more Next Steps they could take to help accomplish what they would like to do. The counselor may need to help the client or group members move from listing general or grandiose Next Steps to listing concrete steps that are realistic and achievable. (See the next strategy for more on goals that are "conceivable, believable, and achievable.") They should try to identify at least one next step for each goal.

Finally, the counselor asks the client(s) to indicate a day or date by which it would be realistic to take each step.

Getting Started may be seen as a values clarification activity that logically follows from an Alternative Search (17), Alternative Action Search (20), or Removing Barriers to Action (22) and precedes the Self-Contract (24). However, it can also be used by itself for its clarifying value or for its educational value in psychoeducational groups.

■ 24. SELF-CONTRACT

Like the Getting Started strategy (23), this activity engages the client in the valuing process of acting—in both considering a concrete action step and deciding whether to commit to taking that step. Whereas getting started provides an opportunity for clients to intellectually consider possible next steps, the Self-Contract makes the action planning much more concrete and immediate. If an individual client or group is ready to think about acting on a goal, plan, or decision, *the self-contract* can help clients move toward real action.

The self-contract works with both individual clients and groups. Picture an individual client who, after a period of confusion and self-doubt, has gotten himself to a place where he is ready to begin looking for work again. The counselor has asked him to engage in an alternative action search (20), and together they have identified a half-dozen possible steps the client could take to begin his job search. The counselor asked him to prioritize the list, and he has identified the three most likely or desirable action steps he might take to begin searching for a job. Now the counselor might introduce the self-contract as follows:

> "I'd like to introduce you to the idea of a 'self-contract' at this point. The self-contract helps you take an idea you are thinking about doing and move it closer to actually doing it. Are you game?... All right, here's how it works. A self-contract sounds or looks like this:

"I will _____
_____
_____ by _____
_____

"So the idea is to choose one of the three ideas you are considering for starting your job search, and write that step in the first blank. You're not actually committing yourself to doing it at this point; you're just stating very concretely what the action step would be."

The counselor may have to help the client put the action step in terms that are very concrete. As we sometimes say, the action step should be

- *conceivable* (one can picture it),
- *believable* (realistic), and
- *achievable* (by the client; the client can do it on his or her own).

So if the client says, "My first step is to find out all the jobs that are available in my field," the counselor might say, "I can't quite picture how you will do that. What will you have to do to find out what jobs are available?" When the client, possibly with the counselor's help, narrows it down to "I will go to the job search office to look at their job postings and Internet database on job openings," that is what the client writes in the blank in the self-contract.

Then the counselor says, "Okay, so you've written down a very specific step you can take to achieve your goal. If you were going to do it—and you're not committing yourself to do it at this point, but just contemplating it—when would you want to do it by?" Once the client thinks about this and possibly explores it with the counselor, the client then writes down a day or date in the space after "by."

Finally, the counselor says, "All right, now comes the big question: Do you want to commit yourself to doing it? It's your choice. If you really feel you are ready to do this, if you are ready to commit yourself to do it, then sign your name at the bottom of the Self-Contract. Remember, if you sign it, it's not a contract with me; I'll be here for you whether you fulfill the contract or not. It's a contract with yourself. Do you want to sign it?"

Clients get the idea. They take it seriously. No one wants to fail to live up to their own expectations of themselves. And even though the contract is with oneself and not the counselor, the client who signs his name has made a sort of public affirmation before the counselor, and that has meaning to the client as well. The counselor is sincere about being there and still being supportive of the client if he fails to fulfill the Self-Contract. Either way, the client learns from the experience, and the results can be explored in further counseling and values clarification.

Self-Contracts can also be done in group settings. Members in a group on loss and bereavement, for example, can be asked to write a self-contract on something they might do to meet their own needs at this point in their life. A Spenders Anonymous group might write Self-Contracts on something they might do to save money. In a couples group (or in couples counseling), a couple might write a joint Self-Contract on something they might do together just for fun. In each case, first they conceive and visualize the idea; then they put a date by which time they would expect to do it; then they decide whether to sign their names or not. At a later meeting of the group, members can share whether they fulfilled their self-contracts, how they felt about the results, and where they want to go from there.

■ 25. WHAT WE KNOW AND WHAT WE WANT TO KNOW

Counselors have always used this activity in its simplest form when they ask an individual client, "What would you like to get from counseling?" "What are your goals?" "How would you like to change?" "What would you like to learn?" or any similar questions that help establish the client's purposes and expectations. What We Know and What We Want to Know serves a similar purpose in group work. It is a good goal-setting activity and helps focus the group's time and attention on topics that are of interest and importance to the group members. The strategy can be used at the beginning of a group or at later stages in the group's development.

The counselor reminds the group of its theme—recovery, careers, sex, health, bereavement, and so on. She holds up an object she brought that symbolizes that theme—an empty liquor bottle, the help-wanted section of the newspaper, a condom, a plate of chocolate chip cookies, a funerary urn, or the like. She then explains, "I'm going to pass around this bottle [or whatever object]. When it comes to you, please tell us one thing you know or think you know on the subject of recovery [or careers, sex, etc.]. If you don't know anything about the subject, then just say 'I pass,' and pass the bottle on to the next person. Okay, Juan, here's the bottle. What's one thing you know about recovery from alcoholism?" As the bottle moves about the room, the counselor can simply thank each person for their contribution or nonverbally acknowledge it, or she can record in a few words or have a group member record each person's contribution on a sheet of newsprint on the board or wall.

As in many values clarification activities, the counselor can take a turn, in this case sharing something she knows about recovery, but being careful to take about the same length of time that other group members took and not have her words sound like a lecture or sermon. If the counselor hears a group member say something he knows that the counselor believes to be inaccurate or harmful, she should still accept the individual's response for now, so as not to discourage participation by correcting the first thing someone said. Later that session or in another group meeting, the counselor can say she has some different information or a different perspective on something someone said, which she'd like to explain or come back to another time.

Once the object has traveled all around the group, the counselor says, "Now that we've shared many things we know or think we know about recovery, I'm going to pass the bottle around the circle one more time, and this time I'd like you to share one thing you'd *like to know* about recovery." Recording the group members' responses is, again, a good way to help them feel that they and their contributions are going to be respected in this group, and the list of things they would like to know provides a potential agenda for future group meetings and discussions.

A shorter version of this strategy includes just one time around the circle, focusing on what the group members would like to know about the subject.

Although the activity lends itself logically to the beginning of a group's time together, it can also be used later in the group's development when a new topic comes up or is being introduced. For example, a group focusing on recovery could focus on "what we know and what we'd like to know about dealing with friends who like to drink" or "what we know and what we'd like to know about handling being alone." As a festive holiday approaches, they could focus on "what we know and what we'd like to know about staying sober over the holiday."

■ 26. VALUES NAME TAGS

This is an excellent strategy for helping a group get to know one another as they engage in values clarification. I often use it at the beginning of a group's life.

The counselor comes prepared with 5 x 7 index cards, masking tape, and marking pens, so that each group member can write his or her name in large letters in the middle of the card. Alternatively, if group members carry notebooks, the counselor can ask them to tear a half sheet of paper from their notebook and use their own pen or pencil to write their names. Either way, the counselor asks them not to fill the card or paper with their name but to leave room around the top and bottom, sides, and corners where they can write some words. The counselor then asks them a series of value-clarifying questions and asks them to write their answers in a particular place on the name card.

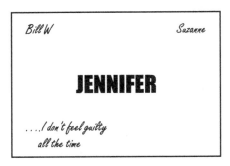

For example, if this was a group meeting around drug and alcohol issues, the counselor might say the following, giving group members a few moments to write their responses to each question before asking them the next question.

I'm going to ask you a series of questions about drugs and alcohol, and I'll ask you to write your answer on a particular part of your card. If it's something you don't want anyone to see, then you can write your answer on the back of the card, so you'll know your answer but no one else will see it. [I might add, "Don't worry about spelling," if it's a group where people might feel self-conscious about their writing.]. Okay, in the upper left corner of your card, write the name of a person you admire in terms of sobriety; that person really has his or her act together when it comes to drugs or alcohol.... In the upper right corner of your name tag, write the initials of a person you think is dangerously addicted. He or she is really in trouble or will be soon.... In the lower right corner, write the best piece of advice you ever got about drugs. Try to keep it to a phrase or sentence.... In the lower left corner, complete this sentence: "The best thing about being sober is _____." Just write whatever words come to mind to finish the sentence.... Finally, all around the name card, wherever you can fit it in, write five "I-N-G words" that describe things about you that you think are important to who you are. For example, I really like to run—for exercise—so I'd write "running" on my card. And communicating with people is really important to me, so I'd write "communicating." So, even if you have to make up a word to do it, put five or so I-N-G words around your card

I typically do a Values Name Tag myself and participate in the next part of the activity.

The counselor then asks participants to take a piece of tape and attach the name tag high on their chest where others can see it. She then asks everyone to stand up and mill around the room, stopping in front of people and reading their name tags. This can be done silently, or people can talk about one corner of their name tag or one I-N-G word with each person they meet. They should be encouraged to read many different name tags and to stop in front of people they don't already know. After milling about for a while (e.g., 5 or 10 minutes, depending on group size), they can get into groups of three, with each person having a couple of minutes to talk about any parts of their name tags that interest them.

Another approach is to have group members sit in their chairs, preferably in a circle where they can see each other's names throughout the session, and go around the circle giving each participant the opportunity to talk about one thing they wrote on their name tags.

Values Name Tags can be general, with group members responding to any value-clarifying questions that might be useful to help people get to know one another and begin using the valuing processes, or, as in the previous and following examples, they can be tailored to a particular theme.

- Something you are proud of regarding (your work, your relationship, money, sex, health, religion/spirituality, how you're dealing with your loss, aging)
- A good role model you had regarding (work, relationships, money, etc.)
- One way you are similar to (or different from) your parents regarding (work, relationships, money, etc.)
- A choice you're facing regarding (your work, your relationship, etc.)
- A habit or ritual you have in relation to (your work, your relationship, etc.)
- Work (a close relationship, money, religion, etc.) is _____

Other strategies, such as Unfinished Sentences (14), Rank Orders (2), and I Wonder Statements (16), also make good questions for a Values Name Tag.

■ 27. WHAT'S IN YOUR WALLET?

This values clarification strategy highlights the valuing processes of prizing and cherishing and public affirmation. Like the Values Name Tag (26) and One-Minute

Autobiography (28), it is a good activity to use near the beginning of a group's life to help participants get to know one another. It also works well a bit later in the group's development to help members move to another level of sharing and trust.

The basic value-clarifying question for this activity is *What is an object in your wallet or purse that shows or stands for something you prize or cherish or is very important to you?* The counselor asks participants: "Look through your wallet or purse and find one or more items—a document, photograph, object, or anything that has significance to you because it represents something you prize or cherish or is very important to you."

Sharing their objects and their meaning can take place in the whole group, in which each member gets a chance to show one item from his or her wallet or purse and explain its significance to the group, or the group can be divided into subgroups of three to six members, in which participants get a chance to show two or three items from their wallet or purse and explain their importance. As always, anyone may pass and just listen to the others.

This activity may be used for values clarification and group cohesion in general, but it can also be applied to a counseling topic relevant to the group. For example, in a group dealing with religion or spirituality, the instruction might be "Find an object in your wallet or purse that has particular meaning to you in terms of religion or spirituality." In a group dealing with one or more health issues, the instruction might be "Find an object in your wallet or purse that has significance to you in terms of your health." One member may show his health insurance card and talk about how much he has sacrificed to be able to afford health coverage. Another might show a picture of her children and talk about how she wants to lose weight so she will be around to see her children grow up and have children of their own. The contents of our wallets and purses are filled with indicators of some of our deepest values. By tapping into that rich source of value indicators, this activity often produces surprisingly meaningful sharing and insight.

■ 28. ONE-MINUTE AUTOBIOGRAPHY

This is a group strategy in which group members share their "autobiographies" with one another in a limited time frame. The autobiography invites participants to reflect on their lives and how their values and character developed.

Depending on the group members' ages and comfort level and on how long the group has been meeting, the time limit can be literally 1 minute, or 2 or 3 minutes. The brief time frame makes it easier for most people to share because they know they cannot possibly fit their life story into 1 or 2 minutes and are therefore not worried about getting it all in or running out of things to say.

A 1- or 2-minute autobiography is an excellent activity for the first session of a group. The general question may be phrased, "In 1 [or 2] minutes, please share with us how you became the person you are, how you developed your values, and who and what influenced you to become who you are. The idea is not to tell every detail of your life but to convey how you became the person you are today. Feel free to say 'I pass' if you would rather not take a turn now." I often give a 1-Minute Autobiography of my own to break the ice and demonstrate how it works.

The 1-Minute Autobiography can also be adapted to the counseling theme or issue that is the focus of the group. For example, "In a 2-minute autobiography, please share with us, from your earliest years on, how you developed your attitudes, habits, and values regarding careers [or drinking, drugs, work, couples' relationships, money, sex, being healthy, religion/spirituality, loss and bereavement, aging, etc.]."

If the group is small enough (up to 15 or so), every person can have a turn. If the group is too big for that, I might have them divide into groups of six or eight so they can share their autobiographies in a small group.

■ 29. PAGES FOR AN AUTOBIOGRAPHY

Counseling and psychotherapy has always been a setting in which clients describe and explore events from earlier in their lives that might have relevance for their current situation. Pages for an Autobiography is a more structured format for gaining greater insight into how our values and value indicators (attitudes, goals, behavior patterns, etc.) developed and recognizing that we have some choice about what to continue or change in the future. (See also Birren & Cochran, 2001.)

Whether in individual counseling or group settings, the counselor asks clients, individually, to spend some time thinking and making notes or writing about how some particular theme was dealt with throughout their childhood and youth. Our 10 sample themes could all serve as topics for an autobiographical "page."

Recovery	Sex
Careers	Health
Work	Religion, Spirituality
Couples	Loss, Bereavement
Money	Aging

For example, the counselor might ask, "How was alcohol dealt with in your home when you grew up? What is your earliest memory about alcohol? Who drank what, how often, and how much? Who abstained? How did it affect the family relationships? What did you observe? What were you aware of? And so on. On your page, spend a few minutes writing or making notes on what you remember about how drinking and alcohol were handled as you grew up." If the theme is bereavement, the counselor might ask, "In your extended family, how were death and bereavement handled? What is your earliest memory around someone in the family dying? What other relatives died during your childhood and teenage years? What funeral customs were followed? How did people mourn? What kinds of emotions were expressed or not? What did you think and feel as you observed these events? How did they influence you? And so on. On your page, spend a few minutes writing or making notes on how death and bereavement were dealt with when you were growing up."

Pages for an Autobiography can be done with individual clients or with groups. Individual clients can share and discuss their page from their autobiography with their counselor. In a group setting, participants can discuss their pages in subgroups and/or the whole group. The activity brings up rich material for the individual and group to process and learn from. In a values clarification context, it gives clients a visceral connection to the source of their value indicators and a realization of how their attitudes, beliefs, and values were influenced as they grew up. By better understanding how they developed their attitudes, beliefs, and behavior patterns, they recognize intuitively that they have some choice as to how they proceed with this issue in the future. It provides an opportunity for them to reauthor the narrative of their life.

Sometimes, particularly in group settings, it helps to begin this activity with a general topic that may be easier and lighter to talk about than the group's theme. This helps establish a nostalgic, accepting tone in the group. General topics that are rich in autobiographical values issues might include the following.

- How each year you spent:
  o Christmas (or other key holidays)
  o New Year's Eve
  o summers
  o first day of school

- Teachers—what your learned from them
- Best friends—why they were, how you broke up
- Exposure to other races, ethnicities, religions
- Hairstyle—all the changes you made
- How you learned:

  o to ride a bike
  o to swim
  o to kiss
  o to play cards
  o manners

After having the group do and discuss one of these Pages for an Autobiography, they can then go on to a page more directly connected to the group's counseling or psychoeducational theme.

◼ 30. ROLE MODEL ANALYSIS

One way to clarify our own values is to examine the role models in our lives who may have influenced our goals, choices, behaviors, and other value indicators. Becoming more aware of how our value indicators and values originated gives us greater choice over whether to continue and commit to those priorities, beliefs, and behavior patterns or whether to modify or change our value indicators or value systems.

Simple value-clarifying questions can be used to invite clients to examine their role models. For example:

- Was he (or she) a role model for you?
- Do you have a role model whose example could guide you at this time?
- Without a male (female) role model at home, where did you go to learn what it means to be a man (woman)?
- Was he (she) a positive or negative role model for you?
- Who was or were your most important role model(s) then?
- Looking back on it, was there another person in your life who could have been a better role model for you?
- When it comes to *work* (or alcohol, money, health, aging, etc.), do you have any role models in your life?

Role Model Analysis takes a basic clarifying question—"Who were your role models?" (or "Who *are* your role models?")—and extends the question into a more elaborate strategy. It can be done individually or in a group.

Explain to the client or group that a role model is someone they admire, someone they look up to, someone they would like to be like, or someone whose example influences them. A person can be a role model in some respects but not in others. A role model can be a positive influence or a negative one. A role model can be alive or dead. A role model can be someone they actually know or someone they have never met. Many types of people can serve as role models, including:

Parent	Friend
Brother, sister	Coworker
Other relative	Employer
Teacher	Author
Coach or team leader	Political figure
Youth group leader	Sports or entertainment figure
Religious leader	

Hand out or ask clients or group members to draw a grid as shown here, with three columns.

Role Model	Personality, Character Trait, or Behavior	Influence
Dad	Reliable, devoted	Being reliable is important to me
Marianne	Friendly, happy	I learned people can be happy
(Regarding alcohol)		
Uncle Bob	Always drunk	Made me want to avoid drinking too much
Jeff	Occasionally drunk	Confused me; should I get drunk sometimes?

Depending on the context, ask them to list up to (a) five current role models; (b) five role models from earlier in their lives, from childhood to young adulthood (or, if younger, until their present age); or (c) five role models past or present in their lives. To adapt the general role model analysis to a particular counseling topic, ask clients to list three or four role models in general in their lives and then list one to three role models when it comes to recovery, careers, relationships, sex, bereavement, or whatever the topic might be. One person can be a role model in both the general and specific categories.

Next, in the second column, ask clients to write down one or two qualities of personality or character or a particular behavior they admire in that person or that impressed or influenced them. You might give an example of your own if that would be helpful in demonstrating how the activity works.

In the third column, they should write a few words to indicate how each of their models influenced them personally, what they learned from that model, or how they are different because of that model's example or influence.

This activity brings up many issues for clients and provides much food for thought and discussion in individual or group counseling.

■ 31. BOARD OF DIRECTORS

Somewhat similar to the Role Model Analysis (30), this strategy has clients examine the sources of their values and value indicators. It encourages them to appreciate some of the inculcation and modeling they have received, to critically evaluate some of their inculcation and modeling, and most of all, to recognize that they are more than the sum of those influences, that ultimately their choices are their own. The Board of Directors can be used in individual or group settings and can be used as a general values clarification experience or applied to particular counseling topics. The general form of the strategy is presented first.

Begin by asking clients or group members to use a whole sheet of paper and to draw the following diagram in the top half of the page.

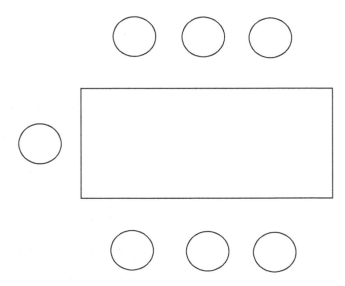

Explain to them the concept of a corporate board of directors—how when a corporation has important choices to make, it calls its board of directors together around a table, and each director contributes his or her ideas and thinking, which helps the board of directors make its best decisions. Continue in the following vein:

"In a way, each person is like a corporation with a Board of Directors. This diagram represents your Board of Directors. Whenever you have an important or difficult decision to make in life, you call together your Board of Directors. The board consists of all those people who have been strong influences on how you think about life's issues, problems, and decisions. For example [give an example of your own], when I have important or hard choices to make in life, I often hear the voices of my _____ and my friend _____ and my college teacher _____, all sort of whispering in my ear and telling me what I should do or what they would do in that situation. So I'm going to write their names or initials next to the circles on my diagram here to indicate that these people often sit on my Board of Directors.

"I'd like you to do the same. See if you can think of four or five or six people who sit on your Board of Directors, whose voices you often hear in the back of your head, whose advice or example comes through to you when you are thinking about what to do. When you think of them, put their initials or name next to one of the circles on these two long sides of your boardroom table.... Keep in mind, you may be glad these people are on your board and welcome their words of wisdom, or you may wish they weren't on your board. But put them down anyway. You may even have someone on your board who is dead or someone you never met but just read or heard about, but if you carry them around in your mind and you hear from them when life gets difficult or you have important choices to make, then put their names down on your Board of Directors.

"Now, you see that the one circle at the head of the table here is still blank. This position is reserved for the chairman or chairwoman of the board. That's *you*; you can write your initials next to that circle. You may not always feel that you are in charge of your board of directors, but you are, or you can take control [now or as you get older (if working with young people)]. So now I would like to ask you some questions about your board."

The counselor then asks one, several, or all of the following questions, possibly writing or posting them on the wall.

- Who sits on your Board of Directors?
- What are one or two things that each member of your board knows about, where you would be wise to listen to their ideas? (Or in what way(s) are you glad they are on your board? or What are their qualifications for being on your board?)
- Which board members do you hope will always serve on your Board of Directors? Why?
- Is there anyone you would like to retire from your board? Why?
- Is there one thing you could suggest to each member of your board that would help him or her be a more effective, better board member?

- Do you feel you are in control of your Board of Directors, or are they or some of them in control of you? When will you be in charge? What advice would you give yourself for how you could convince some of your board that you deserve to have more control?
- Is there anyone else you would like to ask to join your Board of Directors?

In a large group, have members get into small groups (e.g., threes or fours), and give each person a fixed amount of time as the focus person (e.g., 2 minutes each) to talk about his or her board of directors and the answers to your questions. Adjust the size of groups or the time limits to fit their comfort level and how many questions you asked them to consider. Remind them they should feel free to share as much or as little about their Board of Directors as they wish.

To adapt the Board of Directors strategy to any topic an individual or group is focusing on, you can use either of the following approaches.

1. Begin by explaining the concept of the Board of Directors and say that this Board of Directors has some big decisions to make about *drugs* (or careers, work, relationships, money, sex, etc.). Ask them: When it comes to this topic, who sits on their Board of Directors? Adapt any of the subsequent questions as needed to fit the topic.
2. Do the whole Board of Directors strategy as outlined, and then extend the metaphor and the activity further by saying: "You will notice that the seats at the end of the table opposite the chairperson have been left blank. These seats are reserved for consultants to the board. When the board has a particular subject it needs advice and counsel on, it calls in specialists on that subject. Today your board has some decisions to make about drugs (or health, religion, loss, aging, etc.)." Ask if there are any other people beyond their regular board members who fill these seats when that topic comes up. Ask them again which of their board members they'd like to hear more or less from on this subject, and so on with the other questions. Again, allow time for clients to discuss their responses in the group or in subgroups.

Conclude the activity by having clients do I Learned Statements (15) or share any ideas they had about how they could work more effectively with their Board of Directors.

■ 32. CHAIRS (OR DIALOGUE WITH SELF)

This is an activity from the Gestalt therapy repertoire (Pavio & Greenberg, 1995; Polster & Polster, 1999) that can be used as a values clarification strategy with individuals or in groups.

If a client is facing a dilemma between two alternative viewpoints or courses of action, the counselor sets out two chairs for the client (for example, the client's own chair and another empty chair). One chair represents one of the two options, and the other chair represents the other option. The client is asked to sit in one chair and make an argument for choosing that option. Then the client is asked to move to the other chair and explain to the imaginary person in the first chair why the second chair option is better. Then the client moves back to the first chair to answer the second chair, and so on. This continues for as long as it feels or seems productive.

Such a Dialogue With Self highlights many of the pros and cons around any decision-making dilemma and also raises feelings about the issues that may help the values clarification process or that may be suitable to handle in another form of counseling or therapy.

■ STRATEGIES 33 TO 38: LIFE GOALS STRATEGIES

This is a series of values clarification strategies, some of which my colleagues and I learned from Dr. Herb Shepherd many years ago. They can be used separately or together. Individually or cumulatively, the strategies invite clients to examine the meaning of their lives: Where are they in their life's journey? Who are they? What have they accomplished? What has been important to them? Where do they want to go from here? These profound value-clarifying questions are appropriate to any counseling theme because they address our deepest values, and our deepest values give us direction and motivation to deal with any of life's challenges or issues we may be facing.

The strategies can be used with individuals or in a group setting. After each activity, individual clients can share their responses with the counselor and explore the feelings, thoughts, and issues raised by the experience. Group members may share their responses with others in the whole group or subgroups. Indeed, because these are often powerful activities that generate many thoughts and feelings, *it is very important that time be provided for processing these experiences* with the counselor or group. As always, clients and group members can pass on any of these activities. In groups, someone who passes still gets a lot out of doing the activity but not sharing it with others or in listening to others' responses.

■ 33. LIFE LINE

Clients or group members are asked to draw a long horizontal line across a page. On the left end of the line, they write their year of birth. On the right side of the line, they write the year they might be expected to die, based on family longevity, their state of health, or other factors they think are relevant. Then somewhere along the line, they are to write the current year, approximately where it belongs between the two end points.

Birth	This	Death
Year	Year	Year

This is their estimated Life Line, which they are asked to contemplate. Many thoughts and feelings are generated by visualizing and contemplating one's Life Line in this way.

■ 34. WHO ARE YOU?

In a group, the counselor asks for a volunteer to respond to some questions about who they are. The counselor then asks the volunteer, "In a word or two, *Who Are You?*" Group members typically respond with "a teacher," "a mother," "a man," or some other descriptor of an important role or part of their identity. Then the counselor asks, "All right, *who else* are you?" and the person typically responds with another of his or her roles or identities. The counselor then asks a third time, "Who Are You?" and a fourth time, and continues for a total of 6 to 10 rounds, depending on the volunteer's ease of response and apparent level of comfort. Some individuals remain on the level of roles they play in life; others go on to the kind of person they think they are, such as "a kind person" or "someone who cares." The counselor thanks the volunteer for demonstrating how the activity works and then asks all the group members individually to list 8 to 10 answers they would give to the question "*Who Are You?*"

■ 35. EPITAPH

The counselor explains what an Epitaph on a gravestone is and gives a few examples or asks the group members if they can give an example of any epitaphs they have seen for members of their family or friends who have died. She then asks the group members to each draw a simple outline of a gravestone on their paper and write inside the gravestone their name, the year of their birth, a dash, the estimated year of death (see Life Line, 33), and finally, an Epitaph that they hope would be a good and accurate Epitaph for themselves when they eventually die.

Jane Doe
1984-2064
"*Epitaph*"

■ 36. SELF-OBITUARY

Clients or group members are asked to take a full sheet of paper and write on the top their name, followed by a comma, and then "died _____," writing today's date in the blank space. The counselor explains or reminds the client or group about obituaries and what they are meant to contain and convey. She then asks the participants to write their own obituaries as they might appear in a local newspaper if they did, unfortunately, die that day. The counselor can remind participants of the kinds of things that often appear in obituaries, such as the deceased's roles in life, memberships, accomplishments, what they were good at, qualities they were loved or admired for, what they were working on (personal or work goals), cause of death, funeral arrangements, and where flowers or donations may be sent in their memory. (Some counselors like to give the client or group members a prepared obituary form with sentence stems that can be filled in, such as "He will be remembered for _____," "He was working on becoming _____," and so on.) Participants typically need about 15 minutes, more or less, to complete their obituaries. This is one of the most powerful strategies for existential soul searching and values clarification.

■ 37. SELF-EULOGY

In this alternative to the obituary, clients or group members write their own eulogies. A eulogy, of course, is a speech delivered at a funeral or memorial service in which a religious leader, family member, friend, or dignitary describes the life, work, accomplishments, and/or personal qualities of the deceased that he or she will be remembered for. Anecdotes are sometimes included that capture the essence of the deceased loved one particularly well. In this activity, clients may be asked to write their own eulogies as they would like them to be delivered if they were to die today or, alternatively, as they would like them to be delivered after they have lived a long and full life. In a group setting, members may be given the opportunity to read their eulogies aloud to the group, or group members may exchange eulogies and read other members' eulogies aloud.

■ 38. LIFE INVENTORY

In this activity, clients and group members take stock of their life trajectory—past, present, and future. The counselor asks the following value-clarifying questions or ones like them. They may be asked one at a time, posted for all to see, or handed out on a sheet of paper with spaces to write responses or notes after each question.

- What was best about your childhood and youth?
- What was difficult about your childhood and youth?
- What turning points, if any, have there been in your life?
- What are you grateful for at this time in your life?
- What are your strengths (personality, character, skills)?
- What aspects of yourself would you like to develop further?
- What are you proudest of having accomplished or done?
- What would you still like to do?
- Who are the important people in your life?
- What relationships would you like to improve?

Group members may discuss their responses to one or more of the questions in the whole group or in subgroups.

Self-Contract (See Strategy 24)

If a client or group is doing the life goals strategies as a sequence, the Self-Contract is an excellent activity to end with. It transitions from all the thinking, feeling, and reflecting that occurred during the exercises to at least one concrete action step they can take to actualize their life goals. The Self-Contract strategy (24) was previously described in detail.

■ STRATEGIES 39 TO 41: WRITTEN SELF-REFLECTION STRATEGIES

Most values clarification strategies take place right in the counseling session or group and involve clients and group members responding quite spontaneously and verbally. Many activities involve a little writing and reflecting, as when clients list and code their Values Inventory (1) or group members list the three or four items of a Rank Order according to their preference (2). However, this is quite different from extended writing, when individuals have time to really reflect on their feelings and thoughts. Extended writing and reflecting are significant aids to values clarification. As letter writers and diarists of old exemplify, writing and reflecting often lead to deeper insights and richer expression than spontaneous reaction and communication, as valuable as those forms may be.

Three strategies for encouraging this type of deeper reflection through writing are values cards, diaries, and journals.

■ 39. VALUES CARDS

This is more of a group than individual counseling strategy. The counselor gives group members or asks them to purchase a stack of 4 x 6 index cards. She asks them, between group meetings, to take a few minutes to write out on one of the cards any thoughts or feelings they have about the group's theme or topics that have come up in the group or their lives. They can write something as short as one sentence, or they can fill every bit of both sides of the card. But what they write about should be real and have meaning to them; it should reflect what they prize or cherish, their beliefs, opinions, life choices, insights, goals, and concerns. What they write on their Values Card may come out of their own thoughts or free associations or may be in response to something that happened to them or something they read somewhere or saw on television. Although most probably will express themselves in prose, if they feel so inclined, they can write a poem, draw, or tape a picture to the card and explain its meaning to them. They should put their names on the cards.

The counselor further explains that she will read each values card herself before the next group session. (Some counselors also like to make a comment or ask a value-clarifying question on each card, in which case she explains that she will do this. It is a way of establishing or extending the relationship between counselor and each individual group member.) She will also select a few cards to read to the whole group at the beginning of their next session. If they would not want her to read their card aloud, they should simply write, "Do not read to group" on the card, and that wish will be respected.

If group members are unlikely to complete their Values Cards between sessions, some counselors have participants write their cards at the beginning or end of the session. A 4 x 6 index card is not essential either. A 5 x 7 card or half-sheet of paper will do, but I find that 4 x 6 cards are preferable because they are not as intimidating to group members as larger cards or pages, they limit my reading time to a manageable length, and they are easy to handle.

Values Cards not only provide the opportunity for group members to deepen their values clarification process through writing but also provide an interesting, thought-provoking way to begin the next group meeting and honor the introspection and views of individual members. The counselor will try, over time, to read values cards from *all* the group members, even some she disagrees with, as a way of communicating that all honest expressions are valued in the group (providing they follow any guidelines the counselor or group may have established for safe, respectful communication).

I have found that Values Cards often provide an occasion for a group member to say something to me that he has not felt safe saying to me or others face to face. It has sometimes been a vehicle for creating dialogue with a group member who feels isolated or alienated and, by responding on his card or reading the card in the group, it has succeeded in involving or reinvolving the individual in the group (Kouzes & Posner, 2010).

■ 40. VALUES DIARY

A Values Diary extends the writing and reflection to a greater degree than the Values Card. It also provides a cumulative record for the clients or group members to have and keep of their own identity, values development, and personal expression.

The counselor either distributes or asks clients or group members to purchase a diary or notebook. Somewhat like a diary in which one records the events of the day, this diary can be used to *record data* related to the theme of the counseling or psychoeducational group. For example, clients or group members might be asked to record

- each time they are tempted to drink or use drugs (*Recovery*)
- the careers of the various people they meet over the course of a week (*Careers*)
- all the types of work they do over a 2-week period (*Work*)
- each time they give or receive a compliment or appreciation to or from their partner (*Couples*)
- every expenditure, large and small, between sessions (*Money/financial management*)
- each time they engage in sex, including where, when, how, satisfaction (*Sex*)

- everything they eat and drink for a 2-week period (*Health/diet*)
- whenever they think about God or religion (*Religion/spirituality*)
- whenever they feel a sense of loss or grief (*Loss*)
- whenever they feel young or ageless (*Aging*)

Similarly, in a therapy setting, a client working on anger management could record every time he felt angry and what he did about it. Clients in a sexual addictions group could record every time they are tempted to masturbate or view pornography.

The time period for recording this data in the diary can vary from a day to a week to the period between counseling or group sessions to whatever time frame seems appropriate to the situation. The diary soon accumulates important information that leads to insight and that can be worked with further in individual or group settings.

■ 41. VALUES JOURNAL

As with the Values Card and the Values Diary, the Values Journal can be used to record any thoughts or feelings clients or group members have about the group's theme or topics that have come up in the group or their own lives. However, unlike Values Cards, there is no limit to the length of the writing, and unlike the Values Diary, the content need not focus on data per se. Rather, their entries can reflect what they prize or cherish, their feelings, beliefs, opinions, life choices, insights, goals, and concerns. The Values Journal provides an opportunity for reflection, insight, speculation, and wonder. What clients and group members write about should be real and have meaning to them. As with the Values Card, they can use prose writing or, if they feel inspired, write a poem or draw.

Values Journals can be topic specific—for example, a couples journal or a spiritual journal in which the entries are about that particular counseling or group theme—or they can be general, with clients and group members writing about any values-rich topic or areas of interest to them.

Some counselors simply encourage clients or group members to keep a diary or journal, write in it freely as they wish, and if they like, share it with the counselor from time to time. It's entirely optional and informal. Some counselors like to structure the strategy like the Values Card, creating the expectation (or, in some cases, the requirement) that participants will keep a diary or journal. The diary is then used in group discussions and activities, and the counselor periodically collects and reads the diaries and uses them as a means of further, personalized communication with group members.

7

Tara's Case

The Woman Who Was Trapped in Her Job

Tara felt trapped in her job. She had worked at her company for 20 years, held a good position with good salary and benefits, and could retire in 8 years with a solid retirement package. But her work had ceased being meaningful or challenging or even interesting to her. She performed at a more than acceptable level to her company, but she felt she was just going through the motions. The thought of continuing with the status quo for 8 more years was mildly depressing to her. Her male counselor did not think she was clinically depressed but heard her saying that she was seriously unhappy with this stage of her life.

Following the protocol of the clarifying interview (chapter 5), once Tara's dilemma was clarified—"I'm stuck in my job and want to leave it or figure out some way to cope with it"—she and her counselor spent two sessions exploring possible alternatives. The counselor's perception was that Tara was a talented woman who had options. Based on his knowledge of the world of work, he thought she could be attractive to other employers, could start her own business, or, with just a little retraining, could be successful in other fields. But the more they explored alternatives, the more it became clear how much Tara valued security. Her present job met her current and future material needs, and she was reluctant to jeopardize these. Moreover, with family, including elderly parents, in the area, she would not consider moving, which limited her job and career options. The more they explored alternatives and consequences, the more it became clear to them both that Tara did not feel she had a free choice in this important aspect of her life. She felt trapped in a prison partly of her own making.

The interview picks up at that point.

COUNSELOR: You sound pretty discouraged. I'm sure I'd be unhappy, too, if I felt trapped in a job I felt burned out at....

TARA: I *am* discouraged... but I guess I've got to learn to live with it....

COUNSELOR: Well, let's talk about how you're going to live with it. Let's say you're settled on this point: you're going to stick with your job until retirement. Period. Decision made. You can always consider unmaking that decision, but for now, apparently you've thought through the alternatives and you don't see any of them as feasible or better than staying where you are. Is that right?

TARA: That's right. I guess I'm choosing the lesser of the evils.

COUNSELOR: Okay, so having made that decision—you're going to be working at your company for probably the next 8 years—what are your options at this point?

TARA: My options? I'm not sure I understand...

COUNSELOR: Well, you're staying put. How are you going to deal with that?

TARA: What choices do I have? Just suffer through it, I guess.

COUNSELOR: That's certainly one alternative—suffer. In fact, there's probably a whole range of options under suffering. You could just be unhappy, or you could take it further and be depressed, or you could even fall apart totally and have a complete breakdown.

TARA: [Laughs.] Oh, I don't think I'll go that far...

COUNSELOR: Okay, good, but suffering is certainly an alternative. But let's say you set aside suffering for the moment. Are there any other choices you have before you?

TARA: You mean like making the best of it?

COUNSELOR: Yeah, like that.

TARA: Okay, I guess I can make the best of it.

COUNSELOR: How might you do that? What different ways might you make the best of it?

TARA: Like at work?

COUNSELOR: That's one option—trying to make the best of it at work. Before we go back and explore that, can you think of any other approaches outside of work that would help you "make the best of it"?

TARA: ... Well, I suppose making the best of my time when I'm not working.

COUNSELOR: Okay, that's a second direction we can explore. Do any other approaches to making the best of this bad situation come to mind?

TARA: Not really; there's *at work* and *not at work*. I can't think of any other ways to look at it.

COUNSELOR: Might I offer a possible third approach?

TARA: Sure.

COUNSELOR: Maybe you'd like to consider ways to keep your work hours to a minimum and maximize your nonwork hours?

TARA: Well, yeah, I guess...

COUNSELOR: You're not so sure about that?

TARA: No.... I don't know; I can think of some issues, but yeah, I guess it would be worth it to think about that, too.

COUNSELOR: Okay, so other than suffering—instead of or in addition to suffering, we have three alternative approaches to making the best of your situation—during work, when you're not working, and also reconsidering the balance of work and nonwork in your life. [Tara nods in agreement]. Are you ready to explore these?

TARA: Sure. Why not?

COUNSELOR: Do you have a preference for which one we start with?

TARA: Not really, or maybe when I'm not at work.

COUNSELOR: Okay, let's start there.... I'd like to suggest a short activity that might be a good way to get into the subject of making the most of your nonwork life. I'll call it "20 Things I Love to Do When I'm Not at Work." Let's take this piece of paper. I'll divide it in half, like this [he draws a line down the middle from top to bottom]. Okay, on the left side of the page, please make a list of about 20 things, if you can, that you really like or love or enjoy doing outside of work. They can be big things or little things; you just have to really enjoy doing them. They can involve other people or not. Okay? Okay, just put them down in any order you like, whatever comes to mind. I'm not going to see the individual things you write, so feel free to put anything down you want. I'll do something else while you're doing this.

[While the client works, the counselor thinks about what coding questions he will ask Tara when she is done with her list. After a while, the counselor notices that Tara has stopped writing about three quarters of the way down the page, or about 15 items.]

COUNSELOR: How are you doing? Seems like you have quite a few things there. It doesn't matter if you hit exactly 20 or not. By the way, I find it sometimes helps to think in terms of particular friends you like to do things with or particular places you love to go, and that may give you some more ideas....

[After a little longer]

COUNSELOR: All right, you've got a nice long list there. Let's work with that. Divide the right half of the page into four columns.

[The counselor then asks Tara to code her inventory, one column at a time, in terms of which things she loves to do alone (A) or with other people (P); which cost a certain amount of money to do ($); which she thinks she'll love doing for the next 8 years until retirement (8); which she thinks she'll love doing for the next 20 years (20), that is, long after retirement; and when she last did each thing (a day, month, etc.).]

COUNSELOR: So, how did it feel to do this list? And as you look at your list of things you love to do outside of work, what thoughts and feelings come to you?

TARA: Well, I hardly know where to begin. At first it was hard, then I got into the swing of things and lots of ideas occurred to me, and then it got hard again. But as I look at it? I get excited... and scared... and sad... and excited again.

COUNSELOR: That's a lot of feelings....

TARA: Yeah.

COUNSELOR: Could you say more about them?

TARA: Yeah, well, excited because it was fun thinking about these things. I really like or love doing them, so the thought of doing them was very pleasure... pleasure-producing to me. I mean it's a happy thought. I can picture my life outside of work being good, being filled with these activities.

COUNSELOR: You felt "This is a good life."

TARA: Yes—outside of work. But then I got scared, worrying that maybe after a day or a week of doing my boring job, these things wouldn't seem so much fun to do. Maybe I'll be too tired or bummed out and won't have the energy to do these things. And then I got sad....

COUNSELOR: Sad?

TARA: Sad, because I wished I could do these things—and probably other things I didn't think of—and probably other new things I get into—sad at the thought of all the time I'm wasting at work when I could be doing things I really love, like these things.

COUNSELOR: So the contrast between these things you love and the picture of yourself at your current job felt discouraging to you?

TARA: Yes.... But then some of the excitement came back, too, because I thought, "Well, okay, I can't live like this all the time, but I can fill a lot of my evenings and weekends and vacations doing these things, and I really look forward to that."

COUNSELOR: So even though you wish you could spend more of your life doing things like this, it feels good to know you can spend a good portion of your life living like this.

TARA: Right. It does.

COUNSELOR: If you step back from the inventory a bit, how does doing this activity make you feel about your decision to stay at your present job until retirement? Does it confirm that decision, or strengthen it, or cause you to question it?

TARA: [Thinks a while] I'd say it confirms it—and maybe strengthens it a little.

COUNSELOR: Okay. In that case, I'm wondering: is there anything you need to do or want to do to about your nonwork life from this point on to fill it with these and other activities you love to do. I mean, are you using your nonwork time like this [pointing to her inventory] already, or will it just happen on its own, or are there some decisions or changes you're going to need to make now to make your nonwork life what you want it to be?

TARA: I'm doing some of these things now. But there's some I want to do more of. And, you know, I can't spend all of my time on things I love to do. I've got household and other chores I have to do out of work and some obligations to my family I have to fulfill, which I can't say I love doing but I'm committed to doing.

COUNSELOR: I get that. I think I just heard three ways you say you spend time out of work: chores to keep your life and household running, family obligations, and then free time, that is, time when you can do what you really want to do.

TARA: That's right.

COUNSELOR: Any other categories of time like that?

TARA: I can't think of any.

COUNSELOR: Shall we explore these three areas more closely now and also look at balancing between them?

TARA: I guess that makes sense.

COUNSELOR: Okay, but before we do that, I just want to ask you to take a deep breath and tell me: how do you feel right now?

In this and subsequent sessions, the counselor and Tara continued to explore the nonwork time topic, including how Tara might do her chores more efficiently, which family obligations she wanted to affirm and which she might reduce or combine, and how she could adjust her free time to spending less time on unsatisfying couch potato activities and more time doing the things in life she loved to do. Then they returned to another of the three main alternatives (other than suffering) for improving the quality of Tara's life—changing the balance of time between work and nonwork. At one point, the counselor asked Tara:

COUNSELOR: Is it an either-or? Either you work full-time at this job or retire?
TARA: I don't know what you mean.
COUNSELOR: For example, does your company have part-time employees, flex-time opportunities, work-at-home opportunities, or other options like that?
TARA: Oh, I see. Well, I don't know about part-time. I mean, I know we have temps from agencies, but that's different. And I know if you work less than half time, you don't get benefits. I couldn't afford to do that. But are there people who work 20 or 30 hours or 4 days instead of 5 or do some work at home? I'm not really sure.

That led to some research and further problem solving, including whether Tara might work full-time for 5 years, then propose a phase-out plan of working three-quarter time the sixth year, half time the seventh, and quarter time the eighth. Then they returned to the first alternative—ways Tara might make the best of her time at work, how she might make it less boring. This produced some promising ideas generated by Tara herself and two offered by the counselor. This led to an action plan for Tara at work, including talking to her superior about a slight change in job description that promised to provide some new challenges to make her time at work more interesting.

■ COMMENT ON THE CLARIFYING INTERVIEW

This case gives a realistic picture of values clarification counseling and counseling in general. It does not always result in a Hollywood ending. After considerable exploration of alternatives, Tara saw no options she was willing to implement that would allow her to leave her unsatisfying job. She began counseling feeling stuck and discouraged, and two sessions later she still felt stuck and discouraged. Along the way, at times, the counselor felt a little frustrated with Tara, whose low tolerance for risk and high need for security were quite different from the counselor's risk tolerance and value system that put life satisfaction higher than material security. But then the counselor quickly reminded himself that this was about Tara's life, not his, and if financial security was that important to her, so be it. He accepted her for who she was, including her risk tolerance and value system, and would continue to support her in making as much of *her* life as she could.

At that point, values clarification was effective in helping Tara realize she *did* have viable options, even in the context of her present job. As they explored and evaluated alternatives for enriching her life outside of work, her job description at work, and the balance between working and not working in her life, Tara started to feel more in control of her life and more optimistic about the future. She had a plan now—for living her life according to *her* value indicators and making as much of it as she could.

I was struck in reviewing this case how, at times, the counselor looked very much like a person-centered counselor doing his best to understand and communicate his understanding of the client's feelings and views, and at other times the counselor reminded me a little of a trial lawyer, asking the client questions as though he had some destination in mind toward which he was leading her. But that would not be an accurate characterization of the interview. The counselor was *not* trying to guide Tara toward a particular destination. When it became clear to them both that Tara's decision was to stay at her current position, the counselor accepted that and supported her in making the most of it. And when she began exploring ways to get the most of her nonwork life and to make her current job a little more challenging, he had no stake in the particular ways she would do these things. Yet, although he had no specific outcome in mind for Tara, he did have *a process* in mind. He was more interested in *the journey* than the destination. The journey consisted of establishing goals and priorities, considering alternatives, evaluating the pros and cons, making free choices, and planning action to implement her choices. The counselor was definitely guiding her on that journey, and she was a willing, active, and engaged partner in the process.

Whether a counselor will be successful in guiding her client through the clarifying interview process depends on two main factors. First, does the client trust that the counselor is supporting him in finding *his own* best answers, rather than imposing her own ideas or solutions on him? Second, is the counselor sufficiently skillful in her role as facilitator of the clarifying process? Are her questions not loaded, that is, free from implied correct answers? Are her questions interesting to the client, relevant to what he is exploring or wants to explore? Does the counselor convey sufficient empathic understanding? Does she avoid monopolizing? Does she give the client enough time to think before she speaks again? Is she sensitive to when simply listening would be more useful than asking a question? Is her judgment accurate about when it's a good time to move the interview forward or when it would be better to return to a previous stage?

These things do not always show up clearly in a transcript. But apparently the counselor in this case demonstrated enough sincerity about his motives of wanting to support Tara's process rather than impose his own goals on her, and apparently he demonstrated sufficient competence in implementing values clarification questions and strategies that Tara was willing and able to join him on this journey.

And he joined her. They were like partners in a dance. She was willing to follow him on the clarifying process he had in mind—goals, alternatives, consequences, and so on. And he was willing to follow her as she got in touch with her feelings and priorities, as she accepted or rejected her own and his suggestions, as she indicated where *she* wanted to go. By the time the music stopped, she was at a new and better place.

8

Handling Strategic, Values, and Moral Conflicts With Clients

▨ STRATEGIC, VALUE, AND MORAL CONFLICTS

As stated earlier, one of main ways values clarification counselors avoid imposing their own values on their clients is to respond to clients and group members with *nonjudgmental acceptance.* The counselor *does not* communicate approval or disapproval of what the client says, nor try to persuade the client or group member to another point of view or course of action. The counselor *does* ask further clarifying questions to engage the client in using the seven valuing processes to explore the client's feelings, goals, choices, and actions more deeply. The counselor follows this protocol whether she agrees with the client or has a conflict with the client's choices and values. However, the question inevitably arises: is this procedure followed 100% of the time, or *are there any exceptions or limits to the counselor's nonjudgmental acceptance?*

Certainly, there are exceptions and limits. For starters, in keeping with the ethics of the profession and the laws of most jurisdictions in which counselors and psychotherapists practice, there is an ethical obligation for the counselor or therapist to intervene or inform others if a client appears to be in danger of physically harming himself or others. It is also widely accepted that the counselor may establish limits, rules, and guidelines in and around the counseling relationship for the comfort and protection of the counselor, the client, the ongoing professional relationship, and the efficient functioning of the counseling office.

Taking action or setting limits to avoid physical harm or disruptive behavior is one thing; offering nonjudgmental acceptance while the client makes a probably self-destructive personal decision is another. Does the counselor stand by and let that occur? Harming others or society is something else again. Does the counselor accept this as well, assuming physical harm is not involved? To put the question more generally, what does the counselor do when the client is expressing a viewpoint, considering a decision, or contemplating or reporting behavior that appears ill-advised in terms of the counselor's professional judgment or in conflict with the counselor's own values or moral code?

Professional codes of ethics offer limited guidance. All the American Counseling Association's Code of Ethics (2005) says on the topic of values is found in section A4 under the heading of "Avoiding Harm and Imposing Values."

A.4.b. Personal Values. Counselors are aware of their own values, attitudes, beliefs and behaviors and avoid imposing values that are inconsistent with counseling goals. Counselors respect the diversity of clients, trainees, and research participants. (pp. 4–5)

The mandate to "avoid imposing values that are inconsistent with counseling goals" suggests that it is permissible to impose values that *are* consistent with counseling goals. Otherwise, the code would simply have said, "Avoid imposing values," period. One assumes the authors did not do this because, arguably, it is impossible for any counseling approach not to impose some values. I discuss this issue further in chapter 11 in the sections "Values Clarification Is and Is Not Value Free" and "Multicultural Aspects of Values Clarification." For now, I will focus on the practical matter of how a counselor using values clarification implements the approach when there is a conflict of professional judgment, values, or morality between the counselor and the client.

Consider three cases. In the first, a client is experiencing a degree of boredom in his work and is seriously contemplating quitting, yet it appears to you, the counselor, based on everything that you know about the client, that this is an excellent job that achieves many of the client's goals and needs for job satisfaction and financial security, that the current boredom in his work would likely recur in any job after the novelty wore off, and that it would be far wiser to try to improve or tolerate the current situation rather than quit the job. In this case, you and the client have a different judgment on a *strategic issue*. It is not a values conflict. You and the client both want the client to have satisfying work and financial security. But you think the client's leaning toward changing jobs is not a well-thought-out choice for obtaining these values.

The same situation could involve a *values conflict* between you and the client. Let's say the client is paying for his two children to attend college. Let's say it's a time of high unemployment in which it will not be easy for the client to obtain another good-paying job soon, and that if he does not find a new job soon, one or both children may very well have to drop out of college. If you were in this situation, you know how *you* would handle it. You would put your children's education above the small increment in satisfaction you might gain in a new job. You'd rank family responsibility over job satisfaction in this case, whereas your client appears ready to rank them in the opposite order. You don't go as far as saying your client is *wrong*, per se; after all, he's entitled to his own priorities. But you have a lot of difficulty accepting his values choice.

Beyond strategic differences and value conflicts that you might have with a client, there may also be *moral* or *ethical* conflicts. Moral and ethical issues are matters that affect the rights and well-being of others. For example, let us stipulate that the client who is somewhat bored at his job is married, and his wife, who earlier in the marriage worked and helped put him through graduate school, is now attending college herself to upgrade her job skills and employability. Now the client is contemplating a choice that would leave the family without the resources for his wife to continue college, thereby jeopardizing her education and future employability. You don't want to judge your client, but you can't help thinking to yourself, "This is *wrong*! She sacrificed a lot for you so you could get to where you are today. Now she deserves her turn, and if that means your tolerating a little boredom at work, then that's what you *should* do." *Wrong* and *should* are moral-laden words. You know you're not supposed to impose your values on the client, but you have these feelings and values. What are you supposed to do with *them*?

It is not always easy to distinguish between strategic issues, values issues, and moral issues. Does a counselor have a qualm about a client's contemplated action because she doesn't think it will be good for the client or for society? A counselor may not share the client's values on issues like work, partner choice, religion, material values, and the like, but clearly these are personal value choices. If clients make a poor choice in these areas, that is unfortunate, but they may only be hurting themselves. A moral issue potentially arises when the client's contemplated or reported actions are likely to be unfair to others, infringe on the rights of others, or hurt others' well-being.

One person's values issue may be another person's moral or ethical issue. For example, a client's dilemma about whether to have an abortion might be a values issue for one counselor and a moral issue for another. These are not hypothetical situations; value conflicts between clients and counselors occur regularly in counseling and psychotherapy, regardless of whether they are addressed. In group settings, when a client's views and reported or contemplated actions are heard by all the other group members, another dimension is introduced. You might let a particular remark you had a moral qualm about pass in an individual counseling session, but you may feel it needs to be addressed in a group setting where others might be influenced or hurt by it. So, whatever the setting, we come back to the question of how does a counselor or psychotherapist who is using values clarification handle situations in which there is a strategic, values, or moral conflict with the client?

■ A CONTINUUM OF COUNSELING RESPONSES

Actually, the counselor has a continuum of possible responses, from total acceptance to ending the counseling relationship. Although aspects of this continuum are applicable to any counseling approach, my purpose here is to consider the various options from the viewpoint of values clarification counseling. In so doing, I have two purposes: (a) to explore the issue of counselor–client strategic, value, and moral conflicts and (b) to illustrate further how values clarification operates, regardless of whether any such conflicts are involved.

Because the following continuum is organized, in part, according to degree of nonjudgmental acceptance, it leaves off one legitimate option—that of no response. Whether in individual or group settings, a counselor does not have to respond to everything a client says. Especially if the statement is tangential to the issue being discussed, the counselor can ignore the comment or not respond at all, conveying neither acceptance nor nonacceptance of the client or group member's statement. Also, the range of possible responses here is not a hard-and-fast continuum. Whether one option may be to the right or left of another (more or less accepting, more like values clarification or more like values inculcation) may depend on the exact wording of the question, the way it is delivered, how the counselor responds to the answer, the prior relationship, and other contextual factors.

1	2	3	4	5	6	7	8	9	10	11	12	13

Total _____ End the
Acceptance   Relationship
(values clarification)   (could be either)   (teaching; values inculcation)

On this continuum, the responses on the left side are most consistent with the *values clarification* approach. The responses on the right side are more characteristic of *teaching* and *values inculcation*, an educational approach widely used by parents, teachers, clergy, youth leaders, politicians, social activists, advertisers, and others with beliefs, attitudes, or behaviors they would like to instill in their target audience (Kirschenbaum, 1995). Even counselors and therapists, on occasion, especially in psychoeducational groups, may employ teaching and values inculcation—intentionally, when it seems consistent with counseling goals (as in teaching a client or group the benefits of anger management), or unintentionally (as in unawarely smiling at client responses one likes while otherwise remaining neutral).

Following are descriptions of 13 types of response to client statements, in a values clarification context.

1. Total Acceptance—simply acknowledge the contribution as you ordinarily would (with a nod, a smile, an "okay" or "thank you," etc.) and move on, or offer an accepting, empathic attempt to understand the client's statement or meaning.

This and the next two options constitute the vast majority of responses in values clarification. Especially in group settings when many group members are taking a turn responding, the counselor acknowledges all contributions with a simple nonverbal signal or one or two words. If the counselor has a strategic, value, or moral judgment, positive or negative, about a client's self-revelation, she does not indicate it but simply accepts the comment and moves on. She *trusts the process*; that is, she trusts that other group members will offer counterbalancing views and/or that further reflection, growth, and life experiences will further the client's positive development.

Another totally accepting response is an active listening attempt to empathize with or more fully understand what the client said and meant. When a counselor is empathically attuned with and fully accepting of a client, arguably there is no room for strategic thinking or value judgments about the client's communication, at least in the moment. A totally accepting, empathic response can be very clarifying for the client and is consistent with the goals and methods of value clarification. All other places on the continuum of responses, however, involve some degree of evaluation or judgment on the part of the counselor and, to that degree, would not be consistent with a *purely* empathic, accepting, person-centered approach.

2. Ask a Clarifying Question—ask a clarifying question or suggest a values clarification strategy with no hidden agenda, no point you're trying to make.

If the counselor happens to have a strategic, value, or moral judgment about the client's self-revelation, she puts it aside and invites the client to engage in one or more of the seven valuing processes. Again, she trusts in the process, in the core hypothesis that as the client continues to utilize the overall valuing process, it leads to wiser choices and more constructive behavior. She does not feel the need to intervene whenever a client or group member says something with which she has a strategic, values, or moral disagreement. She employs clarifying questions and activities without a motive of correcting or enlightening the client about something he just said.

3. Ask a Clarifying Question to Engage a Valuing Process—ask a question or suggest a strategy to help the client utilize a particular valuing process that appears to be underutilized.

Again, this and the previous two options comprise the vast majority of responses in values clarification. The counselor doesn't use this question or strategy to try to influence the client's thinking or behavior about an issue. Rather, it appears to the counselor that, for example, the client may not have considered any alternatives or thought about the consequences, so the counselor asks a question or proposes a strategy to help the client do that. She asks the client, "Do you think there might be some ways to lessen your boredom at work while still staying with your present employer?" Or "If you leave your job, what might the consequences be for your daughters' education? How concerned are you about this?" The counselor has no stake in whether these questions will change the client's thinking or behavior. Following the core hypothesis of values clarification, she just believes that such questions will increase the likelihood of a good outcome.

4. Ask a Pointed Clarifying Question—ask a clarifying question to help guide the client toward a more enlightened viewpoint or better course of action.

Here a counselor asks a question or suggests a strategy to help the client recognize a mistaken belief he has or see the moral issue or problem in his current or intended behavior or to suggest a wiser viewpoint, better choice, or more effective action, according to the counselor's judgment. The question or strategy might be the very same one as in the previous option, but in this case the counselor has a point to make. She may think leaving the job is a bad idea strategically, so she asks, "Do you see any benefits in looking for and getting a new job before you give notice on your present one?" She may be unhappy at the thought of the daughters' having to leave college because their father left his job, so she asks, "What might be the consequences of leaving your job for your family?" and "You say one negative consequence of leaving your job would be putting your daughters' education at risk. How unhappy would you have to be at work to take that step? If the left side of this line is 'A Tiny Bit' unhappy or bored, the next point is 'Somewhat' unhappy or bored, the next point is 'Very' unhappy or bored, and the other end of the line is 'Totally' miserable, how much unhappiness and boredom might you be willing to tolerate to keep your daughters in college?"

Again, these exact questions could fit in this or the previous two categories, depending on the counselor's intent. If worded and delivered skillfully, the client might not be aware of the counselor's strategic, value, or moral judgment. These may be very helpful value-clarifying questions that the client feels are useful in his valuing process. Arguably, such questions, while subtly imposing the counselor's values ("A man should take care of his family"), may contribute toward counseling goals, that is, toward the client's own goals of having a good job and supporting his family. *However*, if too many of a counselor's clarifying questions fit into this category, if the counselor is repeatedly using clarifying questions to educate and enlighten her clients on the issues being focused on, and if the counselor's nonverbal behavior communicates approval or disapproval, clients and group members are likely to begin to sense this. They will begin to feel that the counselor has an ax to grind and is imposing her own values, and they may become more defensive and less forthcoming in their participation.

I notice that I sometimes ask clients or group members clarifying questions that fall halfway between this and the previous category (between 3 and 4). I hear a client express a viewpoint or intention that I personally or professionally find problematic. I'm sorry, I'm human; sometimes I make value judgments ("I'd never renege on my responsibility to *my* children that way"). Or based on my knowledge and clinical experience, I make a professional judgment ("I think this 'boredom' issue is just going to reproduce itself on your next job, so you'd be better off facing it now and spare your family the stresses of leaving your job"). So I ask, "How would you respond to those who might say to you, 'No job is free from some boredom, and you're taking a big risk of jeopardizing your daughters' education to pursue what may be an unrealistic dream'?" I use the sentence stem "How would you respond to those who might say _____?" to introduce an alternative viewpoint that counters their own, but I do it in a way that's impersonal. They don't have to react to my viewpoint but to some disembodied other or others. I might very well do the same thing with client statements that I agree with or think are wise, just to encourage them to consider alternatives, but in this case I have in mind challenging the client's statement through a pointed clarifying question.

However, any traces of values imposition vanish in my reaction to their response. Whatever they respond, I feel perfectly willing to accept their answer. They thought about the new viewpoint I presented, and they shared their response, utilizing two or three valuing processes—considering an alternative perspective, considering a possible consequence (e.g., "I might end up just as bored in my next job"), and sharing or affirming their position. So I'm content. Whether they stick to their original outlook or continue to mull over the subject, as so often occurs, I feel I've done my job. I can accept them as they are and as they are becoming.

In other words, I hold my own strategic, value, or moral judgment lightly as it applies to my client. I could be wrong. I want the client to consider my pointed clarifying question, but I also really do trust the process. However the client answers, I respond in a way that conveys acceptance, so the client feels "He does accept me as I am. I may have wondered what was behind his question, but in any case, I feel he's on my side, helping me sort this through, not trying to impose his solutions on me."

If, instead, I continue to come back at the client with more pointed value-clarifying questions, it will begin to feel to the client like a lawyerly cross-examination. Then whatever values clarification may have been occurring will probably cease and be replaced by some other process, from defensiveness to passive acceptance to reluctance to participate, none of which furthers the values clarification process.

5. Express a Concern—express your concern about the consequences of the client's actions or intended course of action.

Like Carl Rogers (1961), who popularized the concept of congruence in helping relationships, I believe it is sometimes useful in a counseling or therapeutic relationship for a counselor to share her feelings with the client or group—as long as it passes a number of screens for appropriateness, including expressing the feeling as *one's own* feeling (e.g., "I am troubled by what you said" or "I'd have difficulty trusting you if you did that") without making value judgments about the client ("What you said is troubling" or "You are untrustworthy"). Hence a counselor with a strategic, value, or moral difference with a client may decide to express a concern about what a client said or about a course of action the client is contemplating. Presumably, the counselor has already broached the issue with one or more clarifying questions but did not feel satisfied that the client really considered the issue. So she might say, for example, "I find myself feeling concerned for your daughters in all this, about the possibility of their having to leave college. Do you think you've given this possible outcome enough consideration?" She begins with an honest expression of concern and follows up with a challenging but fair, not necessarily loaded, value-clarifying question.

I have found that clients can usually accept and appreciate my concern for them and their loved ones. As long as this option is not used very often, it can be consistent with the goals of values clarification. In other words, although I have communicated my concern or other feeling to the client, he still trusts that I believe he has to make his own choices and that I am his supportive helper as he sorts through the issues and choices.

6. Offer to Give Information or Opinion—ask whether the client would like further information or your opinion about the subject under discussion.

Even when there is no disagreement with the client about strategy, values, or morality, the counselor may think that the client might benefit from having additional *information* or from hearing the counselor's *opinion* on the topic under consideration. If the counselor knows or has that information herself, she might want to share it with the client. The counselor's opinion could have been incorporated into a pointed clarifying question, but if the client did not seem to get the point or deal thoughtfully with the issues it raised, perhaps the counselor now wants to offer her own opinion more explicitly. When there *is* disagreement with the client about strategy, values, or morals, the counselor is sharing the information or opinion with the hope that it might influence the client's thinking or the client's present or contemplated behavior. So the counselor asks the client whether he would like to hear or read the information she has or hear her opinion. Although most clients will answer affirmatively, this is still a more accepting, less directive action than the following two options.

The extent to which sharing information and opinions with the client is consistent or inconsistent with values clarification is discussed further in options 8 and 9.

7. Suggest Further Information—suggest clients seek further information; suggest resources clients may pursue to help them learn more about the situation or issues.

The counselor does not provide the information in the office or for the client to take home but recommends a book, article, Web site, DVD, organization, or other resource for the client to pursue on his own. For example, she may suggest that the client who is bored with his job visit a particular Web site to check job openings in his field or a particular blog to see strategies that other job seekers are using and the problems they are encountering. The counselor may suggest this information solely to further the client's valuing process by expanding his understanding of alternatives and consequences and, as such, *would* be consistent with the values clarification process. If the counselor has a strategic, value, or moral disagreement with the client, she may suggest this information to encourage the client to consider or adopt her point of view. This *would not* be consistent with the goals of values clarification.

(This option is less accepting and more imposing than the previous one because the counselor does not first ask the client whether he would like more information. It is less nonaccepting and less imposing than the next two because the client does not have to actually follow the counselor's recommendation or can do so cursorily.)

8. Share Information—convey information that might inform or influence the client's view, help the client choose a better course of action, or lessen the negative impact of his contemplated action.

Sharing information with clients or groups resembles teaching a lot more than it resembles values clarification. Yet teaching can serve a values clarification goal. It can be consistent with the valuing processes of considering alternatives and considering consequences. The new information may very well deepen the client's understanding of the relevant topic, including considering alternative perspectives and choices and better understanding the arguments for and against different courses of action. The counselor may offer the information verbally in the session or may give the client a book, article, DVD, or other resource to read or view at home. For example, she may offer the client who is contemplating leaving his job a newspaper article she just read on the difficulty that unemployed workers have in finding a new job in the current economy. The counselor may think the information in this article may help the client think through the consequences of leaving his job (values clarification), or she may think—and hope—that reading the article might help dissuade the client from leaving his job (values inculcation). Hence, sharing information with clients can be more or less consistent with the goals of values clarification, depending on the counselor's motive and how the client receives the information.

The information the counselor shares can include the couns〈
or professional experience with the topic under consideration. T〈
Sharing one's experience for the benefit of another person easily
preaching, and explaining the moral of the story, which all risk 〈
fication into values inculcation.

I believe it is possible for a counselor using values clarification to share information with clients *occasionally* in the spirit of furthering several of the valuing processes (alternatives, consequences, action steps). It should be limited to *occasionally*
because the more frequently this is done, the more the focus of counseling moves
from *the client's process* to the *counselor's information*. In other words, it moves from a
values clarification counselor doing a little teaching to a teacher doing a little values
clarification. This is true even when there is no strategic, values, or moral conflict
with the client. When there is such a conflict, it is that much more likely that the
client will sense that the counselor's information is intended to change his mind or
behavior; he will soon or eventually resist such attempts at influence, and the values
clarification process will cease.

9. Express a Strategic Opinion—share your professional or personal opinions on the issue under discussion, including what the likely consequences of the
client's actions or intended course of action will be and what better courses of
action might be.

"I think you're underestimating the difficulty of finding a job in today's economy."
"You think your wife will understand and support your decision to quit your job? I
think she'll go through the roof!" "From what you've told me, I think you might be
able to improve the situation at your current job." Thus the counselor may express
her difference of strategic opinion with her client. To the extent such an opinion
helps a client hear an alternative viewpoint or consider alternative solutions that he
may have not thoughtfully considered before, this is arguably consistent with the
values clarification process—if it doesn't produce defensiveness and if it quickly
returns to the *client's* valuing process.

Stronger expressions of opinion might include "I think you're making a mistake,"
"I think that's a bad idea because _____," "I think a better choice would be _____," or
expressing strategic agreement, such as "I think that's a good idea" or "That sounds
more likely to succeed to me." In each case, the counselor seems to think the valuing
process is insufficient to help the client make his own best choice, so she needs to tell
the client the better way to think, choose, or act. At some point, when the counselor
begins evaluating the ultimate correctness or incorrectness of a client's choices, this
is clearly inconsistent with the values clarification approach.

However, having departed from the values clarification approach in expressing
her opinion, the counselor can quickly return to it by asking, "How do you feel about
what I just said?" "What parts of what I just said do you agree or disagree with?"
"On a scale of 1 equals strongly disagree to 10 equals strongly agree, how would you
place your reaction to what I just said?" or other questions to reengage the client in
the valuing process.

10. **Share a Value or Value Judgment**—affirm your own values about the topic under consideration, without or with a stated or implied judgment regarding the client's values.

This is another option for counselors that can be done with nonjudgmental acceptance or the opposite. There are times when a counselor can share her values without imposing them, especially in psychoeducational groups (see chapter 3). At times like this, the counselor is not intending to disagree with a particular client or group member, but sharing or affirming her own position on the topic, in the spirit of offering another alternative for consideration, as in "I would put my daughters' education first and change jobs later." This is hard to do in an individual setting without making the client feel judged, but it is possible. It is much easier in group settings, where the counselor can take a turn as one of many group members.

If, however, the counselor expresses her own values in the form of a value judgment about what the client or group member has said ("I really have a different ordering of priorities from what you just expressed. To me, a father and husband's first duty is toward his family"), that is an imposition of the counselor's values on the client or group. It is not consistent with the values clarification approach. It may be an honest statement, but it's not values clarification. Ironically, someone trying to impose his or her values on us sometimes causes cognitive or emotional dissonance in us that can lead to values clarification, but the act of imposing is not values clarification, and it places a counseling relationship at considerable risk, as well as raising ethical concerns.

11. Express a Moral Judgment—present your own moral viewpoint on what the client has been saying or doing.

In this option, the counselor's expression of her moral values is intended to apply not just to herself, but to the client, group members, and possibly others—possibly everyone. Such a moral judgment may be expressed when there is no obvious value conflict with the client or when the counselor feels so strongly about a value or moral conflict she has with a client or group that she chooses to intervene. For example, a counselor may tell a client in an individual or group setting, "That's wrong! A man's first responsibility is toward his family. A person in your situation should tolerate a little boredom at work and keep his secure job to put his daughters through college." I suspect most counselors would be appalled at such an intervention. The counselor is clearly imposing her own personal and moral values on the client or group.

Yet consider an alternate scenario. A group is picking on one of its members, teasing him cruelly for being different. The counselor says, "This is wrong! No person should be treated this way. How would you feel if you were in a group and everyone ganged up on you because you were the only white person, or black person, or short person, or overweight person, or whatever?" We might ask whether this is likely to be an effective intervention or whether another intervention would be better, but I suspect most counselors would *not* be appalled at this counselor's expression of moral outrage and attempt to protect a group member.

In either case, this is not values clarification. Both examples are another method of values education, that of values *inculcation*. Teaching, preaching, and persuading (*even when disguised as clarifying questions*, as in "How would you feel if ____?") are methods of inculcation (Kirschenbaum, 1995). They may or may not be justified in specific instances, but in the last two examples, we are clearly near the end of the continuum representing the opposite of nonjudgmental acceptance.

12. Set a Limit—set a limit as to what behavior you can or cannot accept if the counseling relationship is to continue.

If a counselor's own professional, personal, or moral values make it difficult or impossible for her to accept a client's behavior in or out of counseling, she may want or need to set a limit on what behavior she can accept. A counselor tells her client, "I know you dislike that racial (or religious, etc.) group. I don't feel that way, but I can accept that these are your feelings. But I can't accept your using that slang word to describe people in that group. It upsets me when I hear it, and then I find it difficult to listen to you. If we're going to continue to focus on this topic, I'm going to have to ask you not to use that word. Can you agree to that?" A couples counselor who is working with each partner separately and together tells her client, "I cannot in good conscience continue to work with you both this way unless you tell her about your affair. I feel like a fraud knowing what I know and having to pretend I don't know it. I simply cannot work that way."

In both examples, the counselor is clearly imposing her values on the counseling situation. She is doing it openly, taking responsibility for her actions without vilifying or blaming the client. This is always a risky choice on the counselor's part. It could produce new growth and learning, but it could also end the relationship.

13. End the Relationship or Do Not Begin It—if the client cannot accept your limit or conditions, terminate the counseling relationship, or do not begin it in the first place, if there is a significant enough value or moral conflict.

This is the extreme option, when a counselor's value or moral judgments are so strong that she feels she can no longer work with a client—or chooses not to work with a client to begin with. One sometimes hears counselors and psychotherapists say, "I could not work with a _____ [insert type of client]. I can accept just about any other client, even when their values are different from mine, but I just can't find the acceptance in me to be a good counselor to people like this. In fairness to these clients, they should see another counselor."

Clearly, professional ethics require counselors and therapists to "respect the diversity of clients" (ACA, 2005) and to get supervision and even counseling on *their own issues* that may be blocking them from working effectively with a diverse clientele. Referring clients who are different from the counselor in demographics or values, on occasion, may be in the best interest of the client, but it may also help counselors avoid dealing with their own prejudices or psychological and emotional issues. In other cases, referring clients who are different from the counselor in demographics or values could be seriously detrimental to clients—there may be no other viable services available, and the client may have been rejected enough already in life that another rejection could be very hurtful—and professional ethics would rule against it. These are complicated and controversial issues that go beyond the scope of this discussion.

That said, if a counselor's value or moral conflict with a client's *particular behavior* is strong enough, and if the client has not accommodated any limit the counselor may have set to mitigate the conflict, then ending the counseling relationship remains an option. It is not values clarification, but it is a legitimate option.

The same can be said for not beginning a relationship with a client who seems to want a type of counseling that the counselor is not prepared or willing to provide. It may be that a client wants career or marital counseling and the therapist does not feel qualified in those areas, so she makes a referral for reasons that have nothing to do with value conflicts. However, it may be that a client wants Christian counseling (including praying together and referring to biblical text), reparative therapy (to "treat" the client for his supposed homosexual "disorder"), or other approaches that may not be consistent with the counselor's value system, let alone area of expertise. In such a case, out of respect for the perspective and goals of the client, the counselor might choose not to enter into a counseling relationship and would recommend that the client see a professional who shares the client's values system.

■ TO CLARIFY OR NOT TO CLARIFY

As this continuum of behaviors indicates, counselors and therapists have a wide range of options for responding to clients when strategic, value, and moral conflicts are present. Some response modes—the first three on the continuum—are completely aligned with the values clarification process and constitute most of values clarification practice. Others—numbers 4 to 10—might be consistent with the goals and processes of values clarification, depending on how they are implemented. If a counselor or therapist truly values the valuing process—that is, if the professional truly wants clients or group members to think for themselves and reach their own best decisions—clients will recognize this. Then the counselor can ask the occasional pointed clarifying question, express a concern, share information, share her values, and temporarily otherwise depart from strict nonjudgmental acceptance without fear of jeopardizing the overall values clarification process. The client knows, even when the counselor's values may be different, that she sincerely wants to help him figure out his own best solutions and reacts to her questions and responses in that light. However, all the best counselor intentions in the world will not override too-frequent poor technique. That is why the values clarification counselor needs to limit the proportion of responses in the middle range of the continuum and rely primarily on the first three types of response, which locate the valuing processes consistently within the client.

Not all counselors can manage to do this, even when they think they want to use the values clarification approach. An anecdote can help illustrate this point.

During the time I was writing this chapter, I saw a romantic comedy movie in which Diane Keaton played a divorced, overprotective mother who was unable to refrain from commenting on every last thing her unmarried adult daughter did and didn't do. She had advice on how the daughter should dress, which man she should date, how she should avoid laughing in a particular way if she wanted to attract men, how she should furnish her apartment, and much more. Every time her unmarried daughter and other two daughters called her on this behavior, the mother protested, "But I just want what's best for her!" or "I just want her to be happy!" After being told for the umpteenth time that her daughter was an adult now and needed to make these decisions for herself, the mother reluctantly agreed to mind her own business, but within minutes, she was intervening again, with the justification of "I love you, and I just can't stand by and see you defeat yourself this way."

One did not need to be a counselor or therapist to recognize that the mother had boundary issues and, in addition to sincerely loving her daughter and wanting what was best for her, was imposing her own values on her daughter, not to mention acting out her own unmet emotional needs for a partner. This mother appeared to be constitutionally incapable of nonjudgmentally accepting anything her daughter said or did. She simply could not put aside her own value judgments. She just *knew, all the time,* what was best for her daughter and felt the need to enlighten the young woman every chance she got.

Although clearly a caricature, this overprotective mother provides an object lesson here. Having taught values clarification to thousands of helping professionals, I believe some counselors, therapists, and group leaders should not use values clarification. Like the overprotective mother, although not as extreme, their value judgments are too strong and omnipresent. They cannot resist the urge to correct, enlighten, or otherwise educate their clients as to the better choice, the wiser way to think. They may try to couch their opinions as clarifying questions, but they just don't pull it off. Their questions are almost always loaded with an implied right answer, or the questions are well-worded but always point the client in the same direction, or their nonverbal behavior communicates approval or disapproval. They may be gifted counselors in other approaches, or they may be gifted teachers or preachers, but they should leave values clarification to others or use it only in limited contexts.

All counselors and therapists need to clarify their own values on this issue, because all will eventually have strategic, values, and moral disagreements and conflicts with their clients. It is an appropriate topic for counselor education and supervision or for self-reflection to consider the following values-clarifying questions and strategies.

How judgmental are you?

Anything Goes		Jerry the
Gary _____		Judge
(Totally		(Totally
accepting)		judgmental)

How well can you control your judgments?

! _____	!
Totally—I put them	Not at All—I'm
aside and forget	controlled by them,
about them; client	blurt them out; client
never knows	immediately knows

How would you divide this Pie of Life to indicate the percentages of your responses to clients that fall into categories 1–3, 4–10, and 11–13?

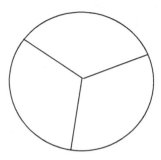

These issues are applicable to all counseling and psychotherapy approaches. In values clarification, they are particularly germane, because if one is too far toward the right of the continuum, one is no longer doing values clarification. How far to the right is too far? (Or how far to the left?) What are appropriate percentages for the 13 different response options? Like all good values clarification strategies, there is no formula, rubric, or benchmark for evaluating one's responses. The value is in the thoughts and feelings that the clarifying questions and strategies raise.

Further examples of values clarification strategies that can be used in counselor and clinical education and supervision and for personal growth—to help counselors and therapists in training to explore some of their own values around counseling issues—are provided in the following chapter.

9 Some Applications of Values Clarification Counseling

There are at least three ways that values clarification can be applied in virtually all types of counseling and psychotherapy:

Goal Setting: Just about the first step in all counseling and therapy settings is clarifying the goals of the counseling or psychotherapy. What are the client's goals? What are the counselor's goals? What are the goals or mandates of others, if any?

- What do you want to get from counseling?
- What are your goals? (How would you rank them in order of importance to you?)
- How committed are you to the process? (On a continuum from 1 to 10, how committed are you?)
- Do you want to be here?
- What would you like to learn?
- Even though you're here against your will, is there anything you want to learn about yourself or anything you'd like to change or improve on?
- Are you willing to go along with these guidelines?
- Can we agree on this contract?

Another form of goal setting involves helping clients clarify their particular goals beyond counseling. Some of this might occur in the initial goal setting, but new goal setting can occur throughout the process, as clients clarify and affirm both short- and long-term goals. Long-term goals might be "I'd like to be free of drugs," "I'd like to get back with my wife," "I'd like to be able to support myself," or "I want to stop feeling depressed." Short-term goals might be "I'd like to go a day with fewer than 10 cigarettes," "I'm going to try to give my wife one compliment a day," "I want to rewrite my resume," or "I want to exercise for 10 minutes every day this week."

Values clarification questions and activities can help clients set these kinds of goals for therapy and life.

Decision Making. In all counseling settings, values clarification questions and activities are helpful when clients are making decisions for their lives.

- What are the different choices available to you? (Rank them in order based on preferred, easiest, best in the short run, best in the long run, etc.)
- What are the pros?
- What are the cons?
- What are the possible or likely consequences?
- What do others think you should do?
- What do you think would be best?
- What additional information do you need?

Action Planning. Values clarification questions and strategies can help clients in all settings put their decisions into action.

- What are the forces that will help you move forward?
- What are the forces that will be obstacles for you?
- How might you overcome these obstacles?
- What actions will you have to take to accomplish this?
- What is the first step you might take?
- Can you do this alone or will you need help?
- When do you want to begin?

To better illustrate how values clarification might work in different kinds of counseling and psychotherapy, including but in addition to goal setting, decision making, and action planning, I will give examples of value-clarifying questions and values clarification strategies for a number of counseling applications:

- career counseling and development
- rehabilitation counseling
- obsessive-compulsive disorder
- human sexuality counseling
- counselor education and supervision
- multicultural and diversity issues
- counselor personal growth and development
- school counseling
- coaching

One goal for this chapter is to show how versatile values clarification questions and strategies are and how they can be created for virtually any setting or any topic one is working on. But please keep in mind:

- These are just a few sample areas of application. Clearly, many other areas could be illustrated, such as couples counseling, pastoral counseling, substance abuse counseling, geriatric counseling, and many other applications that are laden with values issues for clients. Indeed, elsewhere in the book are examples of values clarification with these and other applications.
- These are just a few examples for each application. Many more activities or many more examples of the strategies (rank orders, unfinished sentences, etc.) could be given or created for each topic.
- Discussion often precedes or follows these strategies. The examples here are presented free of context. In actual counseling and psychotherapy, any one of these strategies is likely to be preceded and/or followed by discussion or by other value-clarifying questions or strategies.
- Clients and group members always have the right to pass.
- In group settings, the counselor may sometimes participate in these activities, as discussed in chapter 3.

■ CAREER COUNSELING AND DEVELOPMENT

As Lynne Shallcross (2010) wrote, quoting career counselor Cyndi Doyle, "At its core, career counseling is about helping people find out who they really are. 'It's having a greater understanding of yourself—your interests, your personality, your values, the skills you have—and how that works into how you would like your working world, how you would like to contribute.... It's getting a greater picture of the person and then helping them decide where they want to go with their career'" (p. 32).

In other words, a major part of career counseling is values clarification. Since the 1970s, when values clarification became popular, values clarification activities (whether named as such or not) have been included in most career education programs and texts. Howard Figler (1975, 1979) wrote a career development workbook for college students consisting entirely of values clarification activities. A values clarification approach to career counseling and development helps clients or students:

- clarify their likes and dislikes around work
- clarify their interests and goals for work and career
- understand the various work and career options available to them
- understand the various aspects of different careers, their benefits and burdens, and how these careers match the client's interest and talents
- choose a job or career path that is their own best choice, having evaluated the different influences and pressures upon them
- plan a strategy for seeking and getting the work they choose
- implement their plan for getting that job or preparing for that career

The process in individual counseling may utilize the clarifying interview (chapter 5), moving through the sequence of prizing, choosing, and acting. Whether in individual counseling or a psychoeducational group, the process may also utilize many different values clarification strategies.

Rank Order: Which do you prefer?

_____ Working alone
_____ Working with one other person
_____ Working in a group or on a team

Values Continuum: What are your expectations for how meaningful (or satisfying or enjoyable or financially rewarding) your work will be to you?

Not at all _____ Extremely

Inventory: Make a list of all the kinds of work you have ever done. Code each item as follows: in the first coding column, use an *A* to indicate work that you primarily did *alone* or use an *O* if you primarily did it with *others*. In the second coding column, use an *S* for work you found *satisfying* and a *U* for work you found *unsatisfying*. Next, put a dollar sign ($) next to any of the types of the work you earned money for doing. Next, put a date or month or year when you last did this kind of work. Finally, put *SK* next to any of these kinds of work that required a *skill* that you think would be useful for the kind of work you might want to do in the future. (Now, let's list together all the different skills your various kinds of work required.)

Proud Question/Circle: Can you think of a time when you were proud of some kind of work that you accomplished? (Go around the circle and share or pass.)

■ REHABILITATION COUNSELING

When prisoners are being released from incarceration, substance abusers are leaving a drug treatment program, people with developmental disabilities are moving from their parents' home to supported living in the community, or other populations are making a significant move toward recovery or independence, values clarification can play a helpful role in their goal setting, decision making, and action planning for their next stage.

Clarifying Questions.

- What are your goals for the next stage in your life?
- What are your goals for the first day (first week? first month?) in your new setting?
- What will your biggest challenges be?
- What strengths do you bring to these challenges?
- Who is available to support you?
- Who might undermine your success? How can you avoid that happening?
- What are you concerned about?
- How will you handle _____?
- What will the best thing be about your next stage?
- What have you learned about yourself in the program (in the last year, etc.) that will help you succeed in the coming weeks?

Unfinished Sentences. The previous clarifying questions could easily be turned into unfinished sentences for a group setting. For example, "I'm concerned about _____" or "My biggest challenge will be _____."

Inventory. In the left column, make a list of all the skills, talents, or strengths you have for living independently (or drug free, crime free, etc.) in the coming period in your life. For example, a strength *I* have that helps me be independent is being able to say no to someone if I don't want to do what they're suggesting. So I'd write "saying No" in the first column....

Skill, Talent, Strength	Proud (P)	New (N)	How it will help

Now that you've had time to list some things, let's whip around the circle and give each person a chance to say one skill, talent, or strength they bring to the next phase of their lives. It may remind you of a skill or talent of your own, and you can add that to your list.

Okay, now in the first column, put a *P* next to any of the skills, talents, or strengths you are proud of. In the next column, place an *N* next to any of the skills, talents, or strengths that are new for you, that you would not have put on your list if you had done this a year ago. Finally, in the last column, for three (or five, etc.) of your skills, talents, or strengths, write a few words to indicate where or how this skill or talent or strength is going to help you or come in handy when you move into the community.

Self-Contract. Think of a step you need to take to be successful in the first week of your new situation and complete this self-contract on paper: "By _____ (day), I will _____." You don't have to sign it, but what might it say if you were going to write a self-contract? Okay, now that you've written it out, you can decide if you're ready to sign this. Let's go around the circle and read our self-contracts. You can also tell us if you signed it, if you like. Remember, you can pass.

■ OBSESSIVE-COMPULSIVE DISORDER

Rob Rice, now on the counselor education faculty of St. John Fisher College in Rochester, New York, has many years of experience working with clients with obsessive-compulsive disorders (OCD). He has used the following values clarification activities both with individuals and in group therapy with clients with OCD. He has used these particular activities in this sequence, as in a workshop framework. In the group setting, he participates in each activity, modeling an appropriate response while reinforcing an atmosphere of safety and respect. He also reminds participants that they always have the right to pass, that is, to skip their turn or not participate.

Two-Minute Autobiography. In 2 minutes, please share some parts of your personal history, including elements related to each of your obsessive-compulsive behaviors or something else that you may be struggling with in your lives.

Continuum. On the continuum I've drawn on newsprint on the wall, please write your name at a place on the line that you think accurately describes how your symptoms affect your life. As our workshop continues over the following weeks, feel free to move your name if you feel there are changes occurring in either direction.

My symptoms have absolutely _____ no impact on my life	My symptoms totally control every aspect of my life

Inventory: 20 Things I Love to Do. Make a list of 20 things (or 10 or 15, depending on the age of participants) in life that you really like doing. In the next column, place a B next to each thing that you loved doing before you began experiencing symptoms of OCD. In the next column, place an A next to each thing you came to love *after* you began experiencing symptoms of OCD. Next, place an N next to each thing you can do now, even with your OCD symptoms. Finally, write a day or number of weeks or a month or a number of years next to each of your favorite things to represent the last time you did it.

Favorite Things to Do	Before OCD (B)	After OCD (A)	Now (N)	Last Time
1.				
2.				
3.				
Etc.				

Inventory. On other occasions, Rice has asked clients to do a different inventory: make a list of each of your obsessive-compulsive symptoms. In the next column, write a few words to indicate what you are afraid will happen if you don't engage in that behavior. Next, place a VT or T or NT next to each compulsion to indicate whether you find this compulsion very troublesome, troublesome, or not troublesome. In the last column, place a W next to each compulsion you perceive as weak (i.e., easily broken), an M next to any compulsions you view to be of moderate strength, and an S next to those compulsions that would be especially difficult to break (i.e., would cause an especially strong anxious response).

Compulsion	Fear	Troublesome (VT, T, NT)	Strength (W, M, S)
1.			
2.			
3.			

Clarifying Questions/Group Interview. First, the counselor teaches the group members how to ask value-clarifying questions. Then, each group member gets the opportunity (they may choose to pass) to receive a group interview (5 to 10 minutes) in which the participants ask them clarifying questions about their symptoms and/or other issues in their lives, including questions about alternative behaviors and their consequences. Rice (2004) comments, "This is a critical and necessary therapeutic step for individuals diagnosed with OCD, as it is when they first recognize that their obsessions and compulsions are in some way separate from them and that they have some control in their relationship with their symptoms."

I Learned Statements. Participants use the I Learned ____ sentence stems (I learned that I ____, I relearned that I ____, etc.; see chapter 6, #15) to reflect on what they may have learned or gained from the workshop or values clarification experience.

■ HUMAN SEXUALITY

Counselors and psychotherapists deal with human sexuality in many contexts: sex education in schools, couples counseling, sex therapy, working with sexual offenders, individual clients with sexual issues, counseling around sexual orientation, geriatric sexuality issues, and more. Like every important area of life, sexuality is replete with value judgments and the challenge of reconciling our goals with our choices and behavior. Here are a few values clarification exercises that counselors and psychotherapists have used to explore values issues around sexuality in different settings. Some of these are described as group activities but can be adapted for individual counseling. (Thanks to Rob Rice and Brande Hunt for parts of three of these activities.)

Three-Minute Autobiography. Take no more than 3 minutes to share with the group how you developed your attitudes, beliefs, and values about human sex and sexuality.

Continuum:

How important is sex in human relationships?

How important is sex *for you* in your current relationship or marriage?

Sex is the least
important element ———————————————— important element
of a (my) relationship

Sex is the most
important element
of a (my) relationship

How important to you is sexual ecstasy versus physical/emotional intimacy in sex?

100%
Stimulation ———————————————— Closeness & Orgasm
& Intimacy

100%

Inventory. Make a list of 10 things (more or less) that you love to do in a physical/sexual relationship. In the second column, put an *O* next to those *older* things on your list, that is, things you've loved to do for most of your adult life, or an *N* next to those things that are *newer* on your list, that is, things that you have come to love doing more recently. In the next column, put a *P* next to those things that you think your *partner* also loves to do. Place a + (plus), – (minus), or = (equal) sign next to each activity to indicate if you'd like to do more of this, less of this, or just about the amount or frequency you do it now. In the last column, write a day or month or year or other word next to each item on your list to indicate when you last did it.

Physical/Sexual Things You Love to Do	Old (O) or New (N)	Partner (P)	+ or – or =	Last Time
1.				
2.				
3.				
Etc.				

Now extend your list by adding three (more or less) additional physical/sexual activities that you would like to do or try. In the Partner column, put a check mark next to each item that your partner knows you would like to do. In the last column, put a check mark next to any of these new activities that, in the next month, you would like to talk to your partner about doing.

Value-Clarifying Questions: These can be asked at an appropriate time in individual counseling, can be used in public interviews or group interviews in group settings, or can be used to go around the group circle and give each member a chance to discuss one of them. They could also be turned into unfinished sentences.

- What is one thing you have learned regarding *when* sex is more likely to be enjoyable for you?
- What is one technique or method you have learned for giving pleasure to your partner?
- What is something someone taught you about sex that has been useful to you in your sexual relationship(s)?
- What is something you'd like to ask your partner to do that you've been scared or reluctant to ask?
- What is a sexual turn-on?
- What is a sexual turnoff for you?
- What do you need to do to get yourself in a good frame of mind for sex?
- What is something your partner can do to help you get in a good frame of mind for sex?
- What would be the ideal frequency for you for sex with your partner?
- What is the best way you know to say no to your partner when he or she wants to have sex and you don't?
- What is the best way your partner can say no to you when you want to have sex and he or she doesn't?
- How have your parent's or parents' attitudes or behavior about sexuality affected your own sexual attitudes or behavior?
- Have you ever read any helpful books or articles on sexuality that you would recommend to others?
- What is something you'd like to know about sex or sexuality?
- How much do you and your partner communicate about what gives each of you pleasure?
- Do you ever say things like "Touch higher," "lower," "softer," "harder," and the like—cues to how your partner can increase your pleasure? (How did you learn to do that? Why not?)
- Have you ever considered _____? Why? Why not?

Rank Orders. The first two are based on Morrison and Price (1974).

Which would you rather do next Saturday?

_____ Spend an evening with a close friend
_____ Spend a beautiful day outdoors

_____ Have a good orgasm

If I'm feeling the need or desire for sexual release, I would rather

_____ Masturbate
_____ Have intercourse
_____ Engage in vigorous physical activity

Which do you enjoy most? Rank all in order from most preferred to least.

_____ Face-to-face intercourse with my partner on top
_____ Face-to-face intercourse with me on top
_____ Penis to vagina from the rear
_____ Oral sex
_____ Anal sex

I Learned Statements. At the end of one or more activities, group members complete sentence stems to reflect on what they learned from the experience. After writing out the sentences themselves, they get to share one of their completed sentences with the group and say a bit more about it if they wish.

- I learned that I_____
- I was surprised that I_____
- I was embarrassed about_____
- I was pleased that I_____
- It made me feel_____
- I realized that I_____
- I see that I would like to_____

■ COUNSELOR AND CLINICAL EDUCATION AND SUPERVISION

Using values clarification questions and strategies in the clinical training and supervision of counselors and psychotherapists accomplishes four things.

First, it is important that helping professionals clarify their own values so they can better recognize and deal with value and moral conflicts they may have with their clients (see chapter 8). In the first chapter of his popular textbook on counseling, Gerald Corey (2009) devotes considerable attention to how counselors need to know themselves and be clear about their own values. Second, as the following examples illustrate, values clarification is an excellent tool to help students and trainees think about and explore important issues in counseling theory and practice. Third, clinical training and supervision are good occasions to teach students and trainees about values clarification, which they can then use with their own clients and groups. Fourth, using values clarification in counselor education and supervision gives students a *personal experience* using values clarification. This is particularly important, because it is only by experiencing the values clarification approach firsthand that counselors can really appreciate the effectiveness of the clarifying process and methods. More will be said about this later under "Personal Growth."

Here are a few examples of the use of values clarification in counselor and clinical education and supervision.

Counselor Education/Clinical Training

*Rank Orders:** In a theories course, once students had studied a number of theories of counseling and psychotherapy, the professor asked them to rank-order the following descriptors in terms of which most to least fit their concept of themselves as a counselor or therapist:

_____ An <u>Archaeologist</u>, seeking to uncover the truth in the past
_____ A <u>Buddha</u>, seeking ultimate truth and meaning in life
_____ A <u>Fellow Traveler</u>, being a sympathetic companion on a journey
_____ A <u>Cognitive Scientist</u>, seeking to understand the connection between our thoughts, emotions, and behaviors

The students each gave their ranking and a short explanation or elaboration on the thinking behind their choices. Sometimes they referred to the different theories that seemed compatible with the different ranked choices (e.g., Buddha = existential; Fellow Traveler = person-centered). This was followed by a more general discussion about the theories and their own evolving counselor identities.

In which counseling setting do you feel the most comfortable, and why?

_____ individual counseling
_____ group counseling
_____ psychoeducational groups

Which clients are you most comfortable working with?

_____ a person of a different race
_____ a committed Christian, Jew, Muslim, etc.
_____ a gay or lesbian person
_____ a flirtatious client
_____ an angry client

Alternative Search/Rank Order: You are a school counselor. A student comes to your office and confides that she cheated on her final exam in biology and received an *A* for the course. What would be three (or more) alternative ways of responding to her?

_____   _____
_____   _____
_____   _____

Rank the choices in order to indicate which way you would be most to least likely to respond. Explain your ranking.

Continuum:

What is successful counseling?

*Relationship	Technique
Ronnie _____	Teddy
(It's all about	(It's all about
the therapeutic	the therapeutic
relationship)	techniques)

Counselor Supervision

Stephen Demanchick, now on the counselor education faculty of Nazareth College, Rochester, New York, developed the values clarification activities marked with an asterisk (*) in a workshop he did for school and community counselors who were going to supervise counselor interns. (Some of his ideas are also included in the previous "Counselor Education and Clinical Training" section, also noted with an asterisk.)

Unfinished Sentences. Ask each class or group member to complete the following sentence stems. Then ask each person to share two of their completed sentences with the group. (Of course, they may pass.) Then ask each person to make an "I Learned ____" or "I was surprised by ____" statement, indicating some thought or insight they had from this activity or something that surprised them. Follow this by group discussion.

- An effective counselor is _____
- I hope my supervisee will _____
- Clinical supervision is _____
- Engaging in good supervision would mean _____
- Counselor education programs should _____
- As a supervisor, I plan to _____
- My view of supervision, after this workshop, is _____

Rank Orders:

*As a school counselor, rank these in order of importance during your day.

_____ Individual sessions
_____ Paperwork
_____ Contacting or working with parents
_____ Consulting with teachers

*Ranking these from most to least important, what do you want your supervisees to be most proficient at?

_____ Problem solving
_____ Being empathic
_____ Handling conflicts
_____ Working with family members of clients

Proud Questions. What are three things that you've done professionally that you feel very proud of? What is one thing you did supervising your intern that you feel good about?

Values Continuum: Supervisors in training, thinking back to when you were learning to be a counselor, where would you have been on this continuum? How independent or dependent were you?

*I want to do
everything ————————————————————————— Teach me,
myself   teach me

Pie of Life: How is your time at work spent? Make a list of the six to eight main things you do at work. Then divide the pie into slices representing how much time you spend on each of these.

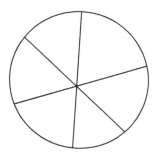

Which parts give you the most satisfaction? Which would you like to increase or decrease in size? Choose two slices, and for each of them, what is one thing you could do to increase or decrease the size of that segment? Are you willing to make a self-contract to do one of those things?

Multicultural and Diversity Issues[1]

This brief workshop utilizes values clarification techniques to help participants begin to view themselves as cultural beings and help them begin to explore how the values they possess as cultural beings may impact their counseling or other work with diverse client populations. This workshop is geared toward counselors in training and practitioner counselors. There are two segments to the workshop: positioning and engagement. *Positioning* refers to helping workshop participants identify and begin to share important aspects of themselves as racial, ethnic, spiritual, socioeconomic, class, sexual, and gender beings. *Engagement* refers to participants exploring how their beliefs will affect their ability to interact with and engage in therapy with various client populations.

---

1. This section was written by Derek Seward, a former doctoral student at the University of Rochester, now on the counselor education faculty in the School of Education, Syracuse University.

Positioning. To help workshop participants (a) begin to consider themselves as cultural beings and (b) elucidate their stance on cultural issues, they are asked to engage in a Rank Order exercise [strategy 2] exploring multicultural topics including race, gender, socioeconomic status, and religion. The facilitator asks each participant to individually complete the rank order exercise, informing participants that they are being asked to make value judgments about cultural issues based on their personal beliefs.

Rank Order Exercise: Please answer the following questions by ranking the choices in order based on your personal beliefs and preferences.

1. What would you rather do?
   _____ attend a foreign film
   _____ attend an art exhibit
   _____ attend spiritual services of a faith other than your own
2. What do you look for in a friend?
   _____ same religious beliefs as yours
   _____ same racial background as you
   _____ same socioeconomic status as you
3. What country would you prefer to live in?
   _____ Haiti
   _____ Iran
   _____ France
4. Which ethnicity would you prefer to be a member of?
   _____ Irish American
   _____ Vietnamese American
   _____ Mexican American
5. I prefer to spend $5 on
   _____ a beverage from Starbucks Coffee
   _____ a can of coffee from a local supermarket
   _____ buying coffee or beverages from a local food pantry or co-op
6. When making an important decision, whom are you most likely to consult?
   _____ a friend
   _____ a family member
   _____ a religious advisor
7. I would prefer to spend 2 hours
   _____ tutoring schoolchildren
   _____ marching in a rally or protest
   _____ helping in a soup kitchen
8. Where are you most likely to go on vacation?
   _____ another country
   _____ within 100 miles of your residence
   _____ within the United States but more than 100 miles from your residence
9. Which would you least like your son or daughter to do?
   _____ marry someone 10 years older

_____ marry someone of a different socioeconomic class
_____ marry someone of a different race or ethnicity
_____ marry someone of a different religion
_____ marry someone of a different sexual orientation (than yours)

10. Which best captures your stance on affirmative action?
_____ it helps and is necessary
_____ it is unnecessary
_____ it is necessary but needs to be altered to be more effective

After participants complete the exercise individually, the facilitator reads each question and asks a few participants to publicly give their rankings and elaborate on their rationale for their selections. Using rank order 2 as an example, participants are asked to consider which cultural aspects—religion, race, or socioeconomic status—they value most or least in a friendship. To begin with, they must first confront how much they do or don't pay attention to such cultural characteristics. As they self-reflect on issues of race, religion, and other diversities, they deconstruct the complex interaction of cultural issues in their daily relationships. In providing an opportunity for participants to share their responses and the rationales behind their choices, participants publicly affirm their own beliefs while providing each other with alternative belief systems.

The second exercise within the positioning section of the workshop is a colonization exercise or "fallout shelter problem" (Simon, Howe, & Kirschenbaum, 1972). This exercise is designed to help participants further explore and identify aspects of culture they prize. The facilitator asks participants to individually identify five people from the list they will take with them on a journey to colonize the moon. Participants must grapple with which cultural aspects they value and the relationship of these to different cultural values. For example, a participant may question if he or she prefers having a gender balance, a diversity of ages, or both.

Colonization Exercise: The earth is dying. Global warming and a depleted oxygen supply have made Earth uninhabitable. You have been selected by the U.S. government to head a group of individuals who are going to colonize the moon. Your task is to select your team. You can choose five people from the following list of possible team members. Keep in mind that Earth is dying and it is certain you will be starting the human race all over again. Consider carefully whom you would include on your team. Keep in mind your race, gender, sexual orientation, religion, and occupation, as you are also going to make the colonization trip.

1. John, 36, librarian, Caucasian
2. Jill, 24, artist, Jewish, paraplegic
3. Doug, 47, medical doctor, Black, Baptist
4. Peggy, 48, CEO of a small software company, Caucasian
5. Emily, 18, high school student, Chinese, lesbian
6. Jorge, 20, college student, Latino, gay
7. Bernice, 65, retired teacher, Native American
8. Henry, 51, farmer, Caucasian, Catholic

9. Simon, 32, carpenter, Native American
10. Ali, 10, student, Chinese, brother of Emily
11. Shaza, 30, radical Islamist woman

After individually completing the colonization exercise, participants assemble in groups of three. Their task is to reach a consensus on which five members from the colonization list they choose to join *the three of them* on the colonization trip, making a total team of eight. To do this, they must share the rationale behind their individual decisions. In additional to publicly affirming their beliefs and values, participants are given glimpses into how their peers' values are similar to and different from theirs. Whole-group discussion may follow, as time permits.

Engagement. In the second portion of the workshop, a variation on the Values Voting exercise [strategy 7] helps workshop participants begin to consider how their beliefs, biases, or values may help or impede their ability to work with certain client populations. The activity consists of participants privately voting yes or no to questions regarding being able to counsel members of various social groups. This exercise confronts participants with how their cultural attitudes and values can enter into the counseling relationship by feeling comfortable or averse to helping a client. To do the exercise, participants are required to question what about their attitudes and values would make it difficult to work with people from different backgrounds or value systems. Also, the activity helps participants identify potential client populations for whom they will need to actively develop strategies or competencies to be able to counsel.

Voting Exercise (adapted from an activity learned from Prof. Kathryn Douthit, University of Rochester). For each of the following people listed, put a "yes" beside the person if you think you would be able to experience enough empathy and compassion to help that person with his or her problems. Put a "no" beside the person if you think that your attitudes, biases, or values would get in the way of your engaging in a helpful counseling relationship with that person.

_____ Veteran
_____ Arab
_____ Gay man
_____ Latino
_____ Lesbian
_____ Native American
_____ African American
_____ Orthodox Jew
_____ Drug dealer
_____ Child molester
_____ Unmarried pregnant teen
_____ Skinhead
_____ Italian
_____ Blind person
_____ Homeless person

_____ Upper-class White person
_____ Gang member
_____ Terrorist
_____ Black militant
_____ Pro-life advocate
_____ Pro-choice advocate
_____ Cigarette company executive
_____ Migrant farm worker
_____ Atheist
_____ Person with a mentally disability
_____ Adulterer

The workshop ends with the facilitator having participants engage in an I Learned exercise [Strategy #15]. The purpose of this exercise is to have participants reflect on their workshop experience, clarify new levels of awareness that have been reached, and terminate the workshop. Specifically, the facilitator asks participants to reflect on their workshop experience and complete the following three sentences: (a) I learned that I _____, (b) I noticed that I _____, and (c) I was surprised that I _____. Participants then have an opportunity to share one of their I learned statements with the group.

■ PERSONAL GROWTH

There are myriad ways that counselors and psychotherapists can use values clarification in their own lives—not just around professional issues, as in the examples in the previous section, but around personal issues. Whether for personal growth and development or to further enrich one's life or to make a practical decision like what new car or appliance to buy, values clarification provides a readily accessible tool that can be used alone or with others. I regularly use values clarification with myself, my family, and friends.

- If my wife and I are on a vacation, on the airplane we might each do an inventory of all the things we want to see and do, code the list in terms of priorities, then share our inventories, and create a joint list and plan.
- If one of us is thinking through a tricky decision, the other might very well offer an opinion, but we're just as likely to ask each other value-clarifying questions.
- If I'm making a big decision, like whether to take on a big project, I might do a 20 Things I Like to Do inventory and consider how the new project will impact my ability to do the things I love.
- If I'm making any decision, large or small, I'll ask myself value-clarifying questions. Just last night, when thinking about whether I wanted to do a particular workshop, I asked myself, "If money were no object [that is, if I had all the money I needed], would I still want to do this workshop?"

- It's not only at Thanksgiving that we go around the table and give each person a chance to complete the unfinished sentence, "I'm thankful for _____ " or "I'm thankful that _____."
- On other occasions with family or friends, one of us might suggest we each take a turn sharing something interesting we're working on or something we're proud of from the previous week. Everyone who wants to gets a turn. It's not a rigid thing; we don't do it all the time. And the gathering still looks more like a group of friends or family enjoying one another than a group counseling session.
- When considering a big purchase and wondering whether it's worth spending all that money on this item, we'll ask, "What else might we spend this much money on? Which would bring the greatest satisfaction? What are the environmental implications (e.g., gas mileage, Energy Star rating)? In what other ways is it consistent or inconsistent with our values?"
- When considering a big move—from the city to the suburbs, from our house to an apartment—we ask ourselves and each other all sorts of value-clarifying questions and make a list of all the pros and cons and consequences we can think of for each choice. What will be the implications for our finances, time spent driving, personal aesthetic satisfaction, health, entertaining friends, having family or friends sleep over, time outdoors, ease of parking, etc.? How can we enhance the positives and mitigate the negatives? On a scale from 1 to 10, where do we stand on each choice?

As these examples illustrate, values clarification comes naturally to us. It is not just a method; it's a way of thinking. It is a good way to show interest in other people and a good way to share what is important to us. Professionals who use values clarification in their lives will be more effective in using it with others. Using it with oneself is good practice that deepens one's skill, experience, and comfort with the approach. The more comfortable we become with the approach and the more natural it feels to us, the more natural it will feel in the counseling setting as well. At times, my colleagues and I have gone so far as to say that, if professionals do not use values clarification in their own lives, it is doubtful that they should use it with others.

That said, I would reiterate a point made earlier—that values clarification isn't the only way to clarify one's values. I often reach a point when I say, "Enough thinking! I'm going for a run." Or I'll sleep on it, or meditate, or consult my gut feelings about what I seem to want to do.

Two further sources containing values clarification activities for personal growth are Simon (1974) and Simon, Howe, and Kirschenbaum (1995).

■ SCHOOL COUNSELING

As I described in chapter 2, there was a period in the 1970s and 1980s when values clarification was oversold as a complete program of moral education and character education in the school, home, and community. As a result, there was a backlash, and values clarification was supplanted by a more robust and defensible character education movement. Gradually, the pendulum swung back a bit, and both supporters and many critics of values clarification came to accept that values clarification could be a useful part of an overall program of values, civic, moral, and character education.

Of course, it is important for one generation to do its best to pass on its most cherished values to future generations. This can be done through a variety of methods for *inculcating values* (which is different from the harsher methods of indoctrinating), by *modeling values*, by teaching *life skills* that are value laden, *and* by using *values clarification* to help young people find personally meaningful values and put their values into practice (Kirschenbaum, 1995).

School counselors who see themselves as having a role in values education, moral education, or character education—especially as they may work with students in classrooms or groups around issues of sex education, career education, bullying, conflict resolution, diversity and tolerance, and other value-laden subjects—should find many helpful skills, activities, and techniques in values clarification, but again, values education and character education are not the subject of this book.

This book is more suited to school counselors who wish to use values clarification *as a counseling tool* with students in individual and group counseling settings and psychoeducational activities. As a counseling tool, values clarification—clarifying questions, clarifying interviews, and clarifying strategies—can play a useful role in helping students with:

- choosing an academic program
- choosing courses
- developing career goals and plans
- balancing schoolwork with extracurricular activities
- implementing better study habits
- handling a conflict with a teacher or other students
- selecting colleges to apply to
- resolving and avoiding disciplinary issues
- getting along with parents
- getting involved in the community and helping others
- dealing with smoking, alcohol, and drugs
- making decisions about sex and sexuality
- responding to bullying
- enhancing personal relationships
- dealing with other areas of social and emotional development

In all these areas and others, values clarification can (a) help students sort through the confusion and conflict in their lives, (b) help them develop a clarity about their purposes that will enable them to be more successful in their schoolwork and lives, and (c) help them move from patterns of apathy, flightiness, overconforming, overdissenting, and poor decision making to purposefulness, consistency, a balance of conformity and individuality, and improved decision making. As long as counselors make it clear that they are using values clarification for these purposes and not as a moral education or character education program (although, again, it may be a tool within such a program), counselors should be on solid ground.

The following is one of many examples of how school counselors can use values clarification in some of the areas listed here. My counseling student Paul Lippa shared with me this "School Interest Inventory" that he and his colleagues developed for students in Greece Arcadia High School near Rochester, New York. Students complete the inventory and share it with their counselor. This serves as a springboard for a first meeting between counselors and their new advisees, for individual counseling, for group counseling, and/or for psychoeducational sessions in which the counselors explore these academic and related issues with the students.

A Little Bit About Me—Interest Inventory

Name:
I live with:
My siblings are (please give names, age, and the school they attend):

Section I: Personal Interests

My hobbies are:
I am very interested in learning more about:
When I grow up, I would like to:

Section II. Academic Interests

The school activity that was most meaningful to me was:
This was most meaningful to me because:
I learn best when I:
The best teacher I ever had was:
He or she was the best teacher because:

When I am in school, the following things help me to be more successful in school (check all that apply):

_____ reducing distractions
_____ use of an agenda or planner book to keep organized
_____ having a goal to spend time each day doing homework
_____ reviewing homework or tests with an adult
_____ speaking to my parent/guardian about how school is going
_____ speaking to some other adult about my problems and successes in school
_____ developing good relationships with my teachers
_____ informing adults about my goals for academic success and career plans
_____ establishing a plan for success and then sticking to it
_____ other (specify)_____

When I am in school, the following areas block me from doing well (check all that apply):

_____ too many distractions with relationships (boyfriends, girlfriends, all friends)
_____ poor study habits

_____ negative peer pressure
_____ incomplete homework
_____ ineffective time management
_____ being bullied
_____ disorganization
_____ school is boring and does not interest me
_____ personality conflict with teachers and/or administrators
_____ putting things off until the last minute
_____ little or no motivation
_____ other (specify) _____

When have you been successful in school and what worked for you?

Section III: Personal Experiences/Relationships/Resolutions
Adults who have been there for me in my life are:
(Please check all that apply to the next questions.)
Do you:

_____ always feel tired
_____ seem stressed out
_____ believe that you can succeed
_____ do enough to just get by
_____ get involved in too much conflict
_____ claim to always be bored
_____ lack a sense of responsibility
_____ feel like you contribute toward helping your family
_____ feel a good deal of anxiety about school-related things (test taking, grades, etc.)
_____ other? (specify) _____

In a similar way to making a New Year's resolution, what are some promises that you are going to try to stick to in order to be successful in high school this year?

In what ways can Arcadia High School adults be of help to you during this upcoming school year?

10 Values Clarification and Other Approaches to Counseling and Psychotherapy

It has often been said that there are hundreds of approaches to counseling and psychotherapy. The goal of this chapter is neither to compare values clarification to all of them nor to attempt an in-depth comparison with any of them. Rather, I will briefly compare values clarification with a limited number of other approaches to counseling and psychotherapy, with the goal of highlighting or further explicating various aspects of values clarification theory and practice. I will begin with some of the classic approaches to counseling and psychotherapy, with which most readers will be familiar, and then consider some relatively newer approaches that have been gaining attention in more recent years.

■ PERSON-CENTERED COUNSELING AND PSYCHOTHERAPY

Values clarification has a great deal in common with the client-centered or person-centered approach developed by Carl Rogers (1951, 1961; Kirschenbaum, 2009). Like the person-centered counselor, the values clarification counselor is prepared to accept the client's values, priorities, and life choices. The counselor does not try to influence the client to stay in or get out of a marriage, to choose a particular job, to lose weight, to move toward or away from one's religious background, or the like. Rather, the counselor has ultimate respect for the client's right to choose his own directions and values. This respect is based on a belief in what Rogers called the "self-actualizing tendency"—the client's innate tendency to grow in positive directions when given a supportive environment. Values clarification shares this basic trust in people—that they can be trusted to guide their own lives as they utilize the valuing process.

There is some similarity with the *process* of person-centered therapy as well. As with person-centered therapy, the process of values clarification stays focused almost exclusively on the client's inner experiencing—what the client prizes and cherishes, the alternatives the client is considering, the actions the client is thinking about taking. However, values clarification is a more directive process than traditional person-centered counseling. Although the counselor does not try to influence the client's decisions in a particular direction, the counselor actively influences the process of counseling. The counselor is saying, in effect, "I think it would be valuable for you to consider what you prize and cherish. I think it may be helpful for you to consider alternatives and consequences, to consider your actual behavior, and so on. Therefore, I am asking you these questions and inviting you to do these values clarification activities." This stance is less person-centered than the classical person-centered counselor, who avoids questions and exercises and relies primarily on empathic listening. Having said that, the values clarification counselor also often uses empathic listening, which is, in itself, an enormously clarifying response that helps the client reflect more deeply on his own thoughts and feelings.

In group psychoeducational sessions—in career education or sexuality education, for example—values clarification would also be more directive than a person-centered approach. In a strictly person-centered group session, the counselor remains the facilitator, responding to the issues and dynamics that came from the group. The values clarification counselor takes a more active teaching or training role, introducing clarifying questions or exercises to further the theme of the group.

■ COGNITIVE-BEHAVIORAL THERAPIES

There are a variety of therapeutic approaches that fit under the umbrella of cognitive-behavioral therapy. Among these, values clarification is highly consistent with rational-emotive-behavioral therapy (REBT), which is discussed in this section, and with reality therapy–choice theory, which is discussed in the following section. Interestingly, Raths, Harmin, and Simon (1966) first developed values clarification at about the same time Albert Ellis (1962, 1994) and William Glasser (1965, 2001) were embarking on their long and important careers. Although most of the energy in the early values clarification work went toward youth development, while Ellis and Glasser developed more far-reaching schools of psychotherapy, there were and are a number of common elements among these approaches.

Both cognitive-behavioral therapy and values clarification are concerned with the integration of affect, cognition, and behavior. On the cognitive side, just as the cognitive-behavioral therapist helps guide the client toward more rational thinking, the values clarification counselor engages the client in a cognitive process for choosing that involves consideration of alternatives and consequences and the influences that may be affecting one's choices. Clarifying questions, rank order exercises, inventories, continuums, and other values clarification strategies are highly cognitive exercises that not only are useful when considering the values issues at hand but also, in effect, teach clients to use these thought processes themselves as a normal part of daily living and decision making. In this sense, both cognitive therapists and values clarification counselors are educating or training clients to think in productive ways.

On the behavioral side, although Ellis evolved gradually from rational therapy to rational-emotive therapy to rational-emotive-behavioral therapy (REBT), acting in a way that contradicts one's irrational thoughts was always an important part of Ellis's self-therapy and therapy with clients. Similarly, values clarification emphasizes taking action to realize one's values in daily living.

Regarding emotion, REBT generally helps clients recognize how their distressful feelings are illogically constructed, how they need not be controlled or guided by them, and how they can be reframed. Values clarification is more concerned with positive feelings of prizing and cherishing and encourages clients to actualize these feelings in their lives. This difference is not surprising. Cognitive-behavioral therapy is *therapy*, which often helps clients deal with distressful emotions. Values clarification is not therapy, but a developmental process for identity development, decision making, and rewarding living.

■ REALITY THERAPY/CHOICE THEORY

If reality therapy/choice theory reflects an "anti-deterministic, present-focused, internal-control, choice-based view of human nature" (Neukrug, 2011, p. 347), the same can be said of values clarification. Both acknowledge the influence of past experience on our thoughts, emotions, and behavior, but they affirm the human ability to transcend past influences through new thinking, decision making, and action.

Like values clarification, reality therapy/choice theory places client choice centrally in both its theory of human functioning and its method for helping clients deal with their issues and move on in their lives. Similarly, both approaches have a strong behavioral component. Glasser always had a clear focus on clients' behavior. "So what are you doing about that?" and "What are you going to do about that?" have been staples of reality therapy. This is consistent with values clarification's everpresent focus on helping clients align their actual behavior with their affective priorities and cognitive choices. On the affective side, reality therapy/choice theory helps clients work through or beyond the distressful feelings that prevent them from achieving their goals. It does this by encouraging positive new ways of thinking and acting, which in turn modify negative feelings.

It is not surprising that many of the questions asked by cognitive-behavioral and reality/choice therapists ("What do you want?" "What's the worst thing that could happen?" "What are you going to do about it?") are very similar to those asked by values clarification counselors. In fact, Robert Wubbolding's (2000) reformulation of reality therapy and choice theory—which includes what the clients *wants*, what the client is *doing* in his life, *evaluating* whether what the client is doing is working, and developing a *plan* of action to better achieve what the client wants—bears a striking similarity to the values clarification process. Similarly, the client's "Quality World" in choice theory is arguably a description of the client's evolving value system.

■ EXISTENTIAL THERAPY

When I was an undergraduate, attending what was then called the New School for Social Research in New York City (now the New School University), I had the privilege of taking a course with Rollo May (1961, 1980)—one of the leading existential psychotherapists of the 20th century. In one of my papers for his course, although I was a junior, I made the rather sophomoric argument that people would experience a lot less existential anguish if they had a good sex life. I believe the good professor wrote "oversimplification" on the paper and gave me a B. Although I will be brief, I shall try not to oversimplify again here.

Many topics for values clarification do not rise to the existential level, but others do. Questions about career choice, decisions about what car to purchase, and dilemmas about money and clothing may be questions about competing priorities. They may be instrumental questions, that is, a means to achieving one's values. But questions about careers, money, possessions, and other value-rich areas *can* also take on existential dimensions. What work do I find meaningful and worth devoting my life to? Can work give me the sense of purpose in life that I seek? How important are material possessions—cars, clothes, a nice house—to me? I know they will not bring me fulfillment in themselves, but can they contribute to the good life I desire? What *is* the good life? What is the *purpose* of life? I value my religious and spiritual life, yet I don't make time for it. Why not? Who am I?

These values questions are existential questions. Who am I? What am I here for? How do I find or create meaning in my life? These are some of the major concerns of existential psychotherapy (Yalom, 1980), and values-clarifying questions and strategies can play a helpful role in seeking and hopefully finding the answers.

This does not mean that values clarification and existential psychotherapy are one and the same. Existential angst and despair, the apprehension of non-being, and a sense of meaninglessness, among other existential issues, may have emotional depth, life history, spiritual emptiness, relationship aspects, a dual diagnostic component, or other dimensions that go beyond life choices and priorities. But usually at least some part of existential work, and often a major part, involves helping the client sort out, discover, or rediscover the values that contribute to a meaningful life. Here values clarification can play a significant role.

Another area of overlap is the focus in existential therapy on freedom and responsibility. Although again these issues may take on profound depth in existential psychotherapy, the valuing process of *choosing freely* provides an opportunity for clients to begin framing their life choices, large and small, in terms of increasing responsibility and authenticity. As Lynn Nowbar (2004) wrote, "The philosophical foundation of Values Clarification is built largely, but not exclusively, on the principles of existentialism, which maintains that existence is prior to essence, meaning that man exists first and then tries to define himself and his purpose in life. The concept of free choice for the individual, clearly emphasized in the Values Clarification approach, has its roots in existentialist philosophy" (n.p.).

■ ADLERIAN THERAPY–INDIVIDUAL PSYCHOLOGY

"Individual Psychology" was first developed in the early 20th century by Alfred Adler, who introduced many of the ideas and themes later furthered by the humanistic psychology and positive psychology movements in the middle and late 20th century (Watts, 2011). Somewhat analogous to the self-actualizing motive described by humanistic psychologists, Adler posited that all humans exhibit an innate striving for mastery, perfection, or superiority, a drive to fulfill their potential, or, as we might put it in values clarification, an intrinsic motivation to clarify and realize their values. But Adler also emphasized that such striving to fulfill one's potential cannot be accomplished in a self-centered, narcissistic manner; it can be fully achieved only when motivated by "community feeling," which contributes to the "social interest." "Thus, true community feeling (i.e., sense of belonging, empathy, caring, compassion, acceptance of others, etc.) results in social interest (i.e., thoughts and behaviors that contribute to the common good....)" (Watts, 2011, p. 43). Adler called this combination of community feeling and social interest *gemeinschaftsgefuhl*, which is "the supreme value for Adlerians" (Watts, 2012).

Similarly, values clarification can be focused solely or primarily on individual satisfaction, or, as I have argued in this book, it can and should also be embedded in relational and social contexts, with individuals consistently considering the origins of their value indicators and the consequences of their choices and behavior not only for themselves but also for their relationships and the wider community, as it exists now and as they would ideally have it. As Adler (1933) put it, "A movement of the individual or a movement of the masses can for us pass as valuable only if it creates values for eternity, for the higher development of all mankind" (p. 52).

Like values clarification, individual psychology "is an optimistic perspective that views people as unique, creative, capable and responsible" (Watts, 2011, p. 44).

■ SOLUTION-FOCUSED BRIEF THERAPY

Solution-focused brief therapy (Berg, 1994; De Jong & Berg, 2002; de Shazer & Dolan, 2007; Guterman, 2006; Murphy, 2008) is strikingly similar to values clarification in a number of ways. In part, this is because solution-focused therapy shares values clarification's optimism about human growth and development, focuses on solutions rather than problems, and focuses on strengths rather than weaknesses. In part, it is because the techniques of solution-focused therapy rely heavily on questions to help clients identify preferred goals, view their situation from an alternative perspective (by considering exceptions and how life would be without their problem), consider alternative solutions, and evaluate coping strategies and solutions. One could almost say that solution-focused therapy is values clarification in a therapeutic context.

Values clarification, like solution-focused therapy, lends itself very well to counseling situations where, for reasons of funding restrictions, institutional guidelines, a mobile client population, or other financial considerations or client factors, relatively few counseling sessions are available. With values clarification, it is possible to get down to business pretty quickly. What are the two or three most likely choices you are considering? Which fit most with your priorities in life? How about this other alternative; would you consider it? What are the pros and cons of the different choices? Which do you lean toward? What would your first step be? How about this? Do you think you'd like to try it? When? How?

Of course, all these questions and others—and each step of the value-clarifying process—can go on for many sessions. In fact, they go on throughout our lives. But in a counseling context, in a single session, 5 sessions, or 10 sessions, it is often possible to make significant progress. Recall the 15-minute example at the beginning of this book, when a young man entered the counselor's office filled with anger and a feeling that he wanted to quit school, explored how he could modify his personal appearance to both feel good about himself and not antagonize others, and left with a plan in mind and a sense of optimism. Granted, it's not always so quick and easy. But the example does illustrate the adaptability and utility of values clarification for brief counseling situations.

■ NARRATIVE THERAPY

... in a therapy of oral tradition, the re-authoring of lives and relationships is achieved primarily, although not exclusively, through a process of questioning. (White & Epston, 1990, p. 17, cited in Neukrug, 2011, p. 402)

Values clarification, like narrative therapy, is primarily, although not exclusively, a process of questioning. Although questions in narrative therapy often focus on externalizing the problem and mapping its effects ("How did this problem come into your life?" "If you were to give a name to the problem, what might it be called?") and identifying unique outcomes or exceptions to the problem ("What would life be like without the problem?" "When was a time that the problem didn't get you down?"), value-clarifying questions are more developmental than therapeutic, engaging clients in using the seven valuing processes around values issues and dilemmas in their lives.

Narrative therapy engages clients in telling their initially problem-saturated stories and then reauthoring those stories into preferred stories (Morgan, 2000). Stories play a part in many values clarification strategies as well, such as the One-Minute Autobiography (#28), Pages From an Autobiography (29), Board of Directors (31), and others. Through such clarifying strategies in which they remember and articulate earlier times and themes in their lives, clients gain a greater awareness of how their value indicators (goals, beliefs, habits, etc.) and values originated. This enables them to step back from their value indicators and begin to ask, "Are these the goals, beliefs, and habits I want to maintain?" This is similar to the process by which clients in narrative therapy step back from their stories and consider whether there are other, more positive stories they would like to adopt. In both cases, there is an assumption that clients can choose their own values or their own stories, that we are not prisoners of our past but active participants in our present and futures.

Narrative therapy has a social-political dimension, in which clients come to recognize those parts of their problems or stories that may have been exacerbated by social and economic inequities in their environment. The same broader issues and dimensions can be raised in the values clarification process through skillful and imaginative clarifying questions.

■ MOTIVATIONAL INTERVIEWING

Motivational interviewing (Miller & Rollnick, 2002) bears a striking similarity to values clarification. Developed in the late 1970s, at the height of values clarification's popularity, and describing itself as a person-centered approach, motivational interviewing shared the humanistic psychology movement's positive view of human potential. Like the person-centered approach and values clarification, it believes that humans are self-motivated to change and grow, that they are often ambivalent about change, and that a collaborative, evocative, and respectful helping relationship can help tip the balance in favor of change. The motivation for change comes from within the client. The counselor or therapist does not need to take sides, which often creates resistance.

The focus of motivational interviewing is consistently on change. The motivational interviewer listens for change talk and responds to it by exploring and reinforcing the client's *desire, ability, reasons, need,* and *commitment* to change. She does this by practicing the microskills of *open questions, affirming, reflecting,* and *summarizing.* The most frequent response is reflecting or listening empathically. The next most frequent response is asking open-ended questions, such as "On a scale of 1 to 10, how important is this to you? Why a 7 and not a 3? What would it take to get to a 7.5?" "What do you think needs to happen?" "What have you done already?" "What do you think you might do about it?" "Would you like me to share a few things that might work for you?" and "How confident are you that you can make that change?"

Arguably, motivational interviewing is a hybrid of person-centered therapy and values clarification. If, in motivational interviewing, the most frequent response is reflective, empathic listening and the second most frequent response is clarifying questions, in values clarification the most frequent response is clarifying questions and the second most frequent response is empathic listening. Motivational interviewing also has its own vocabulary, its questioning technique is adapted to focus more consistently on change, and it includes greater explicit affirmation of the client's strengths, efforts, and motivation toward change. It also has a research program that supports the approach's effectiveness.

■ ACCEPTANCE AND COMMITMENT THERAPY

Stephen Hayes, a founder of acceptance and commitment therapy (Hayes, Strosahl, & Wilson, 2012), describes ACT as one of several of the newer "behavior technologies" that are taking the fields of cognitive and behavioral therapy to a new stage of development. According to Hayes (2004), ACT consists of six processes: "1) establishing psychological acceptance skills; 2) establishing cognitive diffusion skills; 3) distinguishing self-as-context from the conceptualized self; 4) contacting the present moment and establishing self-as-process skills; 5) distinguishing choice from reasoned action (necessary to avoid values clarification from becoming excessively rule governed), clarifying values, and distinguishing them from goals and actions; and 6) teaching committed behavioral persistence and behavioral change strategies linked to [chosen] values" (p. 15). In an accompanying diagram, he calls the fifth and sixth processes values and committed action.

172 ■ VALUES CLARIFICATION

In other words, as Hayes (2004) explains, ACT has two main parts. The first four processes comprise the *acceptance and mindfulness skills*, and the last two constitute the *commitment and behavior change skills*. The first group helps clients be aware and accepting of their inner processes, recognize their feelings and selves as changing phenomena based on context, give up their need for defensiveness but rather hold their self-concepts lightly, not rigidly, and separate from themselves. The second part of ACT has them move ahead with their lives. They don't work hard at changing their feelings and cognitions—inner processes that are the most difficult to change—but they move toward valued goals. ACT "involves a deep interest in what one wants out of life and learning to build larger and larger and larger patterns of effective behavior linked to those goals and values" (p. 17). Describing ACT, as well as dialectical behavioral therapy and integrated behavioral couples therapy, Hayes writes, "Instead of pursuing truth," that is, instead of trying to unravel all the sources and ins and outs of their past problems, "clients are encouraged to become passionately interested in how to live according to their own values, that is, how to accomplish their purposes" (p. 10).

Clearly, values clarification is central to ACT. Although ACT's definition of *value* and *values* is somewhat different than in values clarification, the point is very much the same. Conscious decision making, free choice ("not excessively rule governed"), taking action to live according to one's values, and doing so in consistent "patterns" are all aspects of values clarification that have been embraced by and incorporated into ACT. Not only are the major parts of values clarification's valuing processes included in ACT, so are many of the classic values clarification activities. For example, Hayes (2004) mentions writing one's tombstone epitaph (strategy 35), writing one's eulogy (#37), and examining "barriers to action" (#22) as methods consistent with ACT. The original textbook on ACT (Hayes, Strosahl, & Wilson, 1999) includes other strategies from the original values clarification repertoire (e.g., Simon, Howe, & Kirschenbaum, 1972).

Interestingly, although these and other activities play a significant role in ACT and are clearly featured in the original *Values Clarification Handbook* (Simon, Howe, & Kirschenbaum, 1972, 1979), no references are given to the earlier work. I point this out not to be critical but as an example of how a great many of the values clarification activities have become incorporated in the next generation or two of counseling and psychotherapy theories and practices. It underlines the point that a greater understanding of values clarification concepts and facility with values clarification methods can enhance the practice of counselors and psychotherapists of many schools.

■ APPRECIATIVE INQUIRY

Appreciative inquiry (Cooperrider & Whitney, 2005) was originally developed in business organization settings but has since been extended to coaching and counseling. Like values clarification, it relies primarily on asking open-ended questions to help clients achieve their goals and overcome difficulties. The appreciative inquirer demonstrates an attitude of *open-minded curiosity*, which is an excellent description of the attitude that helps a values clarification counselor be effective.

Appreciative inquiry is based on the premise that humans change and grow more by building on the positive than by focusing on the negative. Hence it focuses on clients' *strengths, vitalities, aspirations,* and *possibilities.* Aspirations, for example, can be explored with questions like these:

- Values: What are my principles? What do I stand for?
- Outcomes: What do I need? What do I want?
- Strengths: What am I good at? What makes me feel strong?
- Behaviors: What activities do I aspire to do consistently?
- Motivators: Why does this matter a lot to me, right now?
- Environments: What support team and structures will facilitate success? (Tschannen-Moren & Tschannen-Moren, 2010, p. 157)

An appreciative interview protocol, adapted to the client's particular situation, asks clients questions about their *best experiences* (e.g., "Can you describe a time when you felt your best, free from any symptom?"), their *core values* ("Tell me some of the things you care most deeply about in this situation"), *supporting conditions* ("Tell me what the key factors are, internal and external, that help you be your best in this situation"), and *three wishes* ("What are your hopes and dreams for the future? If you could make three wishes that would be granted, what would they be?").

One familiar with either values clarification or appreciative inquiry will recognize that scores of questions commonly asked in one approach are also regularly used in the other approach. Moreover, the appreciative, accepting attitude of the counselor asking the questions is similar in both approaches. However, there are also differences based on the conceptual structure of each approach. Values clarification counselors select and create questions based on the seven valuing processes. Appreciative inquiry utilizes questions based on an elegant set of principles in which positive attention in the present (the poetic principle) leads to positive anticipation of the future (anticipatory principle), which leads to positive questions and reflections (simultaneity principle), which lead to positive conversations and interactions (constructivist principle), which lead to positive energy and emotions (positive principle), which lead to positive actions and outcomes. And although both approaches are positive and solution oriented, values clarification may at times use clarifying questions and activities to explore the problem *and* possible solutions, when appreciative inquiry may go directly to the latter.

■ LIFE COACHING

Coaching or life coaching is a growing and sometimes controversial offshoot of professional counseling and consulting (Ivey & Ivey, 2009; Williams & Menendez, 2007). Whatever one thinks of this movement, there is no denying that some counselors coach and some coaches counsel.

Sports coaches, voice coaches, drama coaches, and other such coaches have traditionally played an active and directive role in guiding their clients to achieve higher levels of performance. They instruct, teach, suggest, advise, give feedback, exhort, and otherwise coach clients toward successfully achieving their goals. The goals themselves are usually straightforward—getting better, winning, achieving a part— but not always. A voice coach would be well advised to ascertain whether her client's goal is to sing in high opera or musical comedy or just for his own enjoyment before commencing a coaching program.

I would say that values clarification is the foundation of life coaching. Helping both the client and the coach become clear on the client's goals, options, and action strategies is central to the coaching process, whether in business, professional, or personal settings. As this process goes on, the coach becomes more active in teaching, practicing, and advising. Counseling shifts to coaching.

Yet many stages of coaching can retain a values clarification aspect. One coach might tell a client, "You should do it this way," but another might ask, "Would you consider this alternative? Might this work for you? What if you tried it this way? Would that feel better?" In this way the coach, like the values clarification counselor, is helping the client consider alternatives but not imposing her own preferences or values on the client.

Another aspect of coaching is helping the client implement the new strategies or skills he has learned. There are often internal and external obstacles that make it difficult for clients of coaches to perform as capably as they might. Here again, values clarification strategies can help clients move from their base of knowledge and skill to resolving the real-world implementation challenges they may face.

■ POSITIVE PSYCHOLOGY

Building on the humanistic psychology movement of the later 20th century, the recent positive psychology movement has focused on human well-being—what it is, under what circumstances it naturally occurs, and how to proactively gain more of it (Seligman, Steen, Park, & Peterson, 2005). As part of a varied research and teaching agenda, Peterson and Seligman (2004) cataloged 24 strengths, character traits, or virtues individuals may have—love of learning, open-mindedness, bravery, integrity, kindness, ability to love and be loved, citizenship, humility, spirituality, and so forth—and suggested that becoming aware of one's "signature strengths" and systematically incorporating these into one's life increases the likelihood of experiencing "authentic happiness" (Seligman, 2002). Their "Values in Action Signature Strengths Test" (Values in Action Institute, n.d.) and the teaching-learning activities accompanying it are, in fact, a substantive set of values clarification activities designed to help individuals clarify what they are good at, what is important to them, and how they might build more of this into their lives.

Often mischaracterized as simply a "happiology" (Peterson, 2006), positive psychology is concerned with *all* the components of well-being, which, according to Martin Seligman (2011), consist of positive emotion, engagement, meaning, accomplishment, and positive relationships. All these elements of well-being, I would say, are human values. And with any enumeration of values and virtues comes the necessity of prioritizing and balancing. The singular pursuit of positive emotion, for example, could lead to drug dependency. The singular pursuit of accomplishment could lead to poor relationships and poor health. Values clarification is necessary throughout one's life to balance and maximize all elements of well-being. The insights and exercises of positive psychology and the insights and methods of values clarification go hand in hand.

11 Theory and Research

■ WHAT IS A "VALUE"?

Philosophers, psychologists, educators, and others have long debated the meaning of the terms *value* and *values*. A dictionary, for example, may define a *value* as "a principle, standard, or quality considered worthwhile or desirable" (*American Heritage Dictionary*, 1991). Psychologist Milton Rokeach (1975) defined a *value* as "an enduring belief that a specific model of conduct or end-state of existence is personally or socially preferable to an opposite or converse mode of conduct or end-state of existence." A philosopher might define a *value* as "a belief, grounded in feeling, that predisposes one to act in a certain way," which I have sometimes stated as "a quality or aspect of life that one believes is important, feels strongly about, and acts upon" (Kirschenbaum, 1995, p. 57). Raths, Harmin, and Simon (1966), on the other hand, lengthened the definition by defining a *value* as a part of our life that meets the seven criteria of values clarification. In just these few examples, we see that some definitions of a *value* include a cognitive, affective, and behavioral component, while other definitions include only one or two of these dimensions.

However, others could object that any of these definitions of a *value* are value free, that is, independent of the content of a person's values. They point out that some evil person—a Hitler, for example—might believe that a particular race or religion is inferior. He might feel strongly about his belief and even act on it in a hateful and violent manner. They would argue that calling race superiority a value, like the values of respect and compassion, is an oxymoron, a contradiction. When some people ask, "Does this person have *values*?" they mean, does he or she embody respect, responsibility, honesty, compassion, and comparable *moral virtues*. They cannot easily accept that people can have destructive or evil values. In other words, one's belief about what constitutes good values often colors one's definition of the very term *values*.

■ VALUES CLARIFICATION IS AND IS NOT VALUE FREE

If the seven-criteria definition of a value is value free in the previous sense, does this mean that values clarification as a counseling or developmental approach is value free? It does, and it does not.

Values clarification is consistent with the ethics of the counseling and psychotherapy professions in that the counselor does not impose her values on the client. That is, the counselor does not impose her religious, political, cultural, social, and personal values on the client. Rather, the counselor respects the client's autonomy and encourages the client to make free choices consistent with the client's own evolving values. This commitment to values neutrality is not only theoretical but also built into values clarification practice. The counselor implements the goal of not imposing her values by:

- asking clarifying questions and strategies on topics that are raised by the client, not on topics on which the counselor thinks the client should focus
- framing the questions she asks so there is not an implied right answer
- accepting whatever answers the client gives without argument or disagreement and refraining from verbal or nonverbal behaviors that seem to approve or disapprove of the client's comments and responses (although further clarifying questions are legitimate)
- offering new alternatives for the client's consideration as possibilities, not suggestions or recommendations

Consistent with the values clarification process, the counselor sincerely wants the client to come up with his own choices and develop his own values. In all these ways, values clarification is, indeed, value free.

Yet values clarification is not completely value free. Although some of the earliest presentations on values clarification tended to suggest that the approach was entirely values neutral, after a number of years, leaders in values clarification recognized that "values clarification is not and never has been 'value free'" (Kirschenbaum, Harmin, Howe, & Simon, 1977, p. 744), because *the values clarification process itself* is value laden.

Clearly, values clarification promotes the value of certain types of prizing, choosing, and acting. Prizing and cherishing one's value indicators (beliefs, choices, actions, etc.) is considered *better than* living without enthusiasm and commitment. Considering consequences is regarded as *better than* choosing impulsively or thoughtlessly. Choosing freely is considered *better than* yielding passively to authority or peer pressure. Acting on one's values is considered *better than* merely talking about one's values. Acting consistently is considered *better than* acting flightily and inconsistently. And so on.

We can go a step further. Toward what end are these valuing processes better than their counterparts? Here again, certain value judgments are implicit in each process. If we urge a thoughtful process of weighing pros and cons, then we value *rationality*. If we promote thinking about alternatives, then we value *creativity*. If we uphold free choice, then we value autonomy or *freedom*. If, in our counseling practice, we honor each client's autonomy, then we uphold the value of *respect*. If, in our group counseling or psychoeducational groups, we support each member's right to participate and be listened to with respect, then we support the values of *fairness* and *equality*. If we encourage "no-lose" conflict resolution, then we value *equality and justice*. Some of these values are instrumental and others terminal, to use Milton Rokeach's (1973) terminology. For example, the value of creativity is an instrument or means toward the terminal value of life satisfaction. The value of rationality is instrumental toward the terminal or end value of justice. One might say that the terminal values implicit in the values clarification process include equality, liberty, and the pursuit of happiness, among others.

Therefore, both in theory and in practice, values clarification is and is not value free. I think values clarification practitioners can both publicly affirm and be proud of both sides of this statement. We can be proud of how values clarification is consistent with a very important tenet of our professional ethics—to respect the client's values and not impose our own. And we can be proud of the values implicit in the values clarification approach, values that are most consistent with our democratic tradition.

■ MULTICULTURAL ASPECTS OF VALUES CLARIFICATION

Recognizing the values implicit in the values clarification process brings to the surface the broader issue of the multicultural implications of the values clarification approach. The Founding Fathers in the United States held "these truths to be self-evident, that all men are created equal, that they are endowed by their Creator with certain unalienable Rights, that among these are Life, Liberty and the pursuit of Happiness." Yet equality and freedom are not self-evident truths or primary values in all cultures. The freedom of all people to choose their political, religious, social, and personal values in the pursuit of happiness is not universally embraced—and not always honored even when espoused.

So there is a paradox here. In some ways, values clarification reflects a modern, democratic, individualistic, Western, middle-class worldview that can be seen as inconsistent with some cultures and traditional value systems and less applicable or inapplicable to other cultural, economic, and political contexts in the United States and around the world. At the same time, many traditional cultures and many individuals within those cultures are grappling with their own value conflicts, and values clarification can be a very helpful tool for them to sort through these tensions.

At the heart of potential criticisms about the cultural bias of the values clarification approach is the charge that values clarification is essentially *individualistic*. It is an approach that emphasizes self-actualization ("What do *you* prize and cherish?" "Are you acting upon *your* values?") and, by so doing, appears to ignore or minimize an individual's duty to the family, group, or collective. In this sense, the values clarification approach could be seen as inimical to the filial piety of some traditional cultures, obedience to the church or religion, loyalty to the state, or devotion to any object or cause beyond oneself. Not all cultures or groups value self-actualization as one of their highest values.

Part of this critique gets to the very concept of self implied in values clarification and other branches of humanistic psychology (Cushman, 1990). Sampson (1988) distinguished between "self-contained" individualism and "ensembled" or "embedded" individualism. "Self-contained individualism is characterized by firmly drawn self–other boundaries. Personal control is emphasized and social responsibility takes the form of 'contractual exchange relationships involving reciprocity'"

(p. 20, in Holdstock, 1990, p. 113). Thus engagement with others comes from free choice, because engagement gains the person either some tangible or potential benefits—from material gain to friendship to love to a better, fairer world, which is also ultimately in one's own interest. "Embedded individualism, on the other hand, emphasizes more fluidly drawn self–nonself boundaries and field control. Relationships are noncontractual, mutually obligatory and communal, and as such operate by different rules than those which govern a more contractually oriented approach. Assistance is given and received without it being evaluated in material terms or in terms of an infringement on personal freedom" (p. 20). From a collectivist perspective, life satisfaction is best achieved through a collective rather than individual identity.

It is now widely accepted that the multiculturally competent counselor or therapist seeks to understand and work with the worldview of the client, rather than impose the worldview of the therapist (Sue et al., 1998). The argument that individuals tend to reflect the individualistic or collectivist worldviews of their cultures is also widely accepted. Therefore, critics might say that the values clarification approach reinforces or imposes an individualistic worldview and therefore is less applicable with clients or in cultures that have a collectivist worldview.

Following from this criticism is the charge that, being primarily individualistic rather than collectivist in its orientation, the values clarification approach fails to attend to the social context as both cause of and potential solution for personal difficulties. It, like much of psychology, fosters individual rather than contextual, collective, or political solutions. In so doing, it fails to utilize resources and support structures in the community that may be of help to clients. Moreover, some problems do not have individual solutions but can be solved only through social and political action.

I believe that such a critique of values clarification is only partly correct and more complicated than typically presented. To begin with, recall that the very purpose and structure of the values clarification approach is designed not to impose the counselor's values or worldview upon the client, but to assist the client in realizing the *client's own* values. The many ways that values clarification counselors can minimize counselor-imposed values are discussed throughout this book.

Moreover, the *choosing process* of values clarification is about more than choosing freely. It also includes the consideration of alternatives. Here the counselor has ample opportunities to help clients explore the alternatives that their own social, religious, and cultural backgrounds may offer. In some cases, this even means asking clients to give thoughtful consideration to their family, faith, or other traditional sources of values when the client might be just as inclined to ignore those sources. The process of considering alternative solutions to an individual's dilemma also provides ample opportunities to consider how the client's social support system, community resources, and social and political action could help clients realize their individual and social values. When the counselor asks (if it seems appropriate to the individual and the relationship), "Have you considered asking for your family's help?" or "What would your religion suggest you do?" or "Are you the only one with this issue, or might your coworkers also share your concern and be able to work with you on improving the situation?" the values clarification process reflects a world-view that is both individualistic *and* collective.

Similarly, asking the client to consider the consequences of his actions need not and, in many situations, *should not* involve asking only about the consequences for the client. The counselor might ask, for example, "Okay, you're considering these two choices. Which would be the better choice for you, which would be the better choice from your husband's perspective, and which would be better for your children?" This could be followed, again if appropriate to the situation, by "Is there a third alternative that could include some of the benefits you mentioned for you *and* your wife and children?" By asking clients to consider the pros and cons and consequences of their choices and actions on *others*—their family, group, community—the process validates the communal roots of our values and hopefully increases the likelihood that a client's choices will be based not only on self-interest but also on the welfare of others and of the social order. In this sense, again, values clarification need not and should not be a completely individualistic process. In these ways and others, values clarification can be practiced with multicultural sensitivity.

However, to argue that the methodology of values clarification avoids or minimizes the imposition of the counselor's values and that the choosing process of values clarification can reflect both individual and social values does not alter the reality that values clarification is, to a significant degree, an individualistic approach. The process itself—by validating the individual and his[1] own feelings, thoughts, and perceptions—strongly supports personal autonomy. Consider a client from a culture that is strongly matriarchal or patriarchal or authoritarian who comes to a values clarification counselor. Throughout the client's life, he has been told, "What *you* think doesn't matter. *Your* feelings are not important. You will follow your family or your group's way. You do not have a choice." Now, without the values clarification counselor ever having to say it explicitly, a different message comes across. "What *you* think *does* matter. I am interested in *your* feelings and priorities. What is the path *you* want to follow? How you live your life is *your* choice." The counselor need not say a word against the values or norms of the family or traditional culture; nonetheless, the process of values clarification counseling itself inculcates the values of personal autonomy and individualism. By so doing, it clashes with traditional or totalitarian cultures. In effect, values clarification implies that the individual is at least to some extent his own authority. An individual, of course, may freely choose to give over that authority to a leader, guru, religion, or group—this is the essence of faith—but it is still the individual making that supreme values choice. Thus values clarification is philosophically and psychologically not exclusively, but significantly an individualistic process.

This does not necessarily make values clarification inappropriate or less applicable to cultures or individuals who do not share this orientation. That is because

---

1. Please recall I am handling pronouns in this book by using the female pronoun to refer to the counselor and the male pronoun to refer to the client or person in general.

cultures and individuals are rarely, if ever, all one way or the other—individualistic or collectivist. Cultures, classes, religious groups, and other communities typically have some characteristics that are traditionally collective and others that are individualistic and modern. Likewise, individuals, whether from primarily individualistic or collectivist cultures, hold both individualistic *and* collectivist values and preferences. Societies and the individuals within them are, in fact, often *highly conflicted* over changing values and customs. People do not necessarily subscribe to only one worldview or value system: middle-class values or lower-class values, religious or secular, traditional or modern, individualistic or collectivist, Eastern or Western, black or white. Although one worldview or set of values may be dominant in a person or culture, there are often contrasting views and values that are important parts of their identities, that have meaning to them.

Thus, when generalizations categorizing traditional and Western cultures as collectivist or individualistic were put to the test, Oyserman, Coon, and Kemmelmeier (2002), in several meta-analyses involving from 35 to 50 studies, found that many widely accepted generalizations about different cultural groups did not hold up. For example, in national comparisons, it was true that European Americans were more individualistic and less collectivist in their value orientations than most traditional cultures, but there were many exceptions to this rule. For example, "Truly startling findings emerged for Korea and Japan: Americans were significantly higher in collectivism than Japanese were, and were not significantly different in collectivism from Koreans" (p. 18, quoted in Williams, 2003, p. 371). There were similar findings, both predictable and surprising, in the U.S. comparisons. Although Latino Americans were no different on individualism and higher on collectivism than European Americans, African Americans turned out to be *higher* on individualism and no different on collectivism than European Americans. Summarizing the Oyserman amd colleagues meta-analyses, Williams (2003) wrote, "[W]orldview is not accurately predicted by race, ethnicity or national group ... the inconsistency with which the endorsement of individualism and collectivism follows hypothesized patterns is evidence for the need to be extremely aware of one's own biases when seeking to determine a client's worldview" (p. 372).

These data are entirely consistent with a person-centered or values clarification viewpoint. People are too complex to be viewed primarily in categories. To assume that everyone from a culture shares a set of attributes or values is a different kind of imposition and stereotyping. From a values clarification perspective, then, people's cultural influences—including gender, race, ethnicity, religion, nationality, class, and other important characteristics—may be very important in forming their identities, but persons are more than the sum total of these influences. They must be *treated* as individuals (pun intended). In other words, each client internalizes cultural influences in different ways and struggles with and balances different identities in different ways. A values clarification approach can be useful in helping clients understand and sort out these multicultural issues, as well as other issues of the human condition. Moreover, if a person or client truly has a more collectivist orientation, the mere act of asking that person questions relative to their values does not necessarily challenge, discredit, or dishonor their more collective way of viewing or being in the world. In fact, it gives them an opportunity to affirm their collectivist orientation.

Still, the multicultural literature has provided valuable cautions, insights, and recommendations as to how the values clarification approach, or any approach, might be more effectively implemented in different cultural contexts. Among other dispositions and strategies, counselors wishing to practice with multicultural competence should be knowledgeable about their clients' cultural influences; be respectful of clients' worldviews; find out from the client what his desired goals of counseling are, explain how counseling works, and negotiate a common purpose; understand, respect, and work with the client's understanding about healing; be willing to discuss and even initiate discussion about differences in the counselor's and client's backgrounds; and be willing, within the limits of their own values and abilities, to utilize the clients' resources and cultural traditions insofar as these are meaningful to the client (Sue et al., 1998; Sue & Sue, 2003). Like any counselor, a values clarification practitioner who is unaware of these multicultural issues, ignores them, or implements these measures less than competently will be less effective in multicultural contexts. But when incorporated into a values clarification practice, these multicultural competencies enhance still further those aspects of the values clarification approach that make it particularly appropriate for multicultural applications.

■ RESEARCH ON VALUES CLARIFICATION

Whatever the approach to anything, people want to know, "Does it work?" In counseling and psychotherapy, that question usually means "Does this approach lead to favorable outcomes?" Do people improve in their diagnoses? Do they become less addicted, less depressed, less agoraphobic, less abusive, and so forth? Do their marriages improve? Do they resolve their career dilemmas? Do they find peace of mind? Or, as I have suggested for values clarification, do they develop greater satisfaction and meaning in their lives and do so without any loss in socially constructive behavior?

This discussion of research on values clarification *will* attempt to make three key points: (a) There is a body of research—some *good*, some mediocre—that supports values clarification in counseling, youth work, and educational settings; (b) because values clarification, by itself, is not a form of psychotherapy, there is no reason to expect outcome studies on its effectiveness in reducing diagnostic symptoms; and (c) counseling and therapy approaches that employ a significant amount of values clarification, explicitly or implicitly, are supported by a growing body of scientific research.

Let me begin with a story.

In the early 1980s, a high school elective course called "Skills for Living" (Kirschenbaum & Glaser, 1978) was one of the most widely used "life skills" curricula in the United States. More than a million students, mostly in public schools, had taken the course, and thousands of teachers and counselors had been trained to teach it. The course was permeated with values clarification activities in which students focused on topics like feelings, friends, family, marriage, parenting, money, career, and relationship with the universe, while learning life skills of decision making, communicating, and dealing with feelings. Students, teachers, and parents gave the course their highest praise.

But did it work? The nonprofit group that sponsored the course, Quest, Inc. (later Quest International, currently Lions Quest International), hired an independent university psychologist to evaluate the program (Jurs, 1983). Because teenage drug abuse was of major concern to society then (and now), Quest hoped to find that their life skills curriculum lessened teen drug use. Instead, they found that students who participated in the course had *higher* levels of illegal drug use by the end of the year in which they took the course. Extremely alarmed, Quest ceased offering Skills for Living. The course, one of the most popular of its kind in the country, soon faded into oblivion (although a middle school and elementary school version and a new high school curriculum have lasted for many years with millions of students participating around the world).

But the story doesn't end there. Further analysis of the research results revealed another important finding. Although it was true that students who participated in the course increased their drug usage, the increase was *less than* that of the typical American teenager! In other words, in each year of high school, American teenagers on average increased their use of illegal drugs. Those who went through the Skills for Living course increased their use significantly less than the average teenager (significant both statistically and in effect size).

Was this cause for celebration? Maybe not. Certainly, the values clarification curriculum, if I can call it that, was not a cure-all. But it helped somewhat. If this were a medication being tested and, for example, the new medication reduced the incidence of the disease from 80% to 50%, without apparent negative side effects, that would be a major breakthrough. Doctors would begin prescribing it, and researchers would redouble their efforts to figure out the helpful ingredients in the medication so it could be improved further. In the politically charged world of education (and counseling and psychotherapy), it doesn't and didn't happen that way.

Indeed, by the 1980s, values clarification and related humanistic education methods had become controversial in education and society. Consistent with the social and political movements that were empowering African Americans, women, students, and other previously disenfranchised groups, values clarification supported the autonomous decision making of youth and adults. For those who saw permissiveness running rampant in society, values clarification was part of the problem. No matter that Skills for Living was organized by an evangelical Christian from middle America who had no political agenda and only wanted to employ whatever methods might be helpful to youth. The Skills for Living sponsors were walking a tightrope, and when the headline read, in effect, "High School Course Increases Drug Use," there was no recovering from it.

This story summarizes the research on values clarification in a nutshell. Research reviews on values clarification showed either promising results or no good evidence of improvement, depending on the slant of the reviewer. One's perspective inevitably was influenced by the educational-political context of the time.

I conducted the first serious review of values clarification research since its early years (Kirschenbaum, 1977a), in which 12 older and 24 newer studies were summarized. The results tended to support the generalization that when teachers and counselors went through a competently led training in values clarification, a large percentage of them returned to their classrooms and counseling venues and actually implemented the approach, resulting in young people showing positive change on various dimensions of personal and/or academic growth. My summary of two of the best studies is quoted here to give a sense of the review.

Clarke et al. The largest and most important study on values clarification to date (Clarke et al., 1974) took place in Visalia, California, under the sponsorship of Operation Future, a youth development and delinquency prevention organization with Jay Clarke as director. The population included 851 fifth though tenth graders, two groups of pregnant minors, two church groups, and sixty-five young people on probation. They were surveyed and rated as to their use of various nonprescribed drugs, their perception of themselves in reference to eight character traits associated with lack of value clarity (e.g., apathy, flightiness, etc.) and their school behavior. One significant finding was a high correlation between drug use and several of the low-valuing traits.

In the second part of their study, Clarke et al. measured the effect of values clarification experiences on the character traits and on the students' use of drugs. The effect of the independent variable [values clarification] on the traits was mixed, with some of the experimental groups remaining the same, a few regressing slightly, and several making enormous gains, i.e., becoming less apathetic, etc. In the area of drug use, the gains were unmistakably significant, as indicated in a preliminary report that stated, "For the most part all groups reduced their intake of all drugs with the exception (in some groups) of alcohol." Not only were these results statistically significant, but in many cases the changes were dramatic in degree. Another dramatic set of findings showed how, without the use of values clarification in the control groups, there was a significant decline in the students' social adjustment (p. 28).

Gorsuch, Arno, and Bachelder. An experienced evaluation team conducted a carefully controlled study (Gorsuch, Arno, & Bachelder, 1976) on the effects of an extensive values clarification program sponsored by the Akron, Ohio, and the National YMCA. They found that the values program (with fourth-, fifth-, and sixth-grade boys) led to significant changes in the groups that had the longer exposures to the program—the club groups that met throughout the year versus the brief summer camp experiences, the boys who experienced two years of the program versus one year. This suggests that those short studies—e.g., ten sessions—which show no changes may not be fair tests of the approach.

Although the data are varied, the major changes were in three areas. The boys in the values clarification program, compared to the controls: (1) shifted toward values which children generally see as desirable in their social environment and on which adults generally score higher than children of this age (while one may question the conformity contained within this criterion, Kohlberg suggests that social conformity is a transitional phase necessary to progress to a more internally-controlled ethical system), (2) increased the degree to which they saw as being deviant those behaviors that are normally defined as deviant within our culture, e.g., excessive use of alcohol (the norm is for children to become increasingly tolerant of deviant acts as they grow older), and (3) became more supportive of internalized values as contrasted with basing value decisions solely on external circumstances (clearly a major goal of values clarification) (p. 29).

Although these particular studies were well designed, I was the first to point out that much of the research on values clarification was of poor quality. Most studies had no comparison groups, and many had few participants. Certainly, the results were equivocal. Some studies showed greater changes in the experimental groups; others showed no difference between the experimental and control groups. Some showed changes in the affective area but not the cognitive, some showed the reverse, some showed both, and some showed neither. This is to be expected. Many of the treatments were very brief, involving a few sessions with a group of 30 participants. In many of these studies, the teachers or counselors were using values clarification for the first time, whereas the control-group leaders were using the approaches they had used for years. It is remarkable that so many studies did show positive changes under the circumstances. It is also significant that in no studies did the experimental groups regress or do more poorly than the controls. Whereas the results in any one or a few studies might be termed equivocal, the directionality of the overall findings seemed very consistent. In a situation where one could describe the cup as half full or half empty, I described it as half full.

Later reviews of values clarification research (Cline & Feldmesser, 1983; Leming, 1987) described the cup as half empty or mostly empty. They highlighted the methodological flaws in the research (while elsewhere being less rigorous in their methodological critiques of alternate methods of values, moral, and character development). They neglected to include some studies supportive of values clarification, including the two important and methodologically sound studies just summarized. They included studies in which the treatment variable was not values clarification at all or where the values clarification teachers or counselors were not trained in the approach. They used studies that looked at one dependent variable as evidence that values clarification did not affect a different dependent variable. In the end, they concluded there was no good evidence that values clarification worked.

Actually, I have no problem with that conclusion in spite of how they got to it. Although I still believe there is much promising evidence for the effectiveness of values clarification and its core hypothesis, I also think it is true that an objective reviewer must conclude, as they did, in effect: "The evidence does not show that values clarification works." This is a fair statement, meaning there is not enough good evidence to assert that values clarification works. Stated differently, an objective reviewer could just as easily conclude: "The research does not show that values clarification does not work. Based on the evidence so far, it may or it may not work; we just don't know. More research is needed."

However, it is a short trip from "the evidence does not show that values clarification works" to "the evidence shows that values clarification does not work." The words are the same, in a different order, but the meaning is very different. Unfortunately, many consumers of research—and some reviewers of research who should have known better—made or implied this mistaken leap.

My own view remains as it was earlier. I still view the cup as half full. That is, many promising studies suggest positive outcomes tend to occur when young people and adults go through the values clarification process. They become less apathetic and more purposeful. They learn more in school. They engage in fewer self-destructive behaviors, at least fewer than their cohort without values clarification. Can we say this with certainty based on the findings? No. Far more and far better research is needed to make such claims with any degree of certainty. And much more research is needed to truly understand how values clarification works with different populations in different circumstances. Meanwhile, the lack of any evidence that values clarification is harmful, combined with the positive experience that thousands of counselors, teachers, and others have had with values clarification over several decades, gives me confidence in using and recommending values clarification to enhance one's counseling and psychotherapy practice.

Meanwhile, there is also research in related fields that sheds further light on whether and how values clarification may work. Milton Rokeach (1961, 1975) demonstrated years ago how confronting individuals with discrepancies between their values and behavior tended to lead them to change their behavior toward being more consistent with their values. Lawrence Kohlberg (1968) and his students demonstrated that exposing young people to moral reasoning one level higher than their own tends to raise the lower level of moral reasoning. Values clarification involves both of these processes: helping clients and group members consider the consistencies and inconsistencies between their goals and beliefs and their choices and actions, and helping clients and group members consider alternative perspectives on their beliefs, choices, and behavior.

In a larger sense, all the decades of research on the effectiveness of counseling and psychotherapy also support values clarification. Values clarification counselors are not unique in what they do. All counselors and psychotherapists, in varying ways and varying degrees, involve clients in looking more deeply at their feelings, goals, and beliefs; in thinking about the choices before them; in encouraging them to make choices less encumbered by the pressure of past and present influences; and in helping them take the first tentative steps toward change and growth. In other words, the methods of values clarification are among the methods of counseling and psychotherapy. The skills of a values clarification counselor are among the many and varied skills of the counseling profession.

Perhaps we can go a step further. In the previous chapter, I pointed out the similarities between values clarification and a number of other psychotherapy approaches, particularly solution-focused therapy, motivational interviewing, and acceptance and commitment therapy (ACT). The growing research evidence for the effectiveness of these approaches is impressive. For example, "A recent review of ACT... outcomes, found effectiveness and efficacy studies in depression, psychosis, substance use disorders, chronic pain, eating disorders, work-related stress, and other problems" (Hayes, Masuda, Bissett, Luoma, & Guerrero, 2004, cited in Hayes, 2004, p. 24). Whether acknowledged explicitly, as with ACT, or implicitly, as with solution-focused therapy and motivational interviewing, values clarification plays an important part in the success of these approaches. This has two possible implications. First is that at least some aspects of values clarification do work, since they contribute to positive outcomes in these other approaches. Second, is that practitioners of these approaches that already incorporate values clarification, knowingly or unknowingly, would do well to enhance their facility with values clarification.

Let me be clear here. It is not being proposed that, because other approaches that use values clarification work, therefore values clarification by itself works. Rather I am reinforcing a point made throughout this book—that values clarification, while not a mental health counseling approach by itself, can play a helpful and important part in many different counseling and therapy modalities. It is or should be one of the basic skills of the profession.

At the same time, values clarification has its own priorities, puts greater emphasis on particular methods, and implements these methods in its own particular way. We need much more research to understand in what circumstances values clarification methods will be most effective with which clients. The same could be said of most approaches in the field of counseling and psychotherapy.

■ CONCLUSION

Years ago, one of the authors of *Values Clarification: A Handbook of Practical Strategies for Teachers and Students* (Simon, Howe, & Kirschenbaum, 1972, 1979) received a letter from a reader who wrote, "I've done all the 79 strategies in the book with my students. What do I do now?" Obviously, he had missed the point.

I hope I have made it clear throughout this book that value-clarifying questions, clarifying interviews, and values clarification strategies are not, in themselves, a counseling curriculum that one imposes on a client or group. They are a set of tools and procedures that are designed to accomplish counseling goals. They are intended to be used selectively—for a particular client or group, for a particular issue, for a particular purpose, whether that purpose is to clarify a particular issue or use it to practice the valuing process.

There is an analogy to a carpenter and his or her toolbox. To the extent that the carpenter has a good number of tools in the toolbox and knows which tools serve which purposes and can use those tools skillfully, that carpenter is able to be more successful in building something new or repairing something that needs to be fixed. Similarly, the counselor or therapist who has in her toolbox clarifying questions, the clarifying interview, and a good number of values clarification strategies (not to mention tools from other counseling approaches) will be able to utilize those tools at just the right moment with a particular client or group to further that client or group's exploration of the issue at hand.

The tools or methods of values clarification are particularly useful, because when implemented effectively:

- Values clarification fosters a high degree of involvement in individual and group settings. Clients and group members *enjoy* reflecting about interesting and important issues and sharing their own feelings, beliefs, and actions with others. The combination of evocative activities and involving group formats makes values clarification successful with shy and reluctant participants as well as with verbal and motivated ones.
- Values clarification fosters genuine self-reflection. Because values clarification does not seek to impose the counselor's values on clients or group members, it creates a sense of safety and acceptance that allows clients and group members to reflect nondefensively on their own values and value indicators.
- Values clarification can be used in a wide variety of counseling and psychotherapy settings. Whether in individual counseling, group counseling, career counseling, marriage and family counseling, pastoral counseling, mental health counseling, rehabilitation counseling, grief counseling, geriatric counseling, financial counseling, or many other settings, values clarification can play anything from a major to an important supporting role.
- Values clarification can be used with a wide variety of topics and issues that counselors and clients focus on. Within any of the counseling settings described, value-clarifying questions, values clarification strategies, and the clarifying interview can be used with many of the specific issues, dilemmas, and choices that clients and groups deal with.
- Values clarification has enough structure to provide a road map for practitioners but enough flexibility to allow practitioners infinite opportunities to exercise their own creativity and develop their own examples and variations.
- Values clarification embodies the multicultural competence of accepting the client's cultural worldview, religious beliefs, sexual orientation, and other diverse values, beliefs, and lifestyles.

Moreover, values clarification can be used side by side with other approaches to counseling and psychotherapy. Because the affective, cognitive, and behavioral realms are *all* central to the seven value-clarifying processes, values clarification has much in common with other counseling approaches. Therefore, whatever one's other theoretical orientation or orientations may be, whatever other approaches a counselor or psychotherapist uses, values clarification can enrich one's practice.

All counseling and therapy practices inevitably deal with clients' goals, priorities, decisions, life choices, and values. I hope that this book will be helpful in supporting counselors and psychotherapists as they work with individuals and groups in this important area.

■ REFERENCES

Adler, A. (1933). On the origin of the striving for superiority and of social interest. In J. Carlson and M. Maniacci (Eds.), *Alfred Adler revisited* (pp. 47–56). New York, NY: Routledge.

American Counseling Association. (2005). *ACA code of ethics.* Alexandria, VA: Author.

American Counseling Association. (2010, April 13). *ACAeNews, 12*(7).

American heritage dictionary: Second college edition. (1991). Boston, MA: Houghton Mifflin.

Berg, I. (1994). *Family based services: A solution-focused approach.* New York, NY: W. W. Norton.

Birren, J., & Cochran, K. (2001). *Telling the stories of life through guided autobiography groups.* Baltimore, MD: Johns Hopkins University Press.

Chitaphong, K. (2004). Untitled, unpublished paper for an advanced counseling theories course, Warner Graduate School of Education and Human Development, University of Rochester, NY, 7 pp.

Clarke, J., et al. (1974). *Operation Future: Third annual report.* San Diego, CA: Pennant Educational Materials.

Cline, H., & Feldmesser, R. (1983). *Program evaluation in moral education.* Princeton, NJ: Educational Testing Service.

Cooperrider, D., & Whitney, D. (2005). *Appreciative inquiry: A positive revolution in change.* San Francisco, CA: Berrett-Koehler.

Corey, G. (2009). The counselor: Person and professional. In *Theory and practice of counseling and psychotherapy* (8th ed.) (pp. 16–35). Belmont, CA: Thomson Brooks/Cole.

Cushman, P. (1990). Why the self is empty: Toward a historically situated psychology. *American Psychologist, 45,* 599–611.

De Jong, P., & Berg, I. (2002). *Interviewing for solutions* (2nd ed.). Pacific Grove, CA: Brooks/Cole.

de Shazer, S., & Dolan, Y. (2007). *More than miracles: The state of the art of solution-focused therapy.* Binghamton, NY: Haworth.

Dewey, J. (1909). *Moral principles in education.* Boston, MA: Houghton Mifflin.

Dewey, J. (1939). *Theory of valuation.* Chicago, IL: University of Chicago Press.

Duane, D. (2004, March 21). The Socratic shrink. *The New York Times Magazine, 153,* 34–37.

Elkins, D. (1977). *Clarifying Jewish values: A handbook of value clarification strategies for group leaders, educators, rabbis, teachers, center workers and counselors.* Rochester, NY: Growth Associates.

Ellis, A. (1962). *Reason and emotion in psychotherapy.* Secaucus, NJ: Lyle Stuart.

Ellis, A. (1994). *Rational emotive behavioral therapy.* Amherst, NY: Prometheus.

Festinger, L. (1957). *A theory of cognitive dissonance.* Stanford, CA: Stanford University Press.

Figler, H. (1975, 1979). *A career workbook for liberal arts students* (1st and 2nd eds.). Cranston, RI: Carroll.

Frisch, M. (2006). *Quality of life therapy: Applying a life satisfaction approach to positive psychology and cognitive therapy.* Hoboken, NJ: John Wiley & Sons.

Glaser, B., & Kirschenbaum, H. (1980, May). Using values clarification in counseling settings. *Personnel and Guidance Journal, 58*(9), 569–574.

Glasser, W. (1965). *Reality therapy: A new approach to psychiatry.* New York, NY: Harper and Row.

Glasser, W. (2001). *Counseling with choice theory: The new reality therapy.* New York, NY: HarperCollins.

Gorsuch, R., Arno, D., & Bachelder, R. (1976). *Summary of research and evaluation of the Youth Values Project, 1973–1976.* New York, NY: Akron, Ohio, YMCA and National Board of YMCAs.

Guterman, J. (2006). *Mastering the art of solution-focused counseling.* Alexandria, VA: American Counseling Association.

Harmin, M., Kirschenbaum, H., & Simon, S. (1973). *Clarifying values through subject matter: Applications for the classroom.* Minneapolis, MN: Winston.

Hayes, S. (2004). Acceptance and commitment therapy and the new behavior therapies: Mindfulness, acceptance and relationship. In S. Hayes, V. Follette, & M. Linehan (Eds.), *Mindfulness and acceptance: Expanding the cognitive behavioral tradition* (pp. 1–29). New York, NY: Guilford.

Hayes, S., Strosahl, D., & Wilson, K. (1999). *Acceptance and commitment therapy: An experiential approach to behavioral change.* New York, NY: Guilford.

Hayes, S. C., Masuda, A., Bissett, R., Luoma, J., & Guerrero, L. (2004). DBT, FAP, and ACT: How empirically oriented are the new behavior therapy technologies? *Behavior Therapy, 35,* 35–54.

Hayes, S. C., Strosahl, K. D., & Wilson, K. G. (2012). *Acceptance and commitment therapy, second edition: The process and practice of mindful change.* New York, NY: Guilford.

Holdstock, L. (1990). Can client-centered therapy transcend its monocultural roots? In G. Lietaer, J. Rombauts, & R. Van Balen (Eds.), *Client-centered and experiential psychotherapy in the nineties* (pp. 109–121). Leuven, Belgium: Leuven University Press.

Ivey, A., & Ivey, M. (2009, July). Bringing coaching and coaching skills into professional counseling. *Counseling Today,* 48–51.

Jurs, S. (1983). *An evaluation of Quest's Skills for Living curriculum.* Unpublished.

Kirschenbaum, H. (1973). Beyond values clarification. In H. Kirschenbaum & S. B. Simon, *Readings in values clarification* (pp. 92–110). Minneapolis, MN: Winston.

Kirschenbaum, H. (1975). Clarifying values clarification: Some theoretical issues and a review of research. *Group and Organizational Studies, 1*(1), 99–116.

Kirschenbaum, H. (1977a). *Advanced value clarification.* La Jolla, CA: University Associates.

Kirschenbaum, H. (1977b). An annotated bibliography on values clarification: 1965–1975. In *Advanced value clarification* (pp. 153–187). La Jolla, CA: University Associates.

Kirschenbaum, H. (1995). *100 ways to enhance values and morality in schools and youth settings.* Needham Heights, MA: Allyn and Bacon.

Kirschenbaum, H. (2009). *The life and work of Carl Rogers.* Alexandria, VA: American Counseling Association.

Kirschenbaum, H. (2012). What is "person-centered"? A posthumous conversation with Carl Rogers on the development of the person-centered approach. *Person-Centered and Experiential Psychotherapies, 11*(1), 14–30.

Kirschenbaum, H., & Glaser, B. (1978). *Skills for living.* Findlay, OH: Quest International.

Kirschenbaum, H., Harmin, M., Howe, L., & Simon, S. (1977, June). In defense of values clarification. *Phi Delta Kappan, 58*(10), 743–746.

Knapp, C., & Simon, S. (2000). An interview with Sid Simon: Values education pioneer. *Values Realization Journal, 13*, 6–11.

Kohlberg, L. (1968). The child as a moral philosopher. *Psychology Today, 2*(4), 24–30.

Kouzes, J., & Posner, B. (2010). *The leadership challenge values cards: Facilitator's guide.* San Francisco, CA: Pfeiffer.

Larson, R., & Larson, D. (1976). *Values and faith: Value-clarifying exercises for family and church groups.* Minneapolis: MN: Winston.

Leming, J. (1987, April). Values clarification research: A study of the etiology of a weak educational research program. Paper presented at the annual meeting of the American Educational Research Association, Washington, DC.

Lewin, K. (1943). Defining the "field at a given time." *Psychological Review, 50*, 292–310. Republished in K. Lewin. (1997). *Resolving social conflicts and field theory in social science.* Washington, DC: American Psychological Association.

Marinoff, L. (2003). *The big questions: How philosophy can change your life.* New York, NY: Bloomsbury. (Later retitled *Therapy for the sane: How philosophy can change your life.*)

May, R. (Ed.). (1961). *Existential psychology.* New York, NY: Basic Books.

May, R. (1980). *Psychology and the human dilemma.* New York, NY: Random House.

Merchey, J. (2006). *Living a life of value: A unique anthology of essays on values and ethics by contemporary writers.* San Diego, CA: Values of the Wise Press.

Miller, W. R., & Rollnick, S. (2002). *Motivational interviewing: Preparing people for change* (2nd ed.). New York, NY: Guilford.

Morgan, A. (2000). *What is narrative therapy? An easy-to-read introduction.* Adelaide, Australia: Dulwich Centre.

Morrison, E., & Price, M. U. (1974). *Values in sexuality: A new approach to sex education.* New York, NY: Hart.

Murphy, J. (2008). *Solution-focused counseling in schools* (2nd ed.). Alexandria, VA: American Counseling Association.

Neukrug, E. (2011). *Counseling theory and practice: Instructor's edition.* Belmont, CA: Brooks/Cole-Cengage Learning.

Neukrug, E., & Milliken, T. (2011). Counselors' perceptions of ethical behaviors. *Journal of Counseling and Development, 89*(2), 206–216.

Nowbar, L. (2004). Untitled, unpublished paper for an advanced counseling theories course, Warner Graduate School of Education and Human Development, University of Rochester, NY.

Oyserman, D., Coon, H., & Kemmelmeier, M. (2002). Rethinking individualism and collectivism: Evaluation of theoretical assumptions and meta-analyses. *Psychological Bulletin, 128*, 3–72.

Pavio, S., & Greenberg, L. (1995). Resolving "unfinished business": Efficacy of experiential therapy using empty-chair dialogue. *Journal of Consulting and Clinical Psychology, 63*(3), 419–425.

Peterson, C. (2006). *A primer in positive psychology.* New York, NY: Oxford University Press.

Peterson, C., & Seligman, M. (2004). *Character strengths and virtues: A handbook and classification.* New York, NY: Oxford University Press/Washington, DC: American Psychological Association.

Polster, E., & Polster, M. (1999). *From the radical center: The heart of Gestalt therapy.* Cleveland, OH: The Gestalt Institute of Cleveland Press.

Raths, L. (1972). *Meeting the needs of children.* Columbus, OH: Charles Merrill.

Raths, L., & A. Burrell. (1963). *Understanding the problem child*. West Orange, NJ: Economics Press.

Raths, L., Harmin, M., & Simon, S. B. (1966, 1978). *Values and teaching: Working with values in the classroom* (1st and 2nd eds.). Columbus, OH: C. E. Merrill.

Rice, R. (2004). *Using values clarification to assist in the treatment of OCD*. Unpublished paper, Advanced Counseling Theories course, University of Rochester, NY.

Rogers, C. R. (1951). *Client-centered therapy: Its current practice, implications, and theory*. Boston, MA: Houghton Mifflin.

Rogers, C. R. (1961). *On becoming a person*. Boston, MA: Houghton Mifflin.

Rokeach, M. (1961, 1973). *The nature of human values*. New York, NY: Free Press.

Rokeach, M. (1975). Toward a philosophy of values education. In J. Meyer, B. Burnham, & J. Cholvat (Eds.), *Values education: Theory, practice, problems, prospects*. Waterloo, Ontario: Wilfred Laurier University Press.

Sampson, E. (1988). The debate on individualism: Indigenous psychologies of the individual and their role in personal and social functioning. *American Psychologist, 43*, 15–22.

Seligman, M. (2002). *Authentic happiness: Using the new positive psychology to realize your potential for lasting fulfillment*. New York, NY: Free Press.

Seligman, M. (2011). *Flourish: A visionary new understanding of happiness and well-being*. New York, NY: Free Press.

Seligman, M., Steen, T., Park, N., & Peterson, C. (2005). Positive psychology progress: Empirical validation of interventions. *American Psychologist, 60*, 410–422.

Shallcross, L. (2010, January). A voyage of self-discovery. *Counseling Today*, 32–38.

Shinbaum, V. (2009, May). Getting to the goal. *Counseling Today*, 62–63.

Simon, S. (1974). *Meeting yourself halfway: 31 value clarification strategies for daily living*. Niles, IL: Argus Communications.

Simon, S., Howe, L., & Kirschenbaum, H. (1972, 1979) *Values clarification: A handbook of practical strategies for teachers and students*. New York, NY: Hart Publishing. Currently available from Hadley, MA: Values Press.

Simon, S., Howe, L., & Kirschenbaum, H. (1995). *Values clarification: A practical, action-directed workbook*. New York, NY: Warner.

Stock, G. (1985). *The book of questions*. New York, NY: Workman.

Sue, D., Carter, R., Casas, J., Fouad, N., Ivey, A., Jensen, M.,... Vazquez-Nuttell, E. (1998). *Multicultural counseling competencies: Individual and organizational development*. Thousand Oaks, CA: Sage.

Sue, D. W., & Sue, D. (2003). *Counseling the culturally diverse: Theory and practice* (4th ed.). New York, NY: John Wiley & Sons.

Tschannen-Moran, B., & Tschannen-Moran, M. (2010). *Evocative coaching: Transforming schools one conversation at a time*. San Francisco, CA: Jossey-Bass.

Values in Action Institute. Values in action signature strengths test. Retrieved from http://www.authentichappiness.org.

Watts, R. (2011). On the origin of the striving for superiority and of social interest (1933). In J. Carlson & M. Maniacci (Eds.), *Alfred Adler revisited* (pp. 41–47). New York, NY: Routledge.

Watts, R. (2012, January 10). Personal electronic communication to author.

White, M., & Epston, D. (1990). *Narrative means to therapeutic ends*. New York, NY: W. W. Norton.

Williams, B. (2003). The worldview dimensions of individualism and collectivism: Implications for counseling. *Journal of Counseling and Development, 81*, 370–373.

Williams, P., & Menendez, D. (2007). *Becoming a professional life coach: Lessons from the Institute for Life Coach Training*. New York, NY: W. W. Norton.

Wubbolding, R. (2000). *Reality therapy for the 21st century*. Philadelphia, PA: Brunner-Routledge.

Yalom, I. (1980). *Existential psychotherapy*. New York, NY: Basic Books.

■ INDEX